OBLIVION

Also by Harry J. Maihafer

From the Hudson to the Yalu:
West Point '49 in the Korean War

Brave Decisions:
Moral Courage from the Revolutionary War to Desert Storm

OBLIVION

The Mystery of West Point Cadet Richard Cox

Harry J. Maihafer

BRASSEY'S
Washington

Library of Congress Cataloging-in-Publication Data

Maihafer, Harry J., 1924–
   Oblivion : the mystery of West Point cadet Richard Cox / Harry J.
Maihafer. — 1st ed.
     p. cm.

   1. Cox, Richard Colvin. 2. Military cadets—United States—
Biography. 3. United States Military Academy—Biography.
4. Missing persons—United States. I. Title.
U410.M1C69 1996
327.12′092—dc20
  [B]   96-25098
                                           CIP

ISBN 1-57488-224-4

10 9 8 7 6 5 4 3 2 1

Printed in Canada

With deep appreciation and grateful acknowledgment to Marshall Jacobs. Without his persistent research and his willingness to follow a trail others had long since abandoned, this book could not have been written.

Contents

Prologue

"Hello, is this Harry Maihafer? I'm calling from Miami, Florida, and my name is Marshall Jacobs. You don't know me, but I know who you are."

Who was this guy? A salesman? Someone soliciting a donation? And could I beg off gracefully? As it happened, however, the voice was pleasant, and like most writers I'm always ready—far *too* ready, in fact—to take a break from the grind of actual writing. My caller went on to identify himself as a retired history teacher who had been pursuing a unique research project. Now he needed someone to collaborate on a book based on that research.

"And why me?" I asked.

"Well, I was in a Barnes and Noble bookstore recently and saw a reference to your book about West Pointers in the Korean War. It said you were a West Pointer yourself, and I felt pretty sure you'd be interested in my research. It involves the Military Academy, and specifically it concerns the greatest mystery in West Point history, a cadet who apparently vanished from the face of the earth. Over the years, cadets occasionally disappear for one reason or another—pressure from the plebe system, disappointing love affairs, failing grades, and so on—but they always turn up. Since the Academy was founded in 1802, only one man ever vanished completely."

My interest picked up, but only a little. "Well, I'm in the middle of another book at the moment," I said.

Undeterred, Jacobs pressed on. "I think this project of mine is right up your alley. It's factual, it's not fiction. I've researched it for over eight years, and I've literally left no stone unturned in my research. I've interviewed hundreds of people; I've read FBI files and army CID files. I've corresponded with numerous people. I have been at the Academy many times in the last few years searching the archives, and I might add that I've had the full cooperation of the authorities at West Point."

By now, he at least had my attention. "What started you on all this?" I asked.

"Well, I was a young college student in 1950 when I first read in the newspaper about a cadet who had disappeared from West Point. As a boy, I lived in Newburgh, just up the Hudson from West Point, and I was very familiar with the Academy and with cadet life. I knew this was something unusual—cadets don't just vanish. Even today, if you'll look in your West Point *Register of Graduates,* you'll see under the Class of '52: 'Richard C. Cox—Mysteriously disappeared.' Over the years, frankly, no one has attempted to research his disappearance as I have.

"The more I learned," he said, "the more interested I became. Finally I determined that one day I'd try to solve the mystery. By background, I'm a historian and a researcher, and once I got started, it became an obsession with me. Early in my research, to give you a hint, I found that Cox, before entering the Military Academy, was stationed in Germany in an intelligence unit.

"Now I'm not a literary person," he said, "and I have no desire to write a book myself. That's where you would come in."

I was still unsure about getting involved, and even remained a bit skeptical, but at least I was curious enough to want to hear more. Although I was well occupied with my current project, even working to meet a contract deadline, I was nevertheless planning a brief Florida vacation in the near future. Jacobs and I agreed to meet at that time.

One morning two months later, I left the condo my wife and I had rented in Delray Beach, headed south, and by midmorning was at the Jacobs home north of Miami. Marshall Jacobs turned out to be personable, articulate, and the owner of a fascinating story. We sat in his comfortable living room; I turned on my tape recorder. Nearby were boxes and boxes of files, all neatly labeled.

During the next several hours, methodically and without notes, Jacobs told about the mysterious case of Richard Colvin Cox, the cadet who had vanished, and what he had learned during his extensive, labyrinthine, eight-year investigation. He spoke slowly and deliberately. His tone, rather than conversational, was that of an educator; I could picture him speaking the same way in the classroom.

Personally, I've always been a fan of mystery stories. Now I was hearing a tale that rivaled the best fiction. It had all the elements—international intrigue, murder, cover-ups, dramatic surprises, and dogged detective work.

Before committing myself to a book project, I needed to know more. I borrowed Marshall Jacobs's clipping file, took it home, and read it at leisure. The folder bulged with items about Cox from papers such as the *New York Times* and the *Washington Post*, articles from magazines like *Life* and *True Detective,* even photocopied chapters from a few books. Respected writers had consistently called it one of the top missing-person stories of all time, listing it alongside those of Judge Crater, Amelia Earhart, and Jimmy Hoffa.

Jacobs had implied that he knew what had happened to Cadet Cox. If that was so, this was a book I wanted to write. When I did, I would also write of West Point, my cherished alma mater, the place where the story began.

"This is a funny fancy of yours, M. Poirot."

"It is, perhaps, a little unusual," Poirot agreed cautiously.

"You see," said Hale, "it's all such a long time ago."

Hercule Poirot foresaw that he was going to get a little tired of that particular phrase. He said mildly, "That adds to the difficulty, of course."

"Raking up the past," mused the other. "If there were an object in it, now . . ."

"There is an object."

"What is it?"

"One can enjoy the pusuit of truth for its own sake. I do."

Part One

Chapter 1

Gloom Period

At the end of World War II, America's interest in West Point may have been at an all-time high. In every theater of war, both on land and in the air, West Pointers—members of the Long Gray Line—had served with distinction. A grateful nation was well aware of its contribution to the final victory, and, understandably, West Pointers such as Eisenhower, MacArthur, Bradley, Patton, and Arnold had become national figures.

At West Point itself in those postwar years, significant changes were taking place under the leadership of Maxwell D. Taylor, a brilliant young war hero who had become the Military Academy's fortieth superintendent. Sports fans, meanwhile, were hailing the exploits of Doc Blanchard, Glenn Davis, and other members of Earl Blaik's superb Army football team, which at one point went thirty-two straight games without a defeat. It was not surprising, then, that by 1950 America considered West Point to be a special place.

Despite the foregoing, on one particular morning in 1950—Saturday, January 14, to be exact—the Military Academy, while it might be special, was also deep into what cadets knew as the Gloom Period, the time between Christmas leave and spring break when the Academy was traditionally overhung by a gray cloud of glum monotony.

On this day, as dawn broke and first call sounded for reveille, "gloom" seemed the appropriate term. A chill wind swept down the Hudson Valley, howled as it passed the elevation known as Crow's Nest, and gave an extra shriek as it slashed across the frozen West Point Plain. A bird riding that wind, annoyed by the buffeting and seeking a place of refuge, might have avoided the cadet barracks, flown high past the magnificent cadet chapel, and, soaring still higher, finally come to rest amid the ruins of old Fort Putnam. Under a leaden sky, perched on a crumbling stone wall dating from the Revolutionary War, the bird could have looked down on a sea of gray: the gray, icy waters of the Hudson, flowing slowly past gray stone walls and gray Gothic buildings, and, at this moment completing the picture, a stirring of gray-clad figures.

Down below, at the foot of each stairwell of the barracks, a plebe "minute caller" was sounding off in a loud voice: "Sir, there are five minutes to assembly for reveille. The uniform is dress gray under overcoats. Five minutes, sir!"

Other plebes, the lowly freshmen fourth-classmen, were already out in ranks, shivering at attention with shoulders back and chins tucked in. Most of the seniors—the first-classmen or firsties—however, who considered it a mark of pride to arrive just as the last note of assembly was sounding, were only now reluctantly crawling out of bed and shrugging into their uniforms.

In North Area, room 1943 (nineteenth division of barracks, fourth floor, third room) was home to sophomore—third-classman or yearling—Dick Cox, a twenty-one-year-old from Ohio, and his roommates, Deane Welch and Joe Urschel. Now all three, in the dark, silently dressed and made their way down the stairs and out into ranks. It was also a mark of pride to dress in the dark and stand reveille while half-asleep.

Precisely at 6:00 A.M., as Cox and other members of Company B-2 streamed into ranks, the bandsmen known as "Hell Cats" sounded the final notes of assembly. Reports were rendered with a minimum of delay. First-classman Tom Strider, Cox's squad leader, looked down the line, saw that everyone was on hand, and gave a quick salute to the platoon leader: "All present or accounted for, sir!"

Platoon leaders relayed reports to company commanders, and up the line it went until all cadets were accounted for. The whole process took less than a minute.

Cox, Welch, and Urschel, animated now for the first time, hurried back to their room. They had less than a half-hour to shave, fold up their bedding, clean the room, and get ready for breakfast formation.

"Police call," when rooms had to be swept and wastebaskets put into the hallways, came at 6:20. Five minutes later, the B-2 minute caller, after checking the uniform flags flying at the far corner of North Area, began to call out: "Sir, there are five minutes until assembly for breakfast. The uniform is dress gray under short over-coats. Five minutes, sir!" He repeated this at the four-, three-, and two-minute marks. At the last, he added: "Do not forget to turn off your lights, sir!"

In B-2's section of North Barracks, each division had two ground-floor doors, one leading to the central barracks compound, the other onto a road that ran along the Plain. Reveille had been in the area of barracks; for breakfast formation, B-2 used the alternate door and assembled on the roadway. Moments later, upon command, the company came to attention, executed a right-face, and marched the short distance to Washington Hall. Once inside, Cox and the other cadets moved quickly to their assigned tables and stood silently at attention. Then, from above on the "poop deck," the Cadet Brigade Adjutant gave the drawn-out command to "Taaake seats!" followed instantaneously by a roaring babel of sound. Breakfast—and the cadet day—was under way.

Following breakfast, Cox and his roommates returned to their room and prepared for Saturday classes. For Cox, this included Russian, his hardest subject and the one to which he devoted the most study time. In overall academics, Dick Cox, a serious, hard-working student, was positioned comfortably in the upper third of his class. Moreover, in "aptitude for the service," his tactical offic-ers' and fellow cadets' evaluation of his leadership potential, Cox was the highest-ranking yearling in all of B-2 company.

In midmorning, at the end of his first-hour class, Dick Cox spoke to a classmate who was heading to New York for a track meet in Madison Square Garden. Cox, who had been on the cross-country team the previous fall, had recently joined the track team but hadn't yet qualified for the varsity travel squad. He wished his classmate good luck and then headed back to his room.

His first order of business was to learn from the charge of quar-ters (CQ) whether the company tactical officer had made his morn-ing inspection or, as cadet slang put it, "Has the Tac?" The CQ, Russ Russomano, assured everyone the Tac "had," so rooms that mo-ments before had been picture-perfect could now be tossed into weekend disarray. Joe Urschel, returning to room 1943, saw his roommate Cox already busy, cramming for his late-morning Rus-sian language class.

After Cox's bout with Russian and a noisy noon meal, came Sat-urday inspection. During the spring and fall, Saturdays normally brought parades and reviews. In the winter, however, with the Plain often covered by snow, cadets formed for inspection in the area of the barracks. Sometimes there were also miniature parades, called "Band-Box" reviews, but on this day the Tactical Department was settling for just an inspection.

Cox, Welch, and Urschel began to get ready, putting on gray trousers, spit-shined black shoes, high-collared dress coats, and long gray overcoats with thrown-back capes. Next the roommates helped each other with the tricky adjustment of waist belts, cartridge boxes, and cross-belts, the latter secured by highly polished brass breastplates. They donned their caps, ensured that the visors bore no fingerprints, picked up their rifles, and made their way out to ranks.

Company B-2 came to attention, and the inspection got under way. Actually, there were *several* inspections, by cadet squad leaders and platoon leaders, by the cadet company commander, and by the company tactical officer, Lieutenant Colonel Irvin. Each inspection might result in demerits for shoes or brass improperly shined, for belts wrongly adjusted, and—greatest sin of all—for a less-than-perfect rifle. Lint in bore might bring but a single demerit. Dust or dirt on any of the external parts or in the receiver might bring two or three. The unthinkable, a spot of rust, was worth even more and would bring not only more demerits but probably cause added scrutiny and a few more "gigs" thrown in for good measure.

Dick Cox was a neat, "spoony" cadet, no doubt helped by his previous army experience; he'd risen to the grade of sergeant. He generally made out well at inspections, and this Saturday was no exception. Still, he must have felt good when it was over and he'd gone unscathed. He and the others would now have the rest of the day to themselves.

It was 2 P.M. by the time inspection ended. Returning to barracks, cadets stomped their feet and griped about the amount of time they had spent standing in the cold. Now that they were "liberated," many started for Grant Hall, the cadet reception area, to meet weekend dates. Still others headed for the gym or the field house to watch athletic events, and some, thankful for the chance to do absolutely nothing, returned to their cots and comforters for extra sack time.

In room 1943, where all three roommates were compatible, Dick Cox was probably closer to Deane Welch, who, like Cox, had had prior army service. Joe Urschel, the third roommate, had come to West Point straight out of high school and was possibly a bit intimidated by the older, more mature Cox.

That day Cox, mature or not, made a suggestion to Welch that had the potential of getting them both into trouble. Cox's civilian suits, sent out for cleaning after his return from Christmas leave, were now back. On Monday, before the next inspection, civilian clothes would have to be placed in storage. While they *were* available, though, what about putting them on after taps and slipping out to Newburgh for a little extracurricular fun?

Welch was tempted, to the point that he tried on one of Cox's suits, which turned out to be too large for him. That ended the discussion, quite possibly to Welch's relief. Although he didn't want to be considered "chicken," neither did he relish the thought of getting caught and gathering extra demerits that might result in free-time confinement or in punishment tours walking the area.

With that out of the way, Welch and Cox discussed their "legal" options. Their best bet seemed to be the field house, where there'd be boxing bouts followed by a basketball game with Rutgers. They put on their short overcoats and headed that way. Cox and Welch, like most cadets, were avid sports fans. Red-haired Deane Welch was a New Hampshire native who liked all sports, but his first love was skiing. Dick Cox, when not participating himself, was simply an all-around fan who had once been sports editor of his high school yearbook.

Athletics, of course, were an integral part of the Military Academy, and every cadet had seen MacArthur's words engraved over the entrance to the gym: "Upon the fields of friendly strife are sown the seeds that upon other fields, on other days, will bear the fruits of victory."

Cox, who had played on an army basketball team in Germany, had always liked the sport. Now, from the stands in the field house, he rooted for Army's "roundballers" as they went up against a determined Rutgers squad.

All-American quarterback Arnold Galiffa, a gifted athlete best known for football, was also captain of the basketball team, which lately had been in something of a slump. Several times they had seen early leads disappear, turning likely wins into losses. Today it seemed to be happening again. Bit by bit, the Cadets' sizeable halftime lead had been slipping away. With two minutes to play, Rutgers scored, closing to within a single basket: Army 56, Rutgers 54. The Cadets went into a delay; in 1950, the NCAA rule limiting time of possession had not yet been adopted. Then, as the clock wound down, Galiffa saw an opening, drove for the basket, and scored a layup as time ran out. The final score was Army 58, Rutgers 54.

Cadets in the stands, who had been holding their collective breaths, let out a yell. Chalk one up for Army! Dick Cox and Deane Welch, after joining the victory cheers, emerged from the field house and began climbing back to the level of the Plain, heading for their room in North Area.

Around five, as they neared the cadet barracks, Cox told Welch: "You go on ahead, I want to check my grades in the sally port." On Saturdays, weekly cadet grades were customarily posted behind glass in the arched tunnels, or sally ports, which led into the central barracks compound.

A few minutes later, Cadet John Samotis, a second-classman in Cox's company, saw Cox near the sally port entrance, talking to a neatly dressed civilian, a young man in his twenties whom Samotis had never seen before. From what Samotis could tell, Cox was doing most of the talking. The visitor stood just under six feet, a bit taller than Cox's five-foot-eight, had a clean-cut appearance, and was wearing a coat and tie under a light-colored topcoat. Although Samotis got a fairly good look at the man, he would later wish he had been more observant.

"Hi, Dick," said Samotis as he passed by. Cox acknowledged the greeting, then resumed talking to the civilian visitor. A few minutes later, Cox went to the Company B-2 orderly room and signed out in the departure log. On Saturdays, cadets were eligible for "dining privileges" (D.P.). When invited by a visitor, they could skip the evening meal in the cadet mess hall and have dinner at Hotel Thayer on post. Cox's entry read:

Name	Class	Destination	Authority	Time Out	Time In
Cox, R C	3	D.P. Hotel	Reg	1745	

When Cox returned to room 1943, only Deane Welch was on hand. Joe Urschel, who had been invited to an officer's quarters for dinner, had been gone since early afternoon. Cox told Welch that he had just talked to the same fellow who had been to see him the previous weekend. He then added that the man, whom he referred to only as "my friend," had invited him to have dinner at the hotel.

As Deane got ready to leave for supper formation, Cox began to change clothes. For Saturday evening at the Thayer, a cadet dressed formally, just as he would if he were escorting a date to a hop.

Instead of the more familiar dress gray, one wore F.D. or full dress—the same gray trousers with black stripes down the seam, but the formal jacket with shiny brass buttons and braid.

At 6:15, first call sounded for supper. Three minutes later, Dick Cox, having put on his full-dress coat, was in front of the mirror, buttoning his long gray overcoat.

Deane Welch, putting on his hat and preparing to leave, said, "See you, Dick."

"Yeah," said Cox, "see you. I should be back early—around nine or nine-thirty."

For Cox, it was evidently just another Saturday night, the passage of a few more hours of Gloom Period. He seemed rather lackadaisical; apparently he viewed dining out as merely a way to break the ennui of a dull January weekend.

Soon after Dick Cox signed out for dining privileges in the B-2 orderly room, Lou Bryan, a cheerful yearling from South Carolina, took over as charge of quarters, replacing his classmate Russ Russomano. Bryan's tour of duty, beginning at 6 P.M., would be for the next twenty-four hours. Russomano, a bright, dark-haired New Jerseyite, after sympathizing with Bryan about catching CQ duty on a weekend, grinned and was on his way.

Bryan had an uneventful evening, broken only by the chatter of cadets coming by the orderly room to sign in as they returned from the hop, the movie, or dining privileges. At eleven o'clock, as taps sounded, Bryan checked the departure book. Except for those at the hop, who were authorized to be out later, everyone but Dick Cox had signed in. This included Cox's roommate Urschel, who'd returned at 10:55.

When a hop ended, a cadet was allowed exactly one hour to return to his company orderly room and sign in. Even if he and his date left the dance early, the same restriction applied. Upon leaving the hop, the cadet was honor bound to note the time and then take but a single hour for a gentlemanly goodnight and—if he was lucky—perhaps for a furtive kiss. "Furtive" was the right word—under the Academy's rather puritanical code, "public display of affection" was strictly forbidden.

The hop ended shortly after midnight, and at 1:10 A.M., with the last man from the hop having signed in, Lou Bryan once more checked the departure log. Opposite Cox's name, the "Time In" space remained blank. Bryan shook his head. Dick was running way late, which meant he'd be in for some serious demerits. With that,

Bryan left the orderly room to make his required inspection, specifically to ensure that all was quiet, no radios were playing, and everyone was in bed.

Bryan's footsteps, as he climbed the darkened stairwell of the Nineteenth Division, were the only sounds to break the stillness. As he reached the fourth floor, he was hoping that Cox would be in his room; perhaps, he thought, Dick had merely forgotten to come by the orderly room to sign in. When he opened the door to 1943 and looked in, however, there was no sign of Cox. Moreover, Welch and Urschel were still wide awake and obviously becoming more and more worried.

No, they told Bryan, they had no idea why Dick hadn't returned. He had left for D.P. a little after six and had said he'd be back early. Something must have happened, but what?

After completing his inspection, Bryan phoned the cadet S.O.D. (senior officer-of-the-day) at South Guard Room to say that Cadet Cox, Richard C., Third Class, Company B-2, had not returned from Dining Privileges. Thirty minutes later, now definitely concerned, Bryan made yet another inspection, with the same empty result. He again called the guard room, saying there was still no sign of Cox. This time the report would be relayed to the O.C., the commissioned officer-in-charge on duty that night.

Around 1:30, the O.C., Major Henry Harmeling Jr., West Point '42, returned to his office in cadet headquarters after having made a quick inspection tour of the barracks area. Everything seemed quiet, and he was ready to turn in.

Although Henry Harmeling was still a month shy of his thirtieth birthday, he was already an experienced veteran. As an infantry company commander in Europe, he had gone into battle with the green 106th Division, been caught up in the Battle of the Bulge, been captured, and spent the remaining months of the war in a German prison camp. By this time he'd acquired more than his share of personal experiences and anecdotes; he was about to add still more.

When he received the report about Cox, Henry Harmeling knew it was something out of the ordinary; cadets might often run late, but they never just vanished.

It was a short night. Harmeling was up and dressed by 7:15. His first action was to ask the cadet O.D. if there was any word on Cox.

"No sir, there's not."

Then, said Harmeling, he needed to talk to Cox's roommates. The O.D. called Lou Bryan, the B-2 charge of quarters, who'd also had a short night. Earlier that morning, thinking that Cox might for some reason have slept in the wrong room, he had checked every bed in the company. Bryan had even inspected the trunk room, the storage area for cadets' luggage and civilian clothes, on the off chance that Cox had been locked in by mistake. He had found nothing, and by this time he had run out of ideas.

Bryan told the guard that Cox's roommates were at early chapel; he'd have them report to the O.C. as soon as they returned. By 9:20, Deane Welch and Joe Urschel were in Harmeling's office.

What could they tell him about their missing roommate? Not much, as it turned out. They said Cox had gone on Dining Privileges shortly after six, having been invited out by a man he'd known in the army in Germany. The same man, they said, had also visited Cox the previous weekend.

What did they know about this fellow? Had they met him? They had not. Fact is, they didn't even know his name. Cox had referred to him only as "my friend," although, to tell the truth, he wasn't much of a friend.

What did they mean by that? Well, they had gathered from Cox's few remarks that he didn't really care for this guy and had even complained that the man was taking up too much of his time. Cox, they said, had described his visitor as pretty much of a braggart, a bad apple who had even boasted about having murdered some woman in Germany.

Murdered? Harmeling came to full alert. If he hadn't been worried before, he was now. He'd better get others involved, and quickly. As soon as Welch and Urschel left, Harmeling picked up the phone and dialed the quarters of Colonel Paul Harkins, the Commandant of Cadets.

Lean, sharp-featured Paul Harkins, USMA '29, had been "Com" for a year and a half. At age forty-five, a veteran cavalryman and tanker, he was considered one of the army's most promising officers. In Europe, he had made a name for himself during World War II as one of George Patton's key staff officers. (From 1962 to 1964, as a four-star general, Harkins would serve as overall U.S. Commander in Vietnam.)

For Paul Harkins, this Sunday had started out pretty much as usual. He dressed, had his breakfast, and, when Harmeling called, was preparing to leave for services at the cadet chapel. Harmeling told Harkins what he knew about the missing cadet. Quickly, Commandant Harkins began to give Harmeling a series of instructions.

"Call Colonel Howell, the provost marshal," Harkins said. The provost, said Harkins, should start an investigation at once. He should also notify the New York police as well as the provost marshal in New York—that would be at First Army Headquarters on Governors Island. Harmeling should be sure Cox's company tactical officer was brought into the situation, after which Harmeling had better notify the Cox family.

The provost marshal, thirty-six-year-old Lieutenant Colonel Edwin N. Howell, Military Police Corps, West Point Class of '38, was in effect the Military Academy's "top cop." When Harmeling told him about the missing cadet and relayed the instructions from Harkins, Ed Howell said he'd make the calls and appoint someone to start an immediate investigation.

Next, Harmeling called Lieutenant Colonel Jefferson Irvin, the B-2 company tactical officer. Except for some of the cadets, Jeff Irvin was undoubtedly the man who knew Cox the best, and the O.C.'s message came as a jolt. He found it hard to believe—Dick Cox was one of his best men, the number one yearling in all of B-2.

Henry Harmeling didn't look forward to what he had to do next. At about ten o'clock, he called the long-distance operator and placed a call to Mrs. Rupert (Minnie) Cox, Dick Cox's widowed mother in Mansfield, Ohio. It was a sorry way, Harmeling thought, for a mother to start the day.

Minnie Cox was startled. Why would she be getting a call from some officer at West Point? Gently, Harmeling said he had some disturbing news. Her son Richard had been missing since last evening. Had he tried to contact her?

No, he had not, and no, she had no idea where he might be. Could she offer any explanation as to why he might have wanted to leave the Academy?

Well, she said, there had been some slight disagreement with his girlfriend when Dick was home at Christmas, but she surely didn't think that was serious enough to make him want to come home.

Might he ask when Mrs. Cox had last heard from her son, and had Richard ever mentioned a recent visitor, someone he had served with overseas?

Actually, she said, she had received a letter from Dick just two days ago, on Friday, but he hadn't said anything about a visitor. Harmeling, with little more to add, promised that someone would call as soon as more information became available. Mrs. Cox, in turn, said she'd let the authorities know at once if Dick either called her or showed up at home.

As she hung up the phone, Minnie Cox had a strange sense of foreboding. Her first thought was to call her other children in Mansfield to see if they knew anything. Then she decided against it. Basically, she wanted to be alone. For years, she had been saying that, with God's help and enlightenment, no problem was too much. This was a time for her to draw on her beliefs and to test them.

She took out the last two letters from Dick and read them over. As usual, Dick had done considerable griping about cadet life, and in one letter he'd even asked, only half-seriously, "What would you think if I chucked West Point?" From what she'd heard, though, all cadets griped, and most of them harbored occasional thoughts of resignation. However, in Dick's letters, despite the complaints, there was no indication that he'd planned to desert the Academy. After all, if he wanted to quit the place, he knew very well he only had to submit a letter of resignation. Mainly it appeared that, coming off Christmas leave, he was having trouble getting back into the West Point routine, obviously missing his girlfriend, Betty Timmons, and perhaps feeling a bit sorry for himself.

On Thursday, January 5, soon after he'd returned to West Point, he'd written:

> Slowly I'm getting acclimated again. I don't know if this place is worth the work that you have to go through here, but since everybody—except the cadets—says that it is, I guess I'll have to stick around. I don't think that it's worth it, but it's too late now to make up for what's already been done. . . . I think I've just about talked myself into the idea that I don't like a military life. . . . But being young I'm probably wrong again, so I'll sit tight and study like a good little cadet for another two-and-a-half decades—or is it years? Little difference.
>
> Thanks, Min [his affectionate term for her] for being a perfect mother while I was home. You sure treat me much better than I deserve. Sorry you've got such good competition—not really sorry—but she is kind of nice, don't you think? Not that anybody could think otherwise. . . .

In his last letter, dated Saturday, January 7, he'd written in part: "Don't have any idea what there is to tell about this place, but . . . I guess I can always rave about how lucky you are to get a certain daughter-in-law I'm thinking about—thinking about too much, as a matter of fact. After those years of not knowing she was alive, I finally woke up to the second best thing that ever happened to me— the first being that I'm your son."

These surely weren't the words of someone who was planning to disappear. Mrs. Cox, a strong-willed woman, fought back the tears and said a prayer.

At 10:15 that morning, Colonel Howell's deputy, Warrant Officer Joseph De Lorenzo, called to say he'd been asked by Howell to begin an investigation. After Harmeling filled him in, De Lorenzo said he would like to interview Cox's roommates at cadet headquarters at one o'clock. Harmeling made the arrangements, then began briefing Lieutenant Colonel Ray Marlin, who arrived around 10:30 to relieve him as O.C.

Harmeling told Marlin what had been happening and then turned over his notes, plus the O.C. brassard, a distinctive yellow armband worn on O.C. duty and recognized by all cadets as a symbol of the respected (and often dreaded) Department of Tactics. For Henry Harmeling, it had been a memorable tour of duty.

Like Harkins, Major General Bryant E. Moore had been anticipating an uneventful Sunday. In midmorning, he arrived for services at the cadet chapel, the magnificent structure often called the finest example of Gothic architecture in North America. As he worshiped on this particular morning, he may have been feeling especially thankful for a nation at peace, for the Corps of Cadets, for the Military Academy, and for his own particular role as West Point superintendent. He was the forty-first man to hold that position; his predecessors included such notables as Robert E. Lee and Douglas MacArthur. It had been a year, almost to the day, since Bryant Moore had replaced the charismatic Max Taylor as superintendent. Moore, however, despite a carefully groomed mustache that gave him a somewhat dapper look, would never have been called charismatic. The fifty-five-year-old superintendent, with combat experience in both Europe and the Pacific, was known mostly as an austere disciplinarian with an often abrasive personality. Those who knew him best, however, recognized Moore as a man of outstanding character and as a proven, highly effective officer.

When services ended, Harkins caught up with Moore outside the chapel and told him they had a problem—a yearling named Cox appeared to be missing. Harkins assured the "Supe" he'd keep him posted, and the two agreed, if nothing more was learned, to meet again early Monday to discuss further action.

At 1:00 P.M., Deane Welch and Joe Urschel were back at cadet headquarters, this time to meet with investigator Joe De Lorenzo. They went over what they had told Major Harmeling, including their suspicion of Cox's civilian visitor. Then the questioning took a different tack. De Lorenzo asked if they thought Cox might have left voluntarily.

Not likely, they said. At least they felt positive he hadn't planned to.

But what if he had? Suppose he went to New York, where would he be likely to go? Were there any places he was known to frequent?

Cox, according to the roommates, was like many other cadets. When he went to New York City, he stayed at either the Astor or the Piccadilly Hotel. They had also heard him mention the Lorelei Club. Again, however, they insisted that Cox wouldn't have left on his own.

Despite the assurances from Welch and Urschel, De Lorenzo talked to both military and civil authorities in New York. He asked them to be on the lookout for a cadet named Richard Cox and asked that they specifically check the places mentioned by Cox's roommates, as well as any of the other usual cadet hangouts. They agreed to do so and promised to notify the Academy as soon as they had any leads.

Sunday afternoon, on orders from Colonel Howell, military policemen made spot inspections of the Thayer Hotel and various other places on the post and reservation, but no trace was found of either Cox or his civilian visitor.

Back in B-2 Company, as cadets formed for compulsory Sunday morning chapel, word of Cox's disappearance had spread rapidly. According to his roommates and the CQ, Cox, when he left for D.P. on Saturday evening, had meant to return, meaning there probably had been either foul play or a serious accident of some kind. Tom Strider, Cox's squad leader and a fellow member of the cross-country squad, wondered where Dick might be if he weren't at the hotel, the barracks, or any other obvious place. Could he, for some unknown reason, have decided to go up into the hills and onto one of the cross-country trails? And might Dick be out there now, lying helpless with a twisted ankle or broken leg? Combing the trails was a long shot, but taking any kind of action seemed better than doing nothing at all.

Strider gathered several members of the cross-country team, and together they headed into the hills behind Michie Stadium. Breaking into groups of two or three, they ran along near-frozen, twisting paths, their breaths leaving vapor clouds in the January air and their heads turning left and right as they jogged along, scanning the woods for any sign of Cox. However, their generous, well-meaning efforts were in vain. When they reassembled, no one had a thing to report, not even a clue or a wild guess.

That night at supper, Cadet First Captain John Murphy made an announcement: Third-classman Richard Cox of B-2 Company was missing. Anyone with knowledge of Cox, or of a civilian visitor who had been to see him each of the past two weekends, was asked to come forward and tell what he knew.

Chapter 2

A Visitor Named George

It began as idle chatter, not exactly a rumor, more a tidbit of local news, a conversation piece for the officers, cadets, and soldiers of the post. One of the cadets was said to be missing, and no one knew why. By Monday morning, when it became clear that Cox's disappearance was not simply a rebellious young man playing hooky and rumors of foul play began to emerge, the story gained momentum. Casual gossip was replaced by genuine concern, and those who knew Dick Cox personally now felt a growing apprehension.

Supposedly the missing cadet, a yearling, was one of the top men in his class. Surely he hadn't deserted, so what could it be? Cadets talked about it in their rooms and on the way to class. Faculty members discussed it with each other and with their families. Even in the barracks, it was the main news of the day, and military policemen, the "insiders" who had been on the Sunday afternoon search parties, were happy to gather a group and tell what they knew. Basically, though, they didn't know that much, not even enough to start a decent rumor.

By regulation, every army unit prepares daily what is called a "morning report," an accounting for each of its members. On Monday, January 16, 1950, in the absence of any better information, Richard C. Cox, Cadet Company B-2, was listed on the morning report of the U.S. Corps of Cadets as AWOL, absent without leave.

That same Monday morning, at 11:25, Major Henry Harmeling received a phone call from Mansfield, Ohio. On the line was Mrs. Minnie Cox, asking if there was any more news about her son Richard. Although he was no longer directly involved with the case,

Harmeling was the logical one for her to call, for at this point he was probably the only officer at the Academy whose name she knew.

Minnie Cox, obviously distraught, said neither Dick's fiancée nor anyone in the family had heard from Richard, and with each passing hour they were becoming more and more worried. Harmeling, while he had nothing further to report, tried to be reassuring. The search was continuing, he said, and they would be sure to let her know as soon as any more information became available. Meanwhile, did she herself have any suggestions as to where Richard might be? Was there anyone he might be likely to contact?

Her only suggestion was that someone might try calling Robert Gandert, a student at Brown University in Providence, Rhode Island. Bob Gandert was her son's closest friend, and if Dick contacted anyone, it would probably be Bob. Harmeling said he'd pass this on, and as the conversation wound down, he once again assured her that someone would be in touch.

That same Monday morning, Commandant of Cadets Paul Harkins, the man most responsible for cadets' daily lives, met with Major General Bryant E. Moore, the superintendent, to discuss the Cox case. After that, his first action was to send a telegram officially notifying Mrs. Rupert Cox that her son Richard was missing as of Saturday evening, January 14. The telegram went on to say that an investigation was under way, that it would be continued, and that she would be kept informed.

Harkins then called Ed Howell, the Provost Marshal, and told him to make sure that the public information officer, Lieutenant Colonel Bill Proctor, was brought up to speed. Once people started making inquiries about Cox in New York, reporters were sure to get in the act, so perhaps Proctor should beat them to the punch and issue a brief press release.

Harkins wracked his brain. Was there anything else that might help? What about Cox's roommates meeting with Dr. Spencer, the staff psychologist? By talking to those who knew Cox best, perhaps Spencer could come up with some new insights, either about Cox or about that mysterious visitor. Accordingly, that afternoon Deane Welch and Joe Urschel reported to Spencer's office on the second floor of the gymnasium.

Douglas Spencer occupied a recently created position in the Academy's newest department. Soon after he became superintendent, the scholarly but pragmatic Maxwell Taylor said he thought it ridiculous that the Military Academy, whose primary mission was the development of leaders, had no department specifically dedicated to that purpose. He therefore established the Office of Military Psychology and Leadership (MP&L) and staffed it with a professional psychologist and officer-instructors, the latter mainly combat veterans.* He had to override the objections of tradition-bound professors who felt the new department was not sufficiently "academic." Their objections may have accounted for MP&L, which was part of the Tactical Department and under the commandant of cadets, being housed in the gymnasium rather than in one of the academic buildings.

Welch and Urschel told Spencer about Dick Cox's visitor, who had come to West Point on the weekend of January 7 and 8 and again on January 14, the day Cox disappeared. The man, they said, had annoyed Cox as he bragged of things in his past, things not only brutal but also criminal. Cox, in fact, had told them he was a little afraid of the man and said he was "capable of almost anything." Spencer remarked how unusual it was for one man to visit another man on consecutive weekends, especially when there allegedly was only a casual acquaintance. He also took note of the strange, almost weird, macho boasting. Putting it all together, Spencer decided that the visitor must have had an unnatural attraction toward Cox. His report, rather quaintly worded, contained an opinion that the visitor was probably a "homosexualist."

Visitors to the Military Academy often comment on how smoothly the place seems to run. In no small measure, this is due to the work of many unsung, behind-the-scene soldiers, the members of the crack 1802d Special Regiment—military policemen, food service workers, clerk-typists, drivers, mechanics, enlisted instructors and other proud members of one of the army's finest outfits. On Monday afternoon, 150 soldiers of the 1802d were pulled from their normal duties and given a unique mission. They were to conduct a massive, intensive search. On Sunday, the search for Cox had been necessarily somewhat cursory. Now it would be carried out in earnest.

Every building on the Academy reservation was searched from top to bottom, every barracks, every warehouse, every shed. Even the buildings at nearby Camp Buckner, customarily locked during

* From 1953 to 1956, shortly after the events described, the author served as an instructor in this department.

the winter months, were opened for inspection. Concurrently, special squads of military policemen examined all tunnels, culverts, and known caves, including the dank utility tunnels under Central Area, which over the years had become a part of cadet lore. (Years earlier, a cadet prankster known as "the mole" had won undying fame among future generations of cadets by exploring those tunnels and by tormenting the authorities, popping up his head from time to time and then rapidly disappearing!)

Unfortunately, a recent heavy snowfall kept the operation from being all that the authorities would have liked. Their preference would have been for soldiers to form a skirmish line and then move methodically throughout the Academy's sprawling fifteen thousand acres. Plans were made to resume the search as soon as the snow had melted.

Earlier that day, Warrant Officer Joe De Lorenzo, the man who had interviewed Deane Welch and Joe Urschel, met with his boss, Lieutenant Colonel Ed Howell, to discuss their next move. Clearly they could use some outside help, preferably from people with experience in missing person cases. Howell called First Army headquarters, fifty miles to the south on Governors Island in New York Harbor, and talked to his opposite number, the First Army Provost Marshal. Through civilian police channels, the Provost Marshal's office issued a thirteen-state alarm for Cox. Next, they alerted the Missing Persons Bureau of the New York City Police Department, as well as most of the taxicab companies in the metropolitan area.

To be sure all bases were covered, an informal call was also made to the New York FBI office on Foley Square. It was for information purposes only; at this stage the FBI wasn't involved. Who knew, though? Before this was resolved, J. Edgar Hoover's G-men might very well be asked to take part in the investigation.

Howell next talked to Captain O. E. Wedbush, chief of the First Army Criminal Investigation Division—the CID. Wedbush thus became one of the first CID officers to learn about Richard Cox. In the months ahead, hundreds of other CID men would come to know the name.

Wedbush, as a staff officer with coordination functions, had no operators directly under his control; however, he was able to call upon various CID assets in the First Army area. Wedbush phoned the Tenth CID Detachment, located nearby on Whitehall Street in lower Manhattan, and talked to the unit's commander, Captain Sam Vercoe.

The drab government building at 39 Whitehall was something of a catchall, providing space not only for the Tenth CID but also for recruiting offices, an induction station, a military police section, and a varied assortment of clerical workers. The desks, chairs, and other furnishings were austere, unattractive government issue. The peeling walls were a faint, bilious green. Overall, the setting was unimpressive. Nevertheless, 39 Whitehall housed some of the U.S. Army's top professionals, including the trained criminal investigators of the Tenth CID.

Sam Vercoe, receiving the call from Wedbush, knew this case was something well out of the ordinary, a case that would doubtless receive a great deal of publicity and that would deserve full attention. His people were often asked to locate young AWOL soldiers from places like Fort Dix or Camp Kilmer, but never had they been asked to find a West Point cadet!

Within hours, two of Vercoe's top men, Murray Kaplan and Joseph Cavanaugh, were checking with desk clerks at midtown hotels, especially hotels favored by cadets, including the Astor, the New Yorker, the Wellington, and the Laurelton. The most promising lead came at the Hotel Piccadilly, on Forty-fifth Street just west of Broadway. According to the register, a Cadet Cox had stayed there the previous weekend, January 7 and 8. When Murray Kaplan checked it out, however, he found it had been Cadet First-Classman *Malcolm* Cox. False alarm. Right kind of cadet, wrong man.

Late that afternoon, Captain Vercoe pulled Kaplan and Cavanaugh off the hotel search and said he was assigning them to the Cox case full time. Tomorrow morning, he wanted them to head for West Point and to check in with Lieutenant Colonel Howell, the Provost Marshal.

That evening, based on information Cox's roommates had furnished to Joe De Lorenzo, other CID agents visited nightspots in the city's Yorkville section, including the Cafe Lorelei on East Eighty-sixth Street, supposedly one of Cox's favorite hangouts. There was no sign of Cox at the moment, but they agreed the Lorelei might warrant a full-time stakeout.

In missing person cases, it was generally agreed that the first twenty-four to forty-eight hours were crucial. However, as Monday the sixteenth came to an end, the first forty-eight hours had come and gone, and despite significant effort at West Point and in New York, the search had come up empty. There was no trace whatsoever of Richard Cox.

Early on Tuesday the seventeenth, Murray Kaplan and Joe Cavanaugh were sitting in the Provost Marshal's office at West Point, being briefed by Lieutenant Colonel Ed Howell and Warrant Officer Joe De Lorenzo. By mutual consent, it was agreed that the two CID men would take over the case and would receive all possible support and cooperation from the West Point authorities.

First stop, of course, was to be room 1943 in North Area. Kaplan and Cavanaugh wanted to examine Cox's personal effects. They also wanted to meet Welch and Urschel, Cox's roommates, while details were still fresh in their minds.

That night at supper formation, based on a request from Kaplan, the Cadet First Captain, twenty-three-year-old John Murphy from Staten Island, again urged anyone with information about Cox to come forward and tell what he knew.

In addition to Welch and Urschel, cadets giving statements included Peter Hains and Lou Bryan, the CQs in Cox's company on January 7 and 14, respectively, plus Mauro Maresca and John Samotis, the only ones who had actually seen Cox's visitor. Over the next few days, by putting it all together, Kaplan and Cavanaugh were able to construct a detailed sequence of events.

It had all begun on the afternoon of January 7, a typical Saturday during Gloom Period, and the upperclassmen, who had reluctantly returned from Christmas leave but a few days earlier, were not in the best of humors. Neither were the plebes, who had had the place to themselves while the upperclassmen were away and now had to resume their role of lowly fourth-classmen, being hazed, bracing at meals, and suffering the countless other aggravations of plebe life.

The day was especially gloomy for those who had duties to perform on what should have been a free afternoon, such as Peter Conover Hains, a fourth-generation West Pointer who was charge of quarters in Cadet Company B-2. Hains's great-grandfather, a classmate of George Armstrong Custer, had graduated in 1861, at the beginning of the Civil War, and served with distinction in the Union Army. His grandfather, Class of 1889, had been wounded in the war with Spain and as a brigadier general had served in World War I. More recently, Peter's father, Class of 1924, had served ably in Europe during World War II and worn the stars of a major general.

On this particular afternoon, however, twenty-year-old Peter Hains was not thinking of his illustrious ancestors. He was considering, rather, the personal misfortune of catching CQ duty on a Saturday afternoon.

About 4:45, the phone rang and Hains answered: "Company B-2 orderly room, cadet in charge of quarters speaking, sir."

"Hey, fellow, do you have a Dick Cox in your company?" Hains thought the man's tone was rough and patronizing, almost insulting. Consequently, his reply lacked the supercourtesy normally afforded a visitor.

"Yeah, we do. Hold on while I go get him." A few minutes later, Hains told the caller that Cox was not in his room.

"Well, look, when he comes in, tell him to come on down here to the hotel." Hains asked the man's name.

"Just tell him George called—he'll know who I am. We knew each other in Germany. I'm just up here for a little while, and tell him I'd like to get him a bite to eat."

That ended the call. Hains wrote a brief note and placed it in the mailbox in the orderly room: "Cox, George called. He is at the hotel. CCQ."

About 5:15, Dick Cox came by the orderly room and Hains showed him the message. Cox read the note, looked puzzled, and said something to the effect that he didn't remember anyone named George. However, he said, he guessed he'd "go down there to the hotel and get something to eat."

Shortly thereafter, a civilian visitor came into Grant Hall, the cadet reception area, and approached Junior Officer of the Guard [J.O.G.] Mauro Maresca, a twenty-five-year-old first-classman from New York and a World War II veteran who had been appointed to the Military Academy through the regular army. Maresca, as J.O.G., was there to answer visitors' questions or help them to contact individual cadets.

The visitor asked Maresca if it were possible to get in touch with a cadet he knew. Maresca said it was and asked for the cadet's name. He also asked the man if he knew which company the cadet was in.

"His name is Richard Cox, and he's in B-2." With that, Maresca called the B-2 orderly room and got word to Cox, who by this time was back in his room, that he had a visitor in Grant Hall.

As Cox prepared to leave his room, Deane Welch asked him who the visitor was. He replied, Welch later recalled, that it was "some guy he had known in Germany" and that he wasn't quite sure who it was himself.

About fifteen minutes later, Cox entered Grant Hall and asked if Maresca would please page his visitor. Thereupon, the man, who had been sitting with his back to the J.O.G. desk, came forward and greeted Cox. The two shook hands and acted as though they were glad to see each other. They then moved to a nearby seating area, a spot where a cadet and a visiting guest could chat in private.

As near as Maresca could remember, the civilian was about five-foot-eleven and weighed around 185. He had a fair complexion, a full face, and a short haircut, and he was dressed very neatly. The only article of clothing Maresca could later recall was a light-colored, new-looking topcoat, possibly a belted trench coat.

Cox and the visitor, after talking for five or ten minutes, returned to the clothing rack. Maresca heard the man chide Cox good-naturedly about how he looked in his cadet uniform, giving Maresca the impression that the two hadn't seen each other in quite a while. He vaguely remembered hearing Cox say something about having to change his uniform if they wanted to go get something to eat, an understandable comment. Cox was wearing dress gray; for eating at the Thayer, he'd have to change to full dress, the formal uniform with all the brass buttons. Dick Cox and the visitor left Grant Hall. It was then about 5:40 P.M.

Around seven, Joe Urschel, having just returned from supper, sat down at his desk to write letters. About 7:15, Cox came into the room and Urschel looked up. Dick was wearing only a towel wrapped around his middle, evidently having just taken a shower, and as Urschel put it, he seemed "very happy and carefree." Cox put on his gym trousers, slippers, and gray jacket, then sat down at his desk, and started to write a letter. Before doing so, however, he pulled open his desk drawer, took out a letter from his girlfriend, Betty Timmons, and began reading it over. Moments later, Cox put his head down and fell asleep. (Upon hearing Urschel's testimony, it became clear to Kaplan and Cavanaugh that Dick Cox and his visitor had never made it to the hotel. Cox could not have left the reception area in Grant Hall at 5:40, changed clothes, gone for one of the Thayer's leisurely dinners, and been back in barracks around seven.)

Interestingly, Peter Hains, who lived in room 1932, one floor below Cox, and who had been relieved of his CQ duties a couple of hours earlier, remembered Cox as coming upstairs that evening around eight. At the time, said Hains, Cox was wearing his full dress coat under an unbuttoned long overcoat. When Hains asked Cox about the evening and about the man he had been with, Cox had said, "It was some guy who claims he knew me in Germany.

[Hains thought Cox might have said Vienna.] I don't know who he is."

Because Urschel was definite that Cox had showered and returned to the room by 7:15, Hains was probably mistaken on the time. Rather than at eight, Cox must have come by Hains's room at least an hour earlier. Despite this possible glitch in Peter Hains's memory, the CID men felt he was accurate when he told about the earlier phone call from Cox's visitor, including the name "George." In any case, since Hains said he felt "fairly certain" the man had said "George," and since this was the only name they had to work with, the agents began calling the visitor "George," and they would continue to do so in the coming months, almost as though there were no doubt of it.

Deane Welch, who had been at a Saturday evening movie, returned to the room around 9 P.M. He found both his roommates at their desks—Joe Urschel writing a letter, Dick Cox with his head down, fast asleep. Cox looked so comical in that position that Deane, just for fun, borrowed a camera from classmate Cecil Sykes, who lived one floor below them, and took Dick's picture.

At 9:30, the bugle call for "tattoo" came over the North Area speaker system. At this, Dick Cox woke up. He muttered something unintelligible and, acting disoriented, rushed out into the hallway, leaned over the banister, and shouted something like "Who's there? Who's down there? Is that you, Alice?"

Welch followed Cox into the hallway and guided him back to the room, and, as he did so, he noticed the odor of alcohol. For the first time, he realized his roommate was under the influence.

"Who's Alice?" Deane asked.

"Some girl my friend mentioned." With that, Cox, still acting irrational, went to his cot, which, as usual, had neatly folded blankets and sheets on top of a doubled-up mattress. He tossed the blankets and sheets on the floor, unfolded the mattress, and, still dressed, threw himself down on the mattress and went to sleep.

Cox woke up again around eleven. At this point, Welch and Urschel had him get up and sit in a chair while they made his bed for him. They then helped him into his pajamas and put him back to bed. It was a generous gesture on both their parts, but, after all, that's what roommates were for!

Next morning, Cox was back to normal, apparently having slept off any ill effects of the Saturday drinking. He rose at 9:30, skipped breakfast (a "privilege" available only on Sundays), dressed, and fell out for Protestant chapel formation. The cadet regiments alternated, and this week the Second Regiment, including B-2 Company, attended late service at 10:30. Cox was back in his room around noon, and fifteen minutes later he was preparing to leave again to meet his friend.

There hadn't been much time to talk, and Cox by nature had always been a rather private person. However, his two roommates were quite understandably curious about what had happened to him on Saturday. When they asked, he said he'd signed in early, around suppertime, and had then gone back to his friend. The man, according to Cox, had had a bottle of whiskey in his car, and he'd insisted on Cox taking several drinks. In fact, he wouldn't allow Cox to leave until he did. He had also made Dick promise to meet with him again on Sunday. The remark about "not allowing him to leave" sounded rather odd, but they let it pass.

Cox returned to the room around 5 P.M. in an angry mood, irritated because he had been planning to study during the afternoon, and his visitor had stayed much too long. Cox grumbled that he'd now wasted an entire weekend on the man.

During the next few days, Dick Cox mentioned his visitor a few times, but never by name, even when asked. Always it was "he," "him," or "my friend." Frankly, from the way Cox spoke of him, the guy must have made Dick uncomfortable, as well as being pretty much of a pain. The man, Cox said, was a former ranger who liked to brag about having killed Germans during the war. He had even boasted about cutting off their private parts afterward. Another story he had told Cox was about having gotten a German girl pregnant and then murdering her to prevent her from having the baby. Definitely not a nice fellow.

Then came Saturday the fourteenth, when Cox and Welch had gone to the basketball game between Army and Rutgers, after which "George" had suddenly reappeared, meeting Cox near the sally port and inviting him to dinner at the Thayer. Evidently it had been the same man. The description furnished by John Samotis, who had seen them talking that day, jibed with that given by Mauro Maresca, the guard in Grant Hall. Except for Samotis saying the man had a "dark and rough" complexion and Maresca remembering him as "fair," the other details of height, weight, age, and dress corresponded almost exactly.

And what about that meeting on the fourteenth? Obviously, it wasn't planned, at least not by Cox. "George" must have been loitering near the B-2 barracks, for who knew how long, just waiting for a chance to intercept Dick Cox. But why?

Murray Kaplan and Joe Cavanaugh, talking it over, decided they now knew the sequence of events reasonably well. It wasn't much to go on, but one thing seemed sure: The key to finding Richard Cox was locating "George," or at least learning who he was.

Since "George" had been at the Academy on both Saturday and Sunday, January 7 and 8, he must have been staying somewhere nearby on Saturday night. He might also, of course, have checked in nearby on Saturday the fourteenth, the day of Cox's disappearance. No one of "George's" description had stayed at the Thayer, so the search had to be broadened. Kaplan and Cavanaugh knew they'd need help to do it right. Albert Klein, a CID agent who was based in Poughkeepsie and knew the local area, could help; even better, Lieutenant Harry Sanderson of the New York State Police generously offered to assist.

Sanderson's troopers fanned out from their base in Monroe, New York, to check hotels, motels, and tourist homes in the surrounding counties, including the Bear Mountain Inn, the largest hotel in the area, and places in Highland Falls, Newburgh, Cornwall on Hudson, Beacon, and New Windsor. Also contacted was Chief Gus Laverty of the Palisades Interstate Park. Laverty asked his rangers to be on the lookout for Cox, but cautioned that the Bear Mountain and Harriman State Parks, almost adjacent to West Point, contained some forty-eight thousand acres with thousands of buildings and shacks, so a complete search could take months.

Despite the exhaustive efforts of many people, no trace could be found of anyone like "George" staying nearby on either January 7 and 8 or January 14 and 15, the weekends in question.

At the Military Academy, Kaplan and Cavanaugh began to go through Dick Cox's things—clothing, books, magazines, letters, photographs, personal effects, anything that might provide a clue. In addition to his uniforms and civilian clothes, they found sixty dollars in cash, a check made out to him for twenty-five dollars, and a gold wristwatch his roommates said he particularly valued—all confirming that when he left the room he must have had every intention of returning.

Early on, an intriguing item was found on Cox's desk calendar. Sunday, January 15, the day following his disappearance, was circled in red with a note to "see Kelly." Who was Kelly? Was he the mysterious "George"? It was definitely worth checking.

Carefully they went through Cox's stack of letters, many of which were from Betty Timmons, the hometown girlfriend many considered to be Dick's fiancée. There were also snapshots of Betty, including one in an attractive two-piece bathing suit. She was a fine-looking young woman—nice face, good figure, and a very pretty dimpled smile.

Somewhat to their surprise, they also found letters from several other girls, ones named Jean, Bibbs, Barbara, Virginia, and Sally. Virginia was a student at nearby Vassar; from their addresses, the others also seemed to live within striking distance (or "dating distance") of West Point. He appeared to be quite the ladies' man!

The agents were also interested in a letter from Langhorne, Pennsylvania, a Philadelphia suburb, written to Cox by a Joseph Groner, who was apparently a good friend and also the writer of that twenty-five-dollar check. They passed the information about Groner to Captain Wedbush at First Army. Wedbush, in turn, made a request for someone in the Philadelphia area—perhaps a CID agent from Fort Dix, New Jersey—to interview Groner.

Next morning, Wednesday the eighteenth, the *New York Times* had a brief item about Cox: "WEST POINTER MISSING—Police Called into Search for Youth Gone Since Saturday."

West Point, N.Y., Jan. 17 (AP)—Army and state police authorities today were called in by the United States Military Academy to aid in the search for a cadet missing since Saturday.

A West Point spokesman said that Cadet Richard C. Cox, 22 years old, of Mansfield, Ohio, a sophomore, was last seen by fellow cadets in the academy's Company B, Second Regiment.

When last seen, the academy said, Cadet Cox wore the West Point full dress uniform under a long cadet gray overcoat. He is described as blond, with close-cropped hair. He is five feet, eight inches tall and weighs 158 pounds.

While the *New York Times* had buried the story on an inside page, in Cox's hometown it was major news. A day earlier, Cox's disappearance had made the front page of the *Mansfield News Journal*. Among other things, the Mansfield reporter quoted Richard Cox's mother, Mrs. Rupert F. Cox, as saying that her son was "especially well thought of by his classmates" and that he was "engaged to Miss Betty Timmons of Mansfield, but they had not planned to marry until he completed his West Point training."

"Mrs. Cox," the story went on, "said she believes her son may be suffering from amnesia."

On Thursday the nineteenth, CID agents Paul Eliot, from Fort Dix, and Jim Ryan, from Philadelphia, arrived in Langhorne to interview Joseph "Bud" Groner. The twenty-one-year-old Groner was quite forthcoming and appeared genuinely concerned about Cox's disappearance.

Groner told them he had first met Dick Cox at Camp Kilmer, New Jersey, in February 1947, as he and Cox were in the process of being shipped overseas. They had sailed on the SS *General Howze*, and, after landing in Germany, they had gone together through the replacement depot at Marburg. They were then both assigned to the Sixth Constabulary Squadron in Coburg.

Groner said he had been Cox's closest friend during that time, and Dick's absence came as a shock to him. When they were together overseas, Groner said, Dick was never absent without proper authority, even for short periods of time. Groner said he had last seen Cox in Philadelphia, after the 1948 Army-Navy game, and he had last spoken to him by phone about a month ago, around December 20. He'd also had a letter from Cox just before Christmas; in it, Dick had said he hoped to spend a weekend in Philadelphia some time in January 1950.

What about that twenty-five-dollar check? Groner said it was to reimburse Dick for some football tickets Cox had bought for him. When asked about "George," Groner couldn't remember anyone from Germany by that name. Cox's closest friends during that time, he said, in addition to himself, included a soldier named Cannizio (not sure of spelling) from Brooklyn; a fellow named Millikin, from San Antonio; Marvin Farnwell, from somewhere in New York State; plus Mike Higgins and Ernest Skari, both from Philadelphia.

Groner gave Agent Eliot some snapshots he had of Cox and promised to notify the CID if he heard from Dick or received any other information. They tended to believe him. Later that day, nevertheless, Agent Jim Ryan, who was based in Philadelphia, part of the Second Army area, and therefore responsible for any Pennsylvania follow-up, called the Pennsylvania State Police barracks in Langhorne. Ryan explained the situation to Corporal Charles Jones. Groner, Ryan said, as Cox's best friend, was a likely person for him to call if he needed money. Jones said he would have the Pennsylvania state troopers keep a close watch on the Groner residence. Four days later, Ryan again went to Langhorne. This time Bud

Groner wasn't home, so he talked to Bud's father, who assured him that his son hadn't heard from Cox and that he was sure he'd let the authorities know if he did.

At West Point, Kaplan and Cavanaugh, as professionals, were covering all the bases. They checked with the phone company, the post office, and Western Union to see if Cox had received any telegrams or special deliveries. They even checked the bank in Highland Falls to see if Cox had an account there. Results were all negative.

During the cadet interviews, the agents learned that Cox, for the five months preceding his entry to West Point, had attended the USMA Preparatory School at Stewart Field. During that time, he and other candidates had often gone into Newburgh. The agents talked to several of the cadets who had been at Stewart with Cox, especially Tom Ayers and John Aker, who had probably been his closest friends at the prep school, and asked about places Cox liked to go. Most of these, such as the Green Room in the Hotel Newburgh, or the Hof-Brau on Broadway, were just places to get a drink. The cadets insisted, however, that Cox was a limited drinker, and "consumption of liquor caused him to get drowsy and fall asleep." The cadets also named several local girls Cox and the others had known. They implied that Cox may have known some of them "quite well," though they assured the agents these girls were not prostitutes.

Did Cox ever mention anyone he'd served with in Germany? Well, they said, there was a recruiting sergeant at Stewart Field who had once been seen with Cox. They had been on a bus going to Newburgh when Cox noticed that the sergeant was wearing a Constabulary shoulder patch. Cox, who had been with a Constabulary unit in Germany, struck up a conversation with the sergeant. No one could recall the sergeant's name.

On the nineteenth, Kaplan and Cavanaugh drove to Newburgh, about twenty miles north of West Point, and visited the proprietors of the Green Room, the Hof-Brau, Ryan's Bar and Grill, the Mayflower Bar, and the Caravan, all places mentioned by Cox's friends. None of the owners or bartenders had seen Cox in recent months, but all were cooperative, agreeing to let the agents know if Cox made an appearance.

So far, it seemed to Kaplan and Cavanaugh, the evidence indicated that Dick Cox was a popular, successful cadet, above average both academically and militarily, and one who surely had no reason to disappear. There *was* one disturbing item, however, even an alarming one: an unfinished letter Cox had been writing to Betty Timmons, which showed deep disaffection for the Military Academy. A complaint wasn't unusual, of course. Cadets, almost unanimously, griped about the rigors of Academy life and seemed to enjoy ventilating their frustrations. Doing otherwise probably wouldn't have been normal for them; cadet life was hard. In his letter to Betty, however, Cox had revealed an unusual bitterness.

He had begun angrily, counting off the days as though he couldn't wait for them to pass. "Still God-damned January," he wrote. "Still the G-D first part of it but—the last week of the first part—10th to be more exact." On top of the letter, which was on Academy stationery, he had drawn a face spitting on the words "United States Military Academy."

The letter began with some affectionate thoughts for Betty, even a reference to their pending marriage. He then mentioned a letter he'd written to his mother, whom he always referred to as "Minnie." "I asked Minnie what she'd think—or do—if I'd give this place the boot it deserves, go to a business or insurance school for two years and then sponge off her until I caught onto the cruel ways of the world."

In another portion of the letter, Cox wrote: "Actually though, the thought keeps entering my mind [about leaving West Point], and I've yet to discover what I'll have lost by leaving the dear old corps."

Finally, he said, "I feel like this is the second letter I've written you tonight—one I addressed to Minnie, but it was all about the one thing I care about—not West Point, dearie—just you." Perhaps, the agents thought, that last sentence put it all in perspective, and they shouldn't take the desire to quit too seriously. Maybe it wasn't so much disaffection with West Point as the natural lament of a homesick boy, one just back from Christmas leave and frustrated by the need to be separated from a loving fiancée. Whatever the reason, this showed a different side of Richard Cox. Perhaps, the agents thought, they didn't "know" him as well as they had believed.

On January 23, after Kaplan and Cavanaugh had been at West Point for a full week, there was a meeting in the office of the West Point Provost Marshal, Lieutenant Colonel Ed Howell, for the two agents to bring the authorities up to date on their investigation.

Frankly, despite going through Cox's things and talking to several cadets, including Cox's roommates, they hadn't made much progress, not even enough to develop a proper working theory. Cox might, of course, have left on his own, either willingly or under coercion from "George." If not, to be brutally frank, he had either committed suicide or been murdered.

"George" was probably the only one other than Cox who knew what had happened. Unfortunately, he hadn't come forward, and they hadn't been able to identify him. Finding "George" would continue to be a top priority.

The other priority, it seemed, should be learning more about Dick Cox himself. Was there anything in his background that might have prompted him to desert?

The agents told Howell they had decided to split their forces. Murray Kaplan would stay at West Point, talking to other cadets who knew Dick Cox and trying to find any shred of information that might help. For his part, Joe Cavanaugh would be going to Cox's hometown, Mansfield, Ohio. Whatever the story was, maybe it began not at West Point, but much earlier, in Mansfield. Joe Cavanaugh would try to find out.

Chapter 3

Richard Colvin Cox

A s Joe Cavanaugh traveled to Ohio, he carried with him one of the circulars now being distributed to state troopers, local police officers, and military provost marshals throughout the Northeast. It had a photo of Richard Cox, looking handsome in a cadet white summer uniform, plus certain vital statistics and the legend: "The above pictured and described Cadet was reported missing from the U.S. Military Academy, West Point, New York, on 14 January 1950. He was last seen at 1818 hours, 14 January 1950, on the Military Reservation. If the above cadet is observed or apprehended, hold and notify the local Provost Marshal, who in turn should notify Provost Marshal, First Army, Governors Island, New York (Attn: Chief, CID) by the most expeditious means."

By this time, Cavanaugh probably could have recited the data on Cox by heart: born July 25, 1928; height, five-foot-eight; weight, approximately 165; medium build; brown hair (crew cut); blue eyes; fair complexion; diagonal scar on right elbow.

Joe Cavanaugh was aware that Cox had served in the army before entering West Point, with much of his time spent in Germany close to the Iron Curtain. Vaguely, he may have wondered if that overseas assignment had special significance. Cox had been in the S-2 (intelligence) section of a border Constabulary unit, and with the Cold War on everyone's mind . . .

In this last week of January 1950, it was hard for anyone *not* to think about Communism and the Cold War. During the past few days, following a trial that included the dramatic disclosure of Whittaker Chambers's "pumpkin papers," senior State Department official Alger Hiss had been convicted of perjury and sentenced to five years in jail.

At the White House, President Harry Truman, who had unleashed two deadly A-bombs near the end of World War II, was now debating whether to authorize the manufacture of the still more ghastly H-bombs.

In China, meanwhile, on the very day Cox was reported missing, a mob had stormed and seized a U.S. Consulate. Furious U.S. Congressmen were saying this action doomed any hope China might have of early recognition.

Also in January, Secretary of State Dean Acheson, speaking to the National Press Club, had described the nation's Pacific line of defense. Doing so, he seemed to exclude both Formosa and South Korea. "It must be clear," Acheson said, "that no person can guarantee these areas against military attack." In Moscow, Beijing, and Pyongyang, Acheson's words were interpreted to mean that the United States would not get involved if someone attacked South Korea. This impression was reinforced on January 19, when the House of Representatives defeated a small measure that would have provided five hundred U.S. Army officers to supervise the equipping of South Korean troops.

Joe Cavanaugh, arriving in Mansfield, was met by Bill Colby, a detective on the Mansfield police force, a brother-in-law of Dick Cox, and no relation to the CIA's William Colby. As a first step, Cavanaugh checked into a hotel. Almost immediately he received a phone call from the owner of the local newspaper, berating him for coming to Mansfield and not contacting her first. He hung up on her.

Along with Colby, Cavanaugh headed for the Cox home at 554 Cook Road. Mrs. Cox, the fifty-nine-year-old widow who ran the family insurance business, would normally have been at work, but on this day, wanting to be helpful, she had stayed home. Through her, Cavanaugh could meet the other family members, as well as her son's fiancée and closest friends.

Minnie Cox explained that her husband had died over ten years ago and that her son Richard was the youngest of six children. Besides Richard, there was one other boy; that was twenty-nine-year-old Rupert Jr. The girls were Mary [Mrs. Watson Slabaugh], age thirty-four; Emily [Mrs. Robert Beard], age thirty-three; and the twenty-six-year-old twins, Nancy [Mrs. Albert Allen] and Carolyn [Mrs. William Colby]. The last two, Nancy and Carolyn, were the ones who had always been closest to Dick. On their birthday, February 28, he always phoned home to talk to them, and he'd even done so from Germany.

Colby and Cavanaugh, as fellow lawmen, hit it off immediately, and at one point Colby said he might come east to help in the investigation. On his own, Bill Colby had written the FBI in Washington to ask for their help in finding his brother-in-law, but he'd been told they couldn't enter the case unless it was shown that Cadet Cox had committed a crime or suffered an injury. They had, however, included the case in a pamphlet that was being distributed nationwide. For his part, Cavanaugh assured Colby that the FBI was being kept informed, and he felt sure that at some point they'd be asked to play a part in the investigation.

When he talked to Mrs. Cox, Cavanaugh asked to borrow any snapshots she might have from Dick's time in Germany. If they were lucky, one of them might show the elusive "George." She turned over several pictures, and Cavanaugh was pleased to see that several of them had identifying names written on the back.

Mrs. Cox also showed Cavanaugh a letter she'd received the day before her son's disappearance. Cavanaugh asked to examine not only that one but also any others she might have kept. Among the stack of letters was one written from Germany on December 30, 1947, six months before Dick had entered the Academy and during the time he was seeking an appointment. In the letter, he had expressed some strong reservations about West Point and an army career. "If I go straight to prep school I might make out OK," he had written, "but if I go before a board [of review] I'm afraid they'll discover how much I dislike the Army and throw me out."

In that same letter, he had written, "To tell you the truth, I don't want to go [to West Point] because whether a general or a private, you're still in the Army and I've finally discovered that I don't like the Army or any of its principles or ways, so don't think I'll make too red-hot an officer. I see now that West Point is far from being a bargain."

Was this a forewarning of some future act, or was it only the griping voice of a nineteen-year-old who had suffered a recent military unpleasantness such as guard duty on a weekend or a "chicken" reprimand, and who, on facing a long-term army commitment, was simply getting cold feet?

Cavanaugh next told Mrs. Cox about the "see Kelly" entry on Dick's desk calendar. The only Kelly she could think of was Dick's friend Jim, whose family spelled their name "Kelley." Jim was now a midshipman at Annapolis. The Kelleys lived on Third Street in Mansfield, which was where the Cox family lived when Dick was growing up.

A call was made to Midshipman James Kelley at the U.S. Naval Academy. Kelley, over the phone, said, "The last time I saw Dick was in Mansfield during the holidays. I told him then I would be seeing him the second weekend in February when I was going to West Point on an 'exchange' weekend. Since then I have heard nothing from Dick." Kelley suggested that Dick, in marking the date, had been merely careless, and by mistake he had circled the fifteenth of January rather than of February.

Midshipman Kelley also was asked if Cox had acted unhappy about being at West Point. "No," Kelley said, "in fact he gave me the impression that he planned to continue right on through graduation at the Academy."

Well, Cavanaugh thought, at least that clears up the mystery of the "see Kelly" entry. But it was another promising lead arriving at a dead end.

Cavanaugh had appreciated Minnie Cox's cooperation and eagerness to help. He had also appreciated the woman herself. She was a devout Christian Scientist, a courageous, strong-willed person who had been running a successful business these past ten years and at the same time raising her children. No doubt she was a dominant force in that family, especially with regard to Richard, her youngest. Was it possible that he'd left home and joined the army to escape that dominance? That was speculation, of course, but something to keep in mind.

After talking to Mrs. Cox, the next person Cavanaugh sought out was Betty Timmons, Dick Cox's fiancée. Although Betty and Dick had spent much time alone and confided in each other, she could think of no reason for him to have left the Academy. Some, of course, had heard him complain about the place, and at Christmastime she and Dick had even toyed with the idea of eloping. Once, in fact, they had started driving to Kentucky to get married there, but after thinking it over, they had abandoned the idea and agreed to postpone marriage until after Dick's graduation.

What about the disagreement someone mentioned? Betty said that was just Dick complaining about her friendship with a local boy, a Mansfield football player, but it had been resolved. They had definitely kissed and made up. In his last letter, in fact, after saying how much he missed her, Dick had written how he was counting the days until spring break, when they planned to get together in New York. Almost with a sigh, he had written, "We get off at 3 P.M., the 16th of March—seems like light years away."

In short, everyone agreed that Dick Cox, when they last saw him, fully intended to stay the course and graduate. Finally, after talking to Cox's family, friends, and schoolmates, Joe Cavanaugh had a good picture of Dick Cox's life prior to West Point and probably could have composed a rather fair biography.

Richard Colvin Cox, son of Rupert F. and Minnie Colvin Cox, was the youngest of six children. His father died when Richard was ten. (There had been rumors of suicide, but actually his death resulted from an aggravated diabetic condition. He'd been a practicing Christian Scientist; some said he would have lived much longer had he received proper medical attention.) Richard's mother, Mrs. Minnie Cox, was currently owner and operator of the family business, the Rupert F. Cox Insurance Agency. She was a good person and a good mother who seemed to dote on Richard, her youngest, whom she may have "babied."

Dick Cox attended six years of grammar school and two years of junior high, after which he entered Mansfield High School. He had been class treasurer in his freshman year, class president as a sophomore, and a member of the student council. He was active in intramural sports, the Pep Club, and Hi-Y, and he was also sports editor of the high school annual. The yearbook, which referred to him as one of its "mainstays," listed his nickname as "Harry" and his favorite subject as physics. It appeared he had been not only a popular student but also a very good one, and in 1946, upon graduation, he had been named a member of the National High School Honor Society.

For ten years, no doubt due to his mother's influence, Dick Cox had attended Christian Science Sunday school, although once he left home, he didn't seem to have maintained any church affiliation.

The summer after high school, Cox had worked in Mansfield as a truck driver for the National Ice Company, and in September he enlisted in the army. After his basic training at Fort Knox, he was sent to Germany, where he was assigned to Constabulary units, first in Coburg, then in Schweinfurt, where he was promoted to sergeant. While at Schweinfurt he applied for and received one of the competitive appointments reserved for members of the regular army; actual admission to the Academy, however, depended not only on passing an entrance exam but also on doing well against other army competitors. His mother, meanwhile, had secured for him a congressional appointment from Representative J. Harry McGregor of Ohio, which made the army appointment superfluous. This may have annoyed Cox, who probably would have preferred to gain admission without any help from a protective mother.

Dick Cox returned to the States in early 1948 to attend the West Point Preparatory School at Stewart Field. He was there from February until he entered the Academy in July. When on leave in Mansfield, he renewed his friendship with Betty Timmons, whom he'd dated in high school, and they had planned to marry following his graduation from West Point.

Well, that was it. Richard Cox appeared to be an intelligent, active, and likeable young man, one with a bright future. So where did the investigation go from here—back to finding "George"? For now, Cavanaugh decided he'd done all he could in Mansfield.

Back east, meanwhile, where several additional agents had joined the investigation, there seemed to be one simple, almost obvious, way to identify "George," the man who supposedly had served with Cox in Germany. A telegram went to the army's European Command, asking for the name of any soldier who had been in the same unit as Cox and who had either a first, middle, or last name of "George"—or even a nickname of "George."

A message came back that the units in question had been disbanded; all pertinent personnel records had been sent for storage to the Army Records Center in St. Louis.

The CID now had snapshots of Dick Cox's friends, lent to them by Mrs. Cox and by Bud Groner. At West Point, they showed the photos to Maresca and Samotis, the only cadets who had been able to describe Cox's visitor. Maresca, after studying them, picked out a man who seemed to resemble "George." On the back of the photo, in Cox's handwriting, was the name "Donald Karge."

A telegram was sent to the Adjutant General in Washington, asking for information about Karge. A prompt reply gave the information that Karge was now living in Chicago. After local CID agents went to Karge's home and questioned him, they found he was able to account for all his actions since January 7. He was well corroborated by witnesses, and Karge was eliminated as a suspect.

Ever since hearing of Cox talking to a man wearing a Constabulary patch, supposedly a recruiting sergeant from Stewart Field, the agents had been trying to locate the man. On February 1, an envelope from the Adjutant General's office in Washington arrived with an official photograph of the man in question. He was identified as First Sergeant Marion J. Newcombe, currently stationed at Camp Carson, Colorado. When Maresca and Samotis saw his picture, they were positive that Newcombe could not be the man they had seen, the one everyone now called "George."

Shortly after Joe Cavanaugh arrived back at West Point, the office received a phone call from Philadelphia. A man who said his name was John Perri said he might have seen that missing cadet, the one he'd read about in the papers. Perri said he was walking down Market Street when he and a young man in cadet uniform had bumped into each other. The cadet had apologized and then walked on. This was about 3 P.M. on January 30, and since Cox was the only cadet absent from West Point on that date, the report was taken seriously.

Perri's information was relayed to CID agent Jim Ryan, who was handling the Cox case in the Philadelphia area. On February 1, Ryan talked to Perri, who added a few details to what he'd said on the phone. When the cadet bumped into him, Perri said, he was walking down Market Street, near Sixteenth. The cadet, after apologizing, had resumed walking, in the direction of Fifteenth Street. There was a man walking beside the cadet, but Perri wasn't sure whether the two were together. The other man, according to Perri, was about twenty-eight years old, about five-foot-ten, and weighed around 175 to 180. He had been wearing a brown hat and a brown topcoat. Ryan made the obvious connection—could this have been "George"? Or was Perri just quoting information he had seen in the papers or in a missing person report?

When shown photos of Cox, Perri said he just couldn't be sure if this was the cadet he had seen. Perri went on to tell Ryan that he had been in the army but had been sent home from overseas in October 1944 and given a "blue" discharge, with "blue" presumably referring to some deficiency. He had protested this type of discharge, he said, and it had been changed to "honorable."

Although Ryan had no clear reason to disbelieve Perri, he tended to be skeptical. In his report, he described Perri as an "extremely fat" person, presently unemployed, who was hoping a few dollars would come his way; as the report put it, Perri was seeking "monetary assistance." In other words, this report might be phony. Nevertheless, Ryan passed it on to a detective named Canning in the missing persons bureau of the Philadelphia Police Department. Canning said he'd have the police keep a lookout for anyone answering Cox's description.

Jim Ryan had been busy. Two days earlier, based on a further request from Captain Wedbush at First Army, Ryan had returned to the Groner home in Langhorne. Once again he had asked Groner if he had any ideas about "George." Since they last talked, Groner said, he had remembered a fellow who had been with him and Cox in Marburg. He said the man's name *could* have been "George," but he wasn't sure. In fact, he couldn't even say whether George had been a first or a last name.

Then the questioning took a different turn. Rather pointedly, Ryan asked Groner if he was aware of the penalty for harboring a fugitive, and he went on to ask Groner if he could account for his whereabouts on the weekends of January 7 and 8 and 14 and 15. Bud Groner, who didn't much appreciate this line of questioning, said he certainly could. On both those weekends, he had been on a date with a Miss Laverne Groff of Cornwells Heights, Pennsylvania, and nowhere near West Point!

With the Cox case receiving increased publicity in the New York area, citizens began to phone in tips. Some asked to remain anonymous; others gave their names. One such tip gave a possible reason for Cox to run away. An unmarried girl Cox had known in Newburgh, it was said, was now in a New York hospital's maternity ward and about to give birth. An agent visited the young woman, who said she remembered Cox quite well and had dated him a few times when he was stationed at Stewart Field. However, she went on to say that she had not seen Cox since he became a cadet, and he definitely was *not* the father of her child.

While the Cox story continued to be covered in the New York press, it got even greater coverage in Cox's home state of Ohio. In Columbus, the stories triggered a reaction from a former West Point cadet who was now a part-time student at Ohio State. The young man, who had dropped out of the Academy a year earlier, had known Cox only slightly. When he saw the story in the papers, he had first assumed Cox would turn up in a day or two, but when that didn't happen, he had decided to come forward with a piece of information that might help.

The ex-cadet first called the FBI and was told that they did not yet have authority to investigate the case. He then called *The Columbus Evening Dispatch* and talked to reporter Lester Ealy. In the latter part of 1948, he told Ealy, he had run into Dick Cox at Grant Hall. They had begun talking and discovered that they were both from the same state. During their conversation, Cox had said he was suffering from severe frequent headaches as a result of having struck his head while swimming. As they talked, he said, he had noticed that Cox's eyes kept blinking and his face had an extreme pallor. Cox, when he told him about the head injury, had asked him not to say anything. He feared that if his injury became known, the authorities might release him because of physical disability.

Reporter Ealy called Mrs. Cox in Mansfield to tell her of this new development. Her reaction was one of disbelief. Her son Richard, she said, had never mentioned any such injury. What's more, she pointed out, this conversation supposedly took place in the fall of '48, when Dick was a plebe, and plebes weren't even *allowed* into Grant Hall.

Ealy mentioned this to the former cadet, who, upon reflection, decided the conversation had taken place not *in* Grant Hall but rather in the immediate vicinity. In any case, Ealy told army authorities about the report, and two CID agents from nearby Fort Hayes went to the Ohio State campus in Columbus to interview the student. During the interview, they were impressed by both his manner and his general character. They felt sure he was not a publicity seeker but rather merely someone trying to help.

At West Point on February 8, a meeting was held in the office of Superintendent Bryant E. Moore. On hand with Moore were Colonel Harkins, Lieutenant Colonel Howell, and CID agents Kaplan and Cavanaugh. The group made plans to search the West Point reservation thoroughly, drag Lusk Reservoir, opposite the football stadium, and drain Delafield Pond at the cadet recreation area on post. They also wanted to drag the various lakes and ponds on the reservation but would have to wait because most were still frozen over. Because of recent heavy snowfalls, the ground search also would have to be delayed.

At the same meeting, Moore approved having someone contact a New York radio station to ask for help. Accordingly, on February 9, a call was made to Robert Montgomery, a popular personality on New York station WJZ whose evening program was popular among cadets. More than happy to oblige, Montgomery asked his listeners to be on the lookout for Cox, and for many nights thereafter, he signed off each show by saying: "Richard Cox—call your mother!"

The group that had met on the eighth assembled again in Superintendent Moore's office on February 13. This time they were joined by an FBI agent. Two weeks earlier, Moore had asked for help from the FBI, but so far, while they had cooperated, it had been on an informal basis. On February 11, Cox's congressman, J. Harry McGregor, had phoned the Bureau with a similar request.

Under army regulations, the status of a person missing for thirty days can be changed from AWOL (absent without leave) to that of "deserter." Now that thirty days had passed, Cox technically could be so classified, which enabled the FBI to enter the case. General Moore asked them to do so. The FBI man said he would relay the general's request to his New York office.

Next day, the FBI informed General Moore that the request was approved. They would enter the case officially, conduct an investigation, and assist in every way possible. Soon Kaplan and Cavanaugh, happy for the help, were briefing the FBI on what they had learned to date.

A few days earlier, as part of Operation "Who the hell is George?" CID agent Del Comstock, acting on information received from Europe, had gone to St. Louis. Once there, he had rolled up his sleeves and begun working his way through boxes of dusty files at the Army Records Center. Comstock went over Richard Cox's service record, making notes on dates, places, and units. He then scrutinized the records of those same units, looking for anyone named "George."

It was a boring, tedious, and time-consuming task, but on February 13 he was rewarded. In Cox's file, Comstock found a special order, dated March 1947; paragraph 27 of that order transferred Cox from "C" Troop to Headquarters Troop of the Sixth Constabulary Regiment, Coburg, Germany. Paragraph 28 of the same order showed a Private J. T. George also assigned to the Sixth Constabulary in Coburg.

Further investigation revealed that Private George had returned from overseas four months earlier, in October 1949. He had been discharged December 5, 1949, and reenlisted the following day. He was then assigned to an artillery battery at Fort Benning, Georgia. At present, George was with his unit on amphibious maneuvers at Little Creek Naval Base in Virginia. In George's personnel file, Comstock also found a physical description. Private J. T. George was five-foot-eleven, weighed 150 to 155, and had brown hair, gray eyes, and even features.

Could this be *the* "George"? The physical description seemed to fit, and, to make the discovery even more exciting, *Private George had been on furlough at the beginning of January.*

Del Comstock, returning from St. Louis, teamed up with Joe Cavanaugh. The two headed south, and when Private J. T. George returned from maneuvers, they were waiting for him. Where did he go on furlough? Where was he on the first two weekends in January? Was he at West Point? No, he said, right after reenlisting, he and his wife had left Fort Benning and had driven to his home in Charlestown, Texas. His reenlistment leave had been for only thirty days, and he had returned on time, signing in on January 7. The unit's morning report verified this: J. T. George was listed as present for duty on the seventh. In addition, both his battery and battalion commanders assured the agents that George had been with the unit constantly since his return.

When asked about Cox, George said he couldn't remember him and looked vague. He was also vague when it came to recalling any names, dates, or places from his time in Coburg, making the CID men suspicious. However, when they talked to other members of the unit, they smiled and said that in their opinion the guy *always* sounded vague.

The investigators were disappointed. This lead had been the most promising yet, and once more they had come up empty. So as not to waste the trip entirely, however, Cavanaugh and Comstock, on the way north, made a stop at Langhorne, Pennsylvania, for another session with Bud Groner. Groner, who had had more than his share of CID visitors, nevertheless remained cooperative, telling all he could remember about Dick Cox's friends, traits, and habits—anything that might help the authorities to find his friend. He again gave the names of soldiers who had known Cox, and this time mentioned a new one. In his opinion the one who sounded most like Cox's visitor "George" was Sergeant David Westervelt, who had been Cox's immediate superior in Coburg, and he urged the investigators to check on him.

By now, although Groner didn't know it, he himself was being kept under surveillance, and his phone had been tapped. Similarly, in Ohio, a watch was being kept on both the Cox home and the home of Betty Timmons, with phone taps also placed on each home.

About this time, a surprising call came from the West Point post office. A letter written by Dick Cox had just been returned, marked "undeliverable." The FBI took possession of the letter, opened it, and saw it had been written two months earlier, on December 11, and addressed to Fraulein Rosemary Vogel of Lichtenfels-am-Main, West Germany.

"Today I was looking through some of the pictures I took of Germany," Cox began, "and noticed yours and 'Luty,' so I decided to write." After asking Rosemary if she remembered him, Cox asked if she would be interested in exchanging a few letters.

The FBI found the next part of the letter rather baffling. "I've enclosed two pictures," Cox wrote, "one taken in the air corps barracks at Schweinfurt and the other here at West Point this year." The envelope, however, contained *no* pictures. Had Cox merely forgotten to include them? Had someone removed the photos from the envelope and then resealed it? Moreover, in searching his effects, they had not found the pictures of Germany he had mentioned "looking over."

So far the case had produced little by way of substantive evidence. The CID—and now the FBI—had been hoping for a break, and maybe this would be it. They examined the letter closely for possible clues. Cox had mentioned being with his army friend, Joseph Groner, of visiting Rosemary in the summer of 1947, and of going boating with her and her brother.

Cox also had written that he was studying Russian, including a phrase written in the Cyrillic alphabet that puzzled the FBI, although it was simply "do you understand Russian?"*—elementary for any new student, like *"parlez-vous Français"* for a French beginner. "Not too easy a language," he continued. "Not too good a people to deal with, either."

Cox closed the letter by asking Rosemary Vogel, "What is the Russian situation in Lichtenfels and the vicinity? . . . I'm very interested in the Russian situation, of course, or anything else you'd like to tell me. And let me know if there is anything I can do for you."

The FBI went over the letter again and again. Trying to find any hidden meaning or code, they even had the note studied by cryptographic experts. On the surface, of course, it all seemed rather innocuous. Still, why the sudden interest in Russia and the situation near Lichtenfels? The next step, obviously, would be to turn this over to army investigators in Europe. Their job would be to locate Rosemary Vogel, after which they might learn whether the letter had any special significance.

It was still February when Bud Groner, who had acquired a private pilot's license on the GI Bill, flew to Ohio to visit the Cox family. Since he considered himself to be Dick's closest friend, it seemed

---

*Вы понимаете по-руский?

the right thing to do. Minnie Cox and the others appreciated the visit, needless to say, but they were disappointed that Groner was as much in the dark as they were about Dick's disappearance.

They asked when he had last gotten together with Dick, and he explained that it was after the 1948 Army-Navy game. Although Groner also attended the '49 game, he had not seen Dick on that occasion. Dick, about to go on a trip to Michigan with the cross-country team, had later apologized and said he was sorry they couldn't spend any time together. Still, it had been a great game, at least for Army fans. Led by team captain John Trent and quarter-back Arnold Galiffa, the cadets had scored a lopsided 38-0 victory.

Funny thing about that game, Groner told them. He had asked Dick to buy six tickets for him, but for some reason Dick had sent only five. Then, at the game, in an adjacent seat, evidently using what would have been the sixth of Dick's tickets, was a very attractive young lady, about nineteen years old, five-foot-seven, reddish brown hair, wearing a fur coat. Maybe *she* would know something about Dick. At least they should try to find out who she was.

At this point, Groner, playing detective, had what appeared to be a stroke of luck. As he looked through photo albums at the Cox home, he suddenly found a picture of Cox, another cadet, and the young woman he had seen at the game.

It seemed to Groner that either a CID man or an FBI man had come to his home in Langhorne every two or three days to question him. Now, in Mansfield, he was interviewed once more. Doing his best to be helpful, he mentioned the "mystery girl" at the Army-Navy game. The agents borrowed the photo from Mrs. Cox and sent it back east for follow-up.

The New York papers had continued to cover the Cox case, and one recent story had included photos of Cox's roommates, Deane Welch and Joe Urschel. This may have prompted two very strange letters mailed to Joe Urschel from Greenwich Village. The first letter writer said he wanted to give Urschel a message, namely, that his roommate Cox was at present in Greenwich Village, where he was being held as a "love prisoner."

The second letter writer said he had seen Urschel's picture in the paper and thought Joe was a nice-looking boy; he asked if Urschel would like to spend a weekend in New York with him. Urschel, calling the letters "crackpot," turned them over to the FBI for what-ever use they might be.

On February 28, the Cox twins, Nancy and Carolyn, waited by the phone. This was the day their "little brother" always called to wish them a happy birthday. If Dick was alive somewhere, they felt certain he would try to get in touch. The hours passed, but the telephone never rang. At day's end, each of the twins had the same thought: Their brother was dead; probably he had been murdered. Painful as it was, they felt they might as well accept it.

On March 1, Kaplan and Cavanaugh decided to call it quits at West Point. They told the authorities they would, of course, be continuing the investigation, but for now they felt they had exhausted all leads at the Military Academy.

Meanwhile, at Providence, Rhode Island, other CID agents were interviewing Bob Gandert, a Mansfield boy attending Brown University. According to Minnie Cox, Bob Gandert was one of her son's closest friends.

Like others they had interviewed, Gandert could give no reason for Cox's disappearance. He mentioned, however, that Dick once told him about having testified at a court-martial in Germany. He understood that the unknown individual was later convicted and sent to jail. Wasn't it possible, said Gandert, that the man Dick had testified against had later sought revenge?

By March 13, the snow at West Point had melted enough to make a thorough ground search feasible. Cadets joined garrison troops in combing all fifteen thousand acres of the rugged West Point terrain. Meanwhile, the lakes, ponds, and Lusk Reservoir were being either dragged or drained.

Thanks to the cooperation of Commissioner William O'Brien, a helicopter from the New York City Police Department joined in the search, scanning those areas of the reservation that were inaccessible on foot.

The *New York Times*, reporting the event, called it a "back breaking job, involving mountain climbing in miniature and frequent tumbles into snow-filled ravines." The searchers, it was said, were "literally beating every bush and examining every stone."

The search continued every day for a frustrating, disappointing week. Nothing. At week's end, Provost Marshal Ed Howell, talking to a reporter, said what everyone had felt but no one wanted to admit: "I am convinced it was foul play. . . . I am sure that we shall not find him alive."

On March 14, Military Academy authorities announced that Cadet Richard Cox was being dropped from the rolls as a deserter.

Normally, the announcement said, this would have taken place after he had been absent for thirty days. However, in view of "the unusual nature" of the case, the action had been delayed for an additional month.

On Tuesday, March 20, two boys came to the police station in Garfield, New Jersey. In the Sunday paper, they had seen a story about the missing cadet, and they thought that maybe he had drowned. At least they knew something that made it look that way. What was that? Well, they had been playing on the banks of the Passaic River, and they had found a pair of gray pants with black stripes down the side, the kind cadets wear.

They were asked when this had happened, and they said it had been around 2:30 on Sunday afternoon, January 21, one week after Cox disappeared. There was also a gray sport shirt and some plain black shoes. They hadn't picked up anything, and hadn't mentioned it to anyone. However, when they saw the story in the papers, they decided to come to the police.

The boys showed one of the officers where they had seen the clothes, which meanwhile had disappeared. The Garfield police, after notifying the FBI and nearby police departments, arranged to have the river dredged below the site in question.

On March 21, David Myron Westervelt, one of the men who had served with Cox in Germany, and who Groner felt resembled "George," was interviewed at his home in Bergenfield, New Jersey, by CID agents and a detective from the Bergenfield Police Department.

Westervelt—age twenty-five, five-foot-eleven, 140 pounds, brown hair, slender build, light complexion, a neat dresser—generally fit the description of "George" as given by witnesses Samotis and Maresca. Interest picked up when, through the assistance of the FBI, a background check was obtained, showing that in 1943, at age seventeen, he had been arrested by the FBI for transporting a stolen vehicle across state lines.

Westervelt said he and Cox had both been attached to the Sixth Constabulary in Germany during the months of May, June, and July of 1947. After that, he never saw Cox again, and he hadn't even known Cox was at West Point until he saw an article in a New York newspaper about his being missing.

Westervelt told the agents he had never been to West Point, and on January 14, the night of Cox's disappearance, he was at a wheelchair basketball game in Teaneck, New Jersey, between the Jersey

Wheelers and the Bullovas, along with his wife, aunt, and uncle. By way of confirmation, he showed the agents a program from the game.

When questioned further, Westervelt said he and his wife were supposed to have had dinner that evening with his aunt and uncle and then go to the game. For some reason they did not meet at dinner, but instead the other couple picked them up at their home around 7:30. They then went to the game, which started at eight, stayed until it was over, went to a roadside diner, where they stayed until around 12:30, after which they returned home and went to bed.

Westervelt could not account accurately for his time before 7:30 on that date, but he believed that he and his wife had been together at home from about 5 P.M. and had had dinner at home.

Westervelt's wife, uncle, and aunt all supported his story. Although it seemed unlikely that David Westervelt was "George," the agents took photos of him to send to the New York office. They also felt it might be good to have Westervelt take a polygraph.

With publicity continuing to mount, the powerful J. Edgar Hoover decided to become personally involved. On March 22, a teletype originating in the office of the director and marked URGENT was sent to the special agents in charge of the FBI's New York and Cleveland offices. The final sentence read: "This case must be given expeditious and continuous attention. Bureau should be advised by teletype of all pertinent developments. Hoover."

Chapter 4

An Abundance of Leads

The 1950 Gloom Period came to a close. Spring arrived in the Hudson Valley, snow melted, the Plain turned green, and there was a noticeable lifting of spirits. For cadets, spring meant not only less gloom, more sunshine, and frequent parades, but also a new athletic season. Varsity and intramural sports—baseball, tennis, golf, lacrosse, track—became an integral part of cadet life. It was now also time for spring break, the eagerly anticipated long weekend.

For Betty Timmons, however, it was a time of disappointment. She had last seen Dick Cox on January 1, when she and Dick's mother had driven him to Cleveland and waved goodbye as he caught a train to return to West Point. Before he left, she had promised Dick that she would meet him in New York during spring break; both of them had been counting on it. They had even set the time, 3 P.M. on March 16, although they hadn't yet agreed on a meeting place.

On March 18, a story in the *New York Times* said that everything pointed to Cox having been murdered but added that family and friends were pinning their hopes on the fact that no body had been found. The story went on to say: "Reached at their respective Mansfield (Ohio) homes, widowed Mrs. Rupert Cox, and attractive, 20-year-old Betty Timmons both admitted, however, that the weight of evidence was tipping the scales against what they wanted to believe. 'I can't believe he's dead; I won't believe it,' said Miss Timmons, who was to have come east to West Point this weekend to spend the traditional spring leave as a guest of her fiancé."

After their weekend together, Betty had planned to find a job in New York so she could remain closer to West Point. Then, after Dick disappeared, she and Dick's mother had considered coming east in March to meet with the West Point authorities. They had decided, however, after talking to Bill Colby, to postpone their trip until mid-April, when perhaps something more would be known.

Detective Colby, Dick's brother-in-law, more or less representing the family, had come to West Point in February to see what he could learn and also to chase down a rumor. A Newburgh newspaper had received an anonymous tip that Dick Cox, while in Germany, had witnessed a murder and had testified against the killer. The Newburgh paper had passed this on to the *Toledo Blade*, which in turn relayed it to the *Mansfield News-Journal*. When Colby asked the people at West Point, he was told that the tip was a bit different from what he'd heard. According to the anonymous source, Cox had testified against someone charged only with *complicity* in the murder. Supposedly the soldier had been sentenced to two years of confinement, which meant he would have been released about the time of Cox's disappearance.

Colby learned that reporters had asked the West Point authorities about the tip. At the time, a spokesman had said that the report had been investigated, but that the army was unable to find records of the trial or of Cox's testimony. However, the spokesman said, "There have been a number of unsolved killings in Germany and we are still investigating the story."

Earlier, Minnie Cox had told CID agent Joe Cavanaugh that she had never heard any such tale from Dick; all in all, both the Cox family and the authorities at West Point tended to discount the story.

Mt. Gilead, Ohio, is a small town about twenty miles southwest of Mansfield on State Route 42. At the end of January, a young couple had driven into the Cities Service gas station in Mt. Gilead, and after buying gas, had said they were on their way to Kentucky to elope. They had then asked Lloyd Lust, the attendant, if there was a jewelry store in town where they could buy a ring.

Three days later, the same couple had reappeared at Lust's station, saying they were now back from Kentucky and had just been married. They had purchased four dollars worth of gas, but were unable to pay. The man, saying he'd return soon with the money, had then left a gray tweed topcoat as a security deposit.

In the third week of March, *The Columbus Dispatch* ran an article on Cox that included his picture. In Mt. Gilead, Lloyd Lust, seeing the photo, told himself, "That's the man!"

Lust remembered the couple who had come to his place about six weeks earlier. It wasn't likely he could forget them; the tweed topcoat left as security deposit was still hanging in his station. An agitated Lust called the FBI to say he had news about the missing cadet.

Within hours, FBI agents were in Mt. Gilead, where Lust told them of the couple who had been at his station not once, but twice, the second time after having been married in Kentucky. The agents showed Lust a picture of Dick Cox, and he said it was "identical" to the young fellow he had seen. The man had been driving a maroon station wagon, possibly a Ford, Lust said, and he had written down the license number. Also, on the first visit the man had cashed an American Express traveler's check, which Lust had deposited in his account at the bank. The couple needed the money, Lust explained, because they were heading to a jewelry store to pick out a ring. As he warmed to the story, Lust added that he now "believed he recalled" that the man had signed the check "Richard Cox."

When Lust was shown a photo of Betty Timmons, he didn't think that was the young woman he had seen. In Mansfield, meanwhile, FBI agents verified that Timmons had not left town during the dates in question.

A check with marriage license bureaus in all neighboring Kentucky counties found that no one named Cox had obtained a license there in recent weeks. Also, at Lust's bank, the Mt. Gilead First National, there was no record of a traveler's check having been deposited by Lust, either one endorsed by Cox or by anyone else. A query to American Express, moreover, showed no record of Richard Cox *ever* having purchased or cashed one of their checks. At that, Lust said maybe he hadn't deposited Cox's check; perhaps he had cashed it. Thanks to a Recordac machine, there was a photographic record of all checks processed by First National. Agents, hoping to find the questioned item, and with the help of bank employees, began looking at pictures of every check handled by the bank since January 15. No such check could be found.

At Spencers, Mt. Gilead's only jewelry store, the matter was finally resolved. The jeweler said a young man had indeed bought a wedding band from him on January 30. The man had given the name of Robert Billson, and he said he was from Madison, Ohio. Billson, when located, said that on January 30 he and his wife had eloped. They had stopped in Mt. Gilead for gas and to buy a ring

and had then driven to Covington, Kentucky, where they had obtained a marriage license and then married on February 2. On the
way home, they again stopped in Mt. Gilead for gas and had left
Billson's topcoat as security deposit when they were unable to pay.
Billson's uncle, who had purchased the station wagon for his
nephew, confirmed the story and showed a vehicle registration with
the same license number as that written down by Lust.

The well-meaning Lust was not the best of witnesses. According
to his World War II supervisor at the North Electrical Manufactur-
ing Company, Lust during the war often reported "suspected sabo-
teurs," and none of his reports was ever substantiated. This time
his imagination, rather than being quietly disregarded, had resulted
in widespread publicity. Nearly every paper in Ohio had carried the
story of the Mt. Gilead sighting, with its romantic implication that
Dick Cox had run away from West Point to get married. Now they
had to run a retraction; the search for Cox was back to square one.

On March 24, at the request of the Tenth CID, David Westervelt
came to the office on Whitehall Street in lower Manhattan to take a
polygraph. Despite what seemed to be a good alibi, Westervelt remained a suspect, if for no other reason, because of a past history
that included a 1943 arrest by the FBI. Meanwhile, Cadets Mauro
Maresca and John Samotis, the two who had seen "George," had
been brought to the New York CID offices so they could observe
Westervelt in person.

In both cases, results were inconclusive. The polygraph operator
said there was no way he could establish any intent to deceive.
However, the operator pointed out that certain Westervelt "mannerisms" during the examination could have invalidated the test. The
cadets, for their part, said Westervelt was the "same type" as the
man they had seen, but "they could not state for certain that he is
the same person." Suspicions still lingered, but only faintly.

Back at West Point, investigators said that Delafield Pond was one
of the likeliest places on the Academy reservation to hide a body.
If Cox had been murdered and digging a grave had not been feasible, the killer might well have dropped the body into Delafield's
cold, dark waters. Delafield was a popular cadet recreation and
swimming area that was alive with activity on summer weekends,
but on the winter evening of January 14, it would almost surely
have been deserted.

In the last week of March, post engineers began the process of
draining Delafield. As the last waters ebbed away, Academy offi-

cials, joined by FBI and CID representatives, watched intently. An FBI teletype told the story. On March 31, 1950, FBI agent Scheidt in New York sent this message to Director J. Edgar Hoover in Washington:

DRAINING OF DELAFIELD POND COMPLETED AND THOROUGH SEARCH OF BASIN EFFECTED. NO TRACE OF COX FOUND. DISTRICT ATTORNEY CLARE HOYT, ORANGE COUNTY, NY, REQUESTED THIS OFFICE TO ADVISE HIM IMMEDIATELY IF CADET COX'S BODY SHOULD BE FOUND, SINCE IT IS HIS DESIRE TO HAVE SAME EXAMINED BY A REPRESENTATIVE OF THE NYC MEDICAL EXAMINERS OFFICE. INASMUCH AS PORTION OF WEST POINT RESERVATION STILL REMAINS UNDER THE JURISDICTION OF STATE OF NY, HOYT ADVISED THAT HE BELIEVED A COMPETENT EXAMINATION OF THE BODY SHOULD BE MADE IMMEDIATELY, AND THE QUESTION OF JURISDICTION DETERMINED LATER. MR. HOYT ADVISED THAT BOTH HE AND THE SHERIFF OF ORANGE COUNTY WOULD BE NOTIFIED IN THE EVENT THAT CADET COX'S BODY IS LOCATED EITHER IN WEST POINT OR ANY OTHER SECTION OF ORANGE COUNTY BUT THAT THE QUESTION OF JURISDICTION MUST BE DISCUSSED.

This message suggested that Dick Cox, even if his body was found, would remain a subject of jurisdictional controversy.

Now that Delafield Pond had been drained and found empty, attention turned to other nearby bodies of water. Between April 3 and 8, grappling hooks were used to drag the various lakes and ponds on the West Point reservation. Lusk Reservoir, Long Pond, Round Pond, and Lake Popolopen were all searched with negative results.

As mentioned earlier, Bud Groner, when he was in Mansfield, had found a picture of Cox, a second cadet, and the "mystery girl" from the Army-Navy game. The FBI's Cleveland office obtained the snapshot from Mrs. Cox and forwarded it to New York. When the picture was shown to Cox's friends at West Point, the other cadet was easily recognized. He, in turn, identified the young woman in the photo, who had been dating someone other than Cox, and said the picture had been taken the previous summer at Camp Buckner.

The young lady was interviewed at her home in Albany, New York. She explained that she had been someone else's guest at the game, and she was unable to add anything helpful to the investigation.

Tips of all varieties continued to arrive. A woman in Long Island City said two men representing the Continental Publishing Company came to her home selling magazines. One of them, she said, bore a strong resemblance to Richard Cox. The publishing company was contacted, and the young salesman to whom she referred was located. He bore a slight, but only a slight, resemblance to Cox.

Mrs. Cox received an anonymous letter postmarked Marion, Ohio. The woman who wrote said she had heard Cadet Cox on a radio quiz show sometime after mid-January. It was either, she said, on Walter O'Keefe's *Double or Nothing* show, or Jim Ameche's *Welcome Traveler* program. The writer claimed the participant gave his name as "Cox" and said he was from Mansfield, Ohio. "I am not a crank," the woman wrote, adding, "I know how you feel as I have children and grandchildren. . . . Hope and pray he will return to you well and sound."

As it happened, another woman, Florence Gillman of Amherst, Ohio, had listened to the same programs. Mrs. Gillman, after seeing a story about Cox in the Cleveland *Plain Dealer*, wrote to Detective Bill Colby, mentioned both the *Double or Nothing* and *Welcome Traveler* shows, and said: "It seems to me that I heard the name Cox on a quiz program. . . . The young man said he was a navy cadet and when asked what brought him out there (to California) he said he was on a trip or vacation or something of the kind. I remember thinking 'there is something fishy about that' as I never knew cadets to be allowed to take trips just when they felt like it."

Colby sent a copy of the letter to Joe Cavanaugh with a personal note: "Joe, if you can find time to drop me a line, I would like to know if it was ever definitely established that Cox testified at a court-martial in Germany, or not. Also I would like to know what has developed in the search for 'George,' and what you have learned about the sergeant you suspected. Of course I realize you may not be able to disclose certain facts that your investigation has revealed."

There was still, of course, no record that Cox ever testified at a court-martial. As for the sergeant, presumably Cavanaugh had been referring to David Westervelt, but without mentioning any name.

Interest in Cox had spread nationwide. In New Haven, Connecticut, a man told the FBI he felt he had a duty to report an itinerant restaurant worker named "George" who he believed was the man they were looking for in the Cox case. In Denver, Colorado, the military police learned that two men had applied for a chauffeur's license, and one of them supposedly had given his name as Richard C. Cox.

In Philadelphia, an off-duty bus driver named Regan told the police that on March 17 he saw a young man in cadet uniform at the J&M Restaurant on Broad and Cumberland Streets. He was shown a photo of Cox but said he couldn't be sure if it was the same man. When employees at the restaurant were interviewed, a waitress and a short-order cook remembered seeing someone in a gray, cadet-type uniform, but they couldn't say if it was Cox. The waitress recalled, however, that the man had gold stripping between his teeth and was about six-foot-one, which seemed to rule out the five-foot-eight Richard Cox.

All leads were run down, no matter how unlikely. In response to a request from the FBI, producers of the two radio quiz shows reviewed all program tapes since January, after which they were able to say definitely that no West Point cadet had been on either program. They guessed that the letter writers, after reading about Cox, and with the best of intentions, had combined two separate bits of memory rather ingeniously. There had been a *navy* cadet on one of the Walter O'Keefe shows in early January. Days later, on another program, one of the guests was named Cox. He was *Bert* Cox, a middle-aged, long-time resident of Hollywood.

Investigating some of the leads involved considerable difficulty. The Denver license applicant, *Stanley* Cox, was located only after an extensive search. He and another man had responded to an ad in the *Denver Post*, in which an elderly couple named Berger had said they needed someone to drive them to California. They had done so, and evidently the man was still in California. At some point, perhaps for fun, he may even have told the Bergers that he was a West Point cadet. The Bergers, after being shown a photo of Richard Cox, said it was not the same man.

Back east in New Jersey, bodies were recovered from the Delaware River at two different locations. In view of the cadet-type trousers and shoes seen earlier on a riverbank by two boys (even though it was a different river, the Passaic), there was initial speculation that one of these bodies might be that of Cox. The youngsters who had found the items were shown a pair of West Point trousers and cadet black shoes, borrowed from an ex-cadet who lived nearby, and were asked if they were the same type. The shoes were the same, they said, but the trousers were a bit different. On the ones they

had seen, the black stripe seemed to be wider. Also, they remembered a name had been written inside that pair in indelible ink. It
was six or seven letters long—definitely longer than "Cox"—and
they thought it began with "MA."

Eventually the first drowning victim, whose body had been recovered near Frenchtown, was identified as Charles Dwyer from
Phillipsburg, New Jersey. The second body, recovered near Camden,
remained unidentified, but was ruled out as a Cox possibility because the physical dimensions were quite different and there were
also tattoos on the body. Dredging the Passaic River near Garfield,
where the trousers and shoes had been seen, also proved negative.

One FBI agent, as he scanned the CID files, took note of the report that Cox had struck his head while swimming and subsequently suffered from violent headaches. When he talked to Mrs.
Cox about this, she told him the same thing she had told the CID:
She didn't believe the story. If it had been true, she felt sure Dick
would have mentioned it to her.

What about the family doctor? Would he know? Actually, she
said, she and her family were all practicing Christian Scientists. Consequently, they did not have a family doctor.

Betty Timmons said she, too, disbelieved the story. She and Dick
had been together constantly when he was home on leave. The only
time he had been swimming, he had been with her, and she would
have known if he had hurt himself. Moreover, in his many letters
to her, he had never mentioned headaches.

Then the ex-cadet who had initiated the story called on Minnie
Cox and repeated what he had said earlier—that Dick had frequent
headaches as a result of having hit his head while swimming. He
went on to say that he himself had been hit on the head recently;
he had been assaulted while walking the streets of Columbus, Ohio.
He had also received threatening phone calls from an unknown man
telling him to stay out of the matter concerning the disappearance
of Richard Cox. Mrs. Cox said that the young man appeared to her
to be suffering from a mental disorder, which not only put his story
in perspective but also made it highly suspect.

A new lead came on March 24, when Detective Carey of the New
York City Police Department received a call from a Mrs. DeCarlo,
manager of the Inwood Hotel on Tenth Avenue, who said that the
previous night, around 8:30, two men had come to her hotel, one
of whom she believed to be Richard Cox. The taller of the two had
done all the talking, and when speaking to his friend, he had called

him "Cox." She was emphatic on this point. The taller man wore a lumberjack-type jacket; the shorter (Cox) had on a trench coat. The taller man said he wanted to rent a room for his friend, but when she told him the price, he said that was too much, and he asked directions to the nearest reasonable hotel. She said all nearby hotels cost about the same and suggested they try something in midtown, such as the Sloane House YMCA. Tonight, Mrs. DeCarlo said, she was reading a late newspaper that contained a picture of Cox, and she recognized him as the man who had been at her hotel the previous evening.

Detective Carey called the Brooklyn Army Base and told the Army CID about the report. Pat Kane, the CID investigator who took the call, went immediately to the Sloane House. He checked the register, found no listing for Cox, and then talked to Mr. Derony, the night clerk on duty. He showed Derony several photos of Cox and asked if he had seen the man. The clerk said he had. The night before, shortly after midnight, someone resembling the man in the photos had come into the Sloane House lobby accompanied by a very attractive young woman. The man tried to call a guest at the hotel, but Derony told him no calls to guest rooms were permitted after midnight. The girl then said, "Let's get out of here."

According to Derony, the man wore a short-sleeved shirt and had a trench coat over his left arm. As they talked, Derony noticed that the man had a scar on his right arm. He specifically remembered this, he said, because it was very similar to a scar he had on his own arm.

This information was passed to Agent Joe Cavanaugh, who came to New York the next day, talked first to Agent Pat Kane, and then interviewed Mrs. DeCarlo at the Inwood and night clerk Derony at the Sloane House.

At first it sounded like two different people being described, one accompanied by a taller male friend, and the other by a young woman. In both instances, however, the alleged Cox had a trench coat, one time wearing it, the other time carrying it over his arm. Even more telling, though, seemed to be the scar. Pat Kane insisted that Derony had described the scar without prompting and without seeing the mention of it on the missing person circular. Moreover, said Kane, Derony's scar *did* look like the one described on the circular. Cavanaugh wondered, after so many false alarms, did they now have a truly valid sighting?

On April 3, the Army European Command, on the chance that Cox might have fled to Germany or somewhere else on the Continent, distributed hundreds of wanted circulars, printed in English, German, and French. Next, although Cox had been dropped from the rolls as a deserter for nearly a month, the Department of the Army closed the loop by issuing an official notification. On April 11, Major General Edward Witsell, the U.S. Army Adjutant General, sent the following letter to Mrs. Rupert Cox: "The Department of the Army is deeply concerned over the disappearance of your son from the Military Academy and will continue its efforts to locate him. I have been assured by the Honorable J. Edgar Hoover that the Federal Bureau of Investigation will cooperate fully in this search. I believe that everything possible is being done to solve the mystery of your son's disappearance." Tactfully, the letter did not use the word "deserter."

April turned into May, and the academic year was drawing to a close. May is probably everyone's favorite month at West Point. Days are mild, mostly sunny, and the Academy grounds, groomed to perfection, show to full advantage. Visitors during the month are thrilled by spectacular full-dress parades and reviews, and cadets (while perceiving these same events as penance rather than pleasure) are cheerfully looking forward to graduation and summer leave.

May is also the month when the class yearbook, the *Howitzer*, is published. In the sports section of the 1950 *Howitzer*, there was a picture of the championship 1949 cross-country team. Included in the group photo were Dick Cox, team captain Dick Lewandowski, and Cox's classmate Dick Shea. Special mention was made of Shea, who was becoming known as the finest distance runner in Academy history. Prior to West Point, coincidentally, Cox and Shea, as enlisted men stationed in Germany, had met at an army track meet in Berlin.

Cadets still talked about a member of the Corps disappearing, but as each day passed and nothing more was learned, they spent less and less time wondering, "Whatever happened to Dick Cox?" Almost before they knew it, the academic year had ended, and it was time for the joyful events of "June Week." Proud parents and sweethearts began to arrive, and soon there were the hops, the reviews and award ceremonies on the Plain, and finally the granting of diplomas and commissioning of new lieutenants. On June 6, at the field house, Secretary of the Army Frank Pace gave the commencement address to a class that included football heroes Arnold Galiffa and John Trent, future astronaut Frank Borman, Cox's squad leader Tom Strider, and Mauro Maresca, one of the cadets who had seen the man now known as "George."

Secretary Pace concluded his remarks, and members of the class, one by one in order of academic merit, filed forward to receive their diplomas. As always, the loudest applause was reserved for the last recipient, the class "goat." Then the First Captain, after calling the class to attention one final time, gave the command: "Graduating class— Dismissed!"

The new lieutenants, with a boisterous cheer, hurled their caps high into the air. Their thoughts were of family, sweethearts, weddings, graduation leave, and freedom from the restrictions of cadet life. At that carefree, happy moment, no one was thinking of war.

Nineteen days later, on June 25, North Korean tanks and troops stormed across the Thirty-eighth Parallel. South Korea, an American ally, had been invaded. Within days, President Harry Truman, with the consent of the United Nations Security Council, authorized General MacArthur to use U.S. troops to repel the assault. America was again at war, and soon a majority of the members of USMA '50 would be heading to the Far East.

The FBI agents continued to check hotels and restaurants in the New York area, paying special attention to establishments in the Yorkville section, which Cox was said to have favored. At one of these, the Little Hofbrau on East Eighty-sixth Street, a waitress said she felt sure that Cox was the individual who had dinner there with a young woman in late February and skipped out without paying his bill. The woman was described as being about twenty-six years of age, five-foot-five, and with very dark hair. Could this be the same dark-haired woman who had been with the alleged Cox at the Sloane House?

In Mansfield, Bill Colby continued to help whenever he could. In response to a request from Murray Kaplan, Colby checked the local draft board and found no record of Dick Cox ever receiving a draft card or ever having registered. In a letter telling Kaplan of this, he added, "Sorry to hear that Joe Cavanaugh has resigned from your detachment. Joe impressed me as a very efficient investigator and I know the Cox family was glad to have a man like Joe on the case."

As indicated in Colby's letter, CID agent Joe Cavanaugh, taking the plunge into civilian life, had resigned from the service in late June. According to his friend Kaplan, Joe planned to take a polygraph course and then go into private business. Cavanaugh, as he left the army and the CID, may have felt frustrated. He had spent the past five months actively searching for Richard Cox, had nothing to show for it, and had not even developed any solid theories. However, as he told his partner Kaplan, his private opinion, even if little more than a gut feeling, was that Cox was still alive somewhere, and when he left West Point, he had done so on his own volition.

Publicity on the Cox case was tapering off. While tips continued to filter in, they were fewer and fewer. It seemed unlikely that any more leads would originate at West Point, or even in Mansfield. From this point forward, the search would concentrate on Dick Cox's army career before he entered the Military Academy. The key to the mystery—if, indeed, there was a key—might well lie with those who knew him in Germany.

At the Army Records Center in St. Louis, files were combed in a search for the names and current addresses of the four hundred or more men who had been in one of Cox's overseas units. The FBI and CID now began the laborious process of interviewing each of these men. Perhaps, in exploring Cox's past, they could learn more of his habits and personality, and of anything that might have gotten him into trouble or made him want to desert. It was also possible that one of these men could lead them to the elusive "George."

Using the interviews, investigators began to trace Cox's steps, starting with September of 1946, when he entered the army at Camp Atterbury, Indiana. From there, he was sent to Fort Knox, Kentucky, for basic training. To learn of that period in Cox's life, the best source was his closest army pal, Bud Groner. Cox and Groner first met at Knox, although at the time it was only a casual acquaintance.

In January of 1947, Cox was transferred to Camp Kilmer, New Jersey, to await shipment overseas. At one of the recreation rooms at Kilmer, he and Groner ran into each other and struck up a friendship. On February 6, 1947, the two left the port of embarkation together, sailing on the army transport *General Howze* and arriving at Bremerhaven, Germany, on February 17. From Bremerhaven, they first went to the replacement depot at Marburg and then were assigned to the Sixth Constabulary Regiment in Coburg, near the East German border. Groner joined the maintenance section and Cox the S-2 (intelligence) section of Headquarters Company. Later, Groner also became a member of Headquarters Company when he was chosen to drive the armored car of the regimental commander, Colonel McKinsey.

While they were at Coburg, Cox and Groner spent much of their free time together. For young men away from home for the first time, it was an exciting time, and Coburg was an exciting place. There was much to do, and many opportunities for both fun and trouble, as off-duty soldiers mixed with German civilians and with refugees from the nearby displaced persons camp.

For Cox, working in an intelligence unit, there was even a sense of adventure. The Constabulary's job was to man border posts and run patrols. Across the border, just beyond the barbed wire and minefields and less than a football field away, were frowning East German and Soviet troops, armed with submachine guns and constantly watching the Americans through binoculars and telescopic sights.

It was a lawless atmosphere, with dealings on the black market, plus incidents of assault, theft, rape, and even murder. Some of the crimes went unreported; others resulted in army courts-martial. (Although Cox had told his friend Bob Gandert, his cross-country teammates, and members of his cadet company that he had been a prosecution witness at one such court, no record could be found of his ever having given such testimony.)

Not far from Coburg was the tiny village of Lichtenfels, where Cox had sent the letter to Rosemary Vogel that had been returned marked "undeliverable." Agents began to look for Fraulein Vogel. Cox's letter had said he was enclosing two snapshots of Rosemary, but the envelope, when opened, had contained only the letter. Moreover, no such photos had been found in Cox's personal effects. Was it possible, on the night he disappeared, that he had brought those photos to show to "George"? If so, it might mean that "George" knew Rosemary and vice versa. It was worth checking.

In July 1947, Cox and Groner left Coburg when the Sixth Constabulary was disbanded. Groner went to the Fifty-third Squadron at Schwabach, and Cox to Troop "D" of the Twenty-seventh Constabulary at Schweinfurt. Cox, like everyone who had lived through World War II, remembered the name of Schweinfurt, a town whose ball bearing factory was the target for two of the largest and costliest air raids of all time. On August 17, 1943, 376 bombers of the Eighth Air Force pounded Regensburg and Schweinfurt, where Nazi fighter planes and ball bearings for their engines were manufactured. Sixty of those planes failed to return. Then, on October 14, some two months later, sixty-two more bombers went down during a daylight attack on Schweinfurt, in a raid that proved so costly that missions deep inside Germany without fighter escort had to be suspended.

Although their units were now separated by about one hundred miles, Cox and Groner managed to keep in touch and often spent their free weekends together. While he was at Schweinfurt, a place that was only now beginning to rebuild out of the World War II rubble, Cox, a good athlete, also played on the regimental basketball team, starting most games at guard. At West Point, he sometimes bragged about those days, saying he had had a very good deal, with little to do other than play basketball. One of his associates at Schweinfurt also remembered him as having had an attractive German girlfriend. During this period Cox applied for and received his appointment to the Military Academy.

In January 1948, Cox returned home to attend the West Point preparatory school at Stewart Field. (Groner returned to the States that same month and was discharged from the army on February 11.) Cox, after an enjoyable leave in Mansfield, much of it spent in the company of Betty Timmons, reported to Stewart Field on the fourth of February.

That, in a nutshell, was a quick summary of Cox's enlisted service. What was he like during this period? As agents continued to search for clues, soldiers who had known him were located and interviewed, either at their homes or at various army posts. He was said to be a good soldier, dependable, unassuming, and friendly although something of a loner. People described him as one who liked a good time but who stayed out of trouble—someone who was proud of his reputation and his personal appearance.

Inevitably, though, with multiple interviews came multiple perceptions and a few contradictions. Although Cox seldom gambled, one witness said he had "a strong inclination toward gambling" and "frequently won as much as several hundred dollars." This man's first thought, in fact, when he heard Cox was missing, was that he had become "too involved in gambling," although he couldn't say whether "gambling activities would cause any foul play."

Similarly, most of his friends said Cox was a very poor drinker, that one or two drinks would either make him ill or cause him to fall asleep. Contradicting this, one man said Cox at Schweinfurt "did a lot of drinking and on one or two occasions got into drunken brawls." This same man testified about "a first sergeant connected with 'D' troop in that squadron with whom Cox got into a couple of fist fights." Unfortunately, he did not know the name of the sergeant.

Cox was said to have traded cigarettes on the black market but only in a minor way, and he was basically quite honest, a "straight arrow." A different picture emerged, however, via a sworn statement from Private James Daly, a military policeman who had known Cox on the *General Howze*. Sent to Coburg for a month's special training, Daly had shared a room with Cox and several others. Daly testified:

> During said training period, all the occupants of our room were in the field with the exception of Cox (at the time still Pvt. or Pfc.) However, during this period, the rear board of my wall locker was pulled out and four cartons of ships stores (Chesterfields) were removed from it. Upon discovering the theft I immediately notified the Charge of Quarters [who] reported the matter to 1st Lt. Jacks, the Duty Officer at the time. 1st Lt. Jacks made an immediate search and strangely enough four cartons of ships stores cigarettes (Chesterfields) were found in Pvt. or Pfc. Cox's footlocker, oddly enough the latter was out of cigarettes the previous evening. That evening he asked me for money to buy cigarettes, but I believe I gave him a package of cigarettes instead. I related this to Lt. Jacks at the time, however, not being able to prove that the cigarettes found in Cox's locker were mine, the matter was dropped. After this I stayed clear of Cox, as I did not trust him.

Another discordant note came when someone questioned Cox's sexual orientation, beginning with the comment by the West Point staff psychologist that Cox's visitor was probably a "homosexualist." Then, too, there were those two weird letters sent to Joe Urschel from Greenwich Village, one of which hinted that Cox was being held there as a "love prisoner." It read in part:

> Could it be possible that your roommate, Richard C. Cox, is the victim of a cracy [sic] homo-sexualist who likes Military boys, with nice shapes? . . . and being that a lot of you lads have nice shapes they prey on these lads. . . . There are three men who make Union Square Park on 14th Street their place of hangout and they prey on young men from 20 to 24 for their sexual desires. I . . . heard them remark that the lads from West Point have nice asses . . . the one who passed that remark, his

name is George . . . if an investigation were made . . . you'll
have Richard C. Cox's lover, who lured him into homo-sexu-
ality, and keeping him prisoner. . . .

The Greenwich Village letters were generally ignored. More attention was given to a report saying that Cox, at a New Year's Eve
party in Mansfield, had been seen dancing with another man. In a
letter to Murray Kaplan, however, Bill Colby explained this:

> In regards to a party at the 40 et 8 Club here in Mansfield,
> which was attended by Richard Cox during his Christmas
> leave, I believe that I may be able to clear up the facts involved
> . . . later in the evening we all went to the 40 et 8 Club, of
> which I am a member, for the purpose of dancing. We spent
> perhaps an hour there, during which time some of the girls in
> our party danced with each other. Shortly before we left and
> in a spirit of "horseplay," some of the men in our crowd
> danced a few steps with other men in our crowd. . . . Drinks
> had been served during the evening, and the dancing episode
> was a little innocent fun, to which no importance was attached
> either at the time of occurrence or now.

Homosexuality didn't seem to be a factor. Bud Groner, as well
as Cox's roommates Welch and Urschel, the ones who knew him
best, insisted that Cox had never given the slightest indication
in that direction—quite the contrary, in fact. There was good
evidence that Cox, when stationed at Stewart Field, had been
intimate with one or more young women from Newburgh. There
was also a sworn statement, by a cadet who had been a close
friend, that told of Cox picking up girls in New York, sometimes
in the Astor Bar, and bringing them to his hotel room.

The FBI and CID continued to question Groner, who was
working that summer at his father's gas station. Often an agent,
without identifying himself, would arrive, strike up a conversation, and ask what he knew about his friend Cox. It was annoy-
ing, but through it all, Groner kept his composure and continued his efforts to be helpful. He said he knew Cox well enough
to feel positive that his friend was not homosexual. Moreover, he
was sure Cox had never testified at a court-martial; if he had, he
believed Cox would have told him about it. He was also confi-
dent that Cox had no close friends named "George" or "Alice."
As for that visitor, Groner still believed it sounded like Sergeant

David Westervelt, who had been Cox's immediate supervisor in Coburg.

On September 14, David Westervelt, who was now residing in New Milford, New Jersey, was again interviewed by the CID. They asked if he had heard from any former members of the Sixth Constabulary, ones who might have known Cox in Germany. Westervelt said he had not.

The power of suggestion is a wondrous thing. On October 11, the Reverend H. Weston Brown was in Boston at the Tremont Street Post Office, looking at a Provost Marshal "wanted" circular about Richard Cox that was posted on the wall.

As he was finishing his business, Reverend Brown saw a brown-haired man in a tweed suit walking out of the post office. He thought it might be Cox, even though he had seen the man only from the rear. Brown, becoming excited, returned to the desk and asked the clerk on duty if he had noticed the man in the tweed suit who had just left. It was Cox, the Reverend said, the one whose picture was on the wall in the lobby. Joe Kelleher, the clerk on duty, said he remembered selling the man some stamps, but otherwise he hadn't really noticed him.

The next day, agents from the Boston CID interviewed both the Reverend Brown and post office employee Joe Kelleher. Brown said he felt sure the man he saw was Richard Cox, although he couldn't say how he was able to identify him by seeing him only from the rear. Kelleher, for his part, said he hadn't paid any particular attention to the young man when he sold him the stamps, so he wasn't in any position to corroborate Reverend Brown's observations. The agents, although skeptical, thanked Reverend Brown for his cooperation and promised to be on the lookout.

In September 1950, as another academic year began at West Point, cadets still talked of Richard Cox. Many decided he probably had been murdered. No doubt his body would turn up someday. Then again, maybe his corpse had been tossed into the Hudson River, in which case it might by this time have drifted well out to sea.

On a more cheerful note, the football team that fall was again crushing all opposition. It looked as though the "Black Knights" were heading for another undefeated season, possibly another national championship.

Despite football, academics, and the other distractions of West Point life, cadets were paying close attention to the war raging in

Korea. Casualty lists now included the names of young lieutenants who had but recently been fellow members of the corps. That past summer, the U.S. Eighth Army, fighting for its very life, had fallen back to the Naktong River and held a thin defense line based on the port city of Pusan. General Walton Walker, the Eighth Army commander, had issued a statement saying it was "stand or die." If the Pusan Perimeter crumbles, Walker said, "we'll see the worst bloodbath Americans have ever known." This statement had very little sales appeal for the newly graduated cadets hurrying forward to join the team.

Before the year was out, the casualty list contained the name of Lieutenant John Trent, "Big John" to his friends, the All-American end and captain of the previous year's Army team. Suddenly football seemed less important, and the true mission of the Military Academy was brought into sharper focus, along with the Academy motto of Duty, Honor, Country.

Chapter 5

An Abundance of Trails

A s 1951 began, the Corps of Cadets staged a review for the departing superintendent, Major General Bryant E. Moore. Moore, who had been closely involved with the Cox investigation from the start, was heading to Korea for a key assignment. His replacement was Major General Frederick A. Irving. (Tragically, only five weeks after leaving West Point, Moore suffered a fatal heart attack shortly after a helicopter in which he was riding crashed into the frozen Han River.)

Korea, of course, was on the nation's mind that winter, and as the casualty lists continued to mount, *Life* magazine ran a story titled "Once More We're Taking a Hell of a Beating." One of the photos showed a young soldier holding a newly washed pair of "long johns" that had frozen solid. The accompanying caption identified him as Sergeant Cox of the Seventh Division artillery "somewhere in Korea."

As a result of the photo, Lieutenant Colonel Ed Howell, the West Point provost marshal, received a letter from State College, Pennsylvania, written by Lieutenant Al Haussemann, Jr., USMA '46, pointing out that Sergeant Cox, in the *Life* photo, was a dead ringer for Richard Cox, the missing cadet.

Howell showed the picture to Cox's roommates, Deane Welch and Joe Urschel. They looked at the picture, handed it back and forth, and then looked again. Yes, they said, it *could* be Dick. There was a striking resemblance, in fact. This was exciting! Had Cox, after running away from the Academy for some reason, then joined the army and shipped out to Korea?

At *Life's* editorial offices in Rockefeller Center, Mary Alves checked the files and said the picture had been taken by photographer Hank Walker. According to Walker's notes, the young man in the picture was Sergeant Shelley Cox, Battery "C," Seventh Division Artillery.

The FBI headquarters in Washington, which had *Richard* Cox's fingerprints on file, obtained *Shelley* Cox's fingerprint cards from the Army Adjutant General. A comparison check was made, and on December 29 it was announced that results were negative. This, however, was not good enough.

Based on a request from the FBI, the Adjutant General in Washington asked the Commanding General, Far East Command, to track down Sergeant Cox and have him fingerprinted. The sergeant, no doubt more than happy for a chance to leave his frontline firing battery for a few hours, was driven to a rear area location. Two sets of fingerprint cards were prepared and, per instructions, were mailed "by the most expeditious means" to West Point.

From West Point, the cards were forwarded to the FBI in Washington. The prints were compared, and once again results were negative. Finally, it was conclusive. Shelley and Richard Cox were definitely two different people.

On January 11, 1951, Minnie Cox wrote a letter to Colonel Paul Harkins, the commandant of cadets. Whenever she had been questioned by investigators, either CID or FBI, they had always asked for any details about Richard that might be helpful, no matter how insignificant they might seem at first glance. In her letter, she said she had just recalled something that might be important.

When her son Dick was in Germany, she said, and after he had applied for West Point, he had read in the army paper *Stars and Stripes* about West Point entrance exams being held. He showed the item to his commanding officer, who realized that Cox should have been notified. If he hadn't happened to see the item himself, he would have missed out on the exam and thereby missed his chance of attending the Academy.

The officer, upset about the communication breakdown, told Cox that "someone will pay for this mistake." Wasn't it possible, Mrs. Cox asked, that her son's complaint had gotten someone in trouble, and that whoever it was had later sought revenge?

Harkins discussed the letter with CID agent Murray Kaplan. Meanwhile, the Cleveland FBI office sent an agent to Mansfield to interview Mrs. Cox about this and any other incidents she might recall. Frankly, however, they didn't think that any "trouble" caused by Cox's complaint would have been serious enough to incite revenge.

Commandant Harkins, in addition to the Cox case and the normal operations of the Military Academy, had something else on his mind at the moment—providing security for a distinguished guest: NATO Commander Dwight Eisenhower was at the Hotel Thayer, writing a speech for delivery to Congress, one whose theme was the need to support NATO with both troops and equipment. He was using the familiar West Point surroundings both for "sanctuary" and for some much-needed privacy.

Federal agents that month continued to locate and question soldiers who had known Cox prior to West Point. They became even more active following a communication on January 22 from the director himself: "RICHARD COLVIN COX, CADET SERIAL # C DASH EIGHT ONE THREE TWO, U. S. MILITARY ACADEMY, WEST POINT, N.Y. MISSING PERSON. YOU ARE INSTRUCTED TO GIVE THIS CASE CLOSE ATTENTION AND TO SEE THAT AUXILIARY OFFICES HANDLE ALL LOGICAL LEADS IMMEDIATELY. HOOVER."

On the first anniversary of Cox's disappearance, J. Harry McGregor, the congressman who had appointed Cox to the Military Academy, called the FBI and asked about the status of the investigation.

In Washington, there is nothing like a congressional inquiry to generate rapid response. Almost immediately, an FBI agent named Rosen paid a personal call on McGregor; his report of the meeting in the congressman's office read in part: "I explained the Bureau's activity in this matter and he was highly pleased to know we had been investigating the case and were presently conducting an extensive inquiry into the matter. He said, of course, he was greatly concerned because his constituents considered this of great local interest and were following the matter with him." Tactfully, Rosen did not mention that earlier in the month the army had changed Cox's status from the nonjudgmental "Missing Person" to something with a pejorative ring to it. Cox was now classified as "Fugitive Deserter."

In early 1951, after many innocuous interviews and much spinning of wheels, there was a sudden development. Two interviews, it seemed, contained information of a sensational nature, enough to launch the Cox investigators on a brand new line of inquiry.

A soldier in Detroit, who had known Dick Cox in Germany, said he had last seen him in April of 1948. On that occasion he had run into Cox, quite by accident, at Tony Pastor's nightclub in Greenwich Village. Cox at the time said he was stationed at Stewart Field, preparing to take the West Point entrance exams. Since Pastor's was a place known to be favored by homosexuals, each man was surprised to see the other.

The soldier, in town for the night, told Cox he was staying at the Dixie Hotel. Later, he said, Cox came to the hotel, knocked on the door of his room, and asked if he could stay. During the night, he said, they had had sex.

In another interview, a man who had been with Cox at Stewart Field, and was now an admitted homosexual, claimed that he and Cox had had sexual relations while they were at the prep school. He also said that Cox, even after entering the Academy, had been very closely associated with other homosexuals and with one man in particular. This witness's opinion was that Cox's disappearance was related to his homosexual activities.

Who, they asked, was the "one man in particular"? This identity he refused to disclose, saying it was a question of honor. The man in question was now on active duty as a commissioned officer, and he felt that giving out this information could jeopardize the man's career.

The questioning continued, and finally the witness relented, but only a bit. He would give them the names of six people who were "closely associated" with Cox, but cautioned that not all of them were homosexual. One of the six, however, was the "special friend."*

In other words, Cox, although known to have had affairs with women, had also been attracted to men. This bisexuality, the agents realized, put a different spin on things and quite possibly had some direct relationship to Cox's disappearance. In future interviews, they decided, agents would try to learn about any other homosexual episodes involving Cox. The FBI field offices received a confidential memo: "It is to be noted that two separate unrelated witnesses have provided information that they had engaged in homosexual

---

* These six names, plus the name of the soldier interviewed in Detroit, appear in the formerly confidential, but now declassified, CID files in the author's possession. No purpose would be served by listing them here.

activity with Cox." The memo advised, however, that any inquiries along these lines would have to be handled with extreme discretion.

Following this new line of inquiry, agents began contacting what they liked to call their New York "confidential informants," particularly those from Greenwich Village. Meanwhile, places that Cox was alleged to have visited were put under surveillance.

Soon they began receiving tips from people claiming to have seen Cox in the New York City area during the winter of 1950 and early in 1951. There was also a report, for some reason previously given little attention, that indicated how Cox might have reached New York City. On the date of his disappearance, a bus owned and operated by the Westwood Transportation Company of Little Ferry, New Jersey, and chartered by the Mohawk Bus Company of Highland Falls (the town just outside the West Point gate) had left Highland Falls at 6:45 P.M. The driver of the bus reportedly stated that one of the ten passengers on his bus that evening was a West Point cadet who left the bus in New York City.

On February 8, 1951, Murray Kaplan met with an FBI agent at the post office building in Suffern, New York, where the FBI maintained a field office. They compared notes on the Cox investigation, and Kaplan no doubt mentioned that he'd now been on the case for more than a year. Nevertheless, the dry language of his report only hinted at his frustration.

"Continued investigation by this office," Kaplan wrote, "in close coordination with the Federal Bureau of Investigation, New York State Police and other law enforcement agencies, has not determined the whereabouts of Cadet COX to date." Rather hopefully, however, his report added: "Several minor leads were revealed, and will be developed by the FBI."

The FBI, going over the CID files, turned its attention once again to the letter Cox had written to Rosemary Vogel, the letter returned as "undeliverable" in which Cox had asked questions about Russians and the Russian zone. Surely, they thought, it couldn't be that hard to find the young lady, who might well know something, if not about Dick Cox, then perhaps about his visitor "George."

Cox's letter had mentioned his friend Bud Groner, who had been with him when he'd met Rosemary and her brother Luty. They again talked to Groner, who said a few weeks earlier he'd received a letter from Rosemary, dated January 10, 1951. In it, she had said she was unmarried and that she "was desirous of visiting America."

Groner remembered the family quite well, including Rosemary's father, Herr Vogel, who he said was the local schoolmaster in the village of Koesten.

In view of Rosemary's statement, it was possible, the agents thought, that Rosemary had already left Germany for the United States. A check was made with the Immigration and Naturalization Service, which found that in 1947 a departure bond had been filed by the soldier fiancée of a Rosemarie Vogel, supposedly so she could come to Chicago. (In the FBI files of the case, the soldier's name has been deleted.)

On February 12, 1951, a message went to the FBI's Chicago office: "ASCERTAIN WHETHER [soldier's name] FIANCEE ENTERED THIS COUNTRY AND WHETHER SHE IS IDENTICAL WITH THE ROSEMARIE VOGEL WHOM COX MET IN LICHTENFELS. IF SHE HAS NOT ENTERED THIS COUNTRY, ASCERTAIN REASON AND DETERMINE [soldier's] WHEREABOUTS ON JAN. SEVEN AND FOURTEEN, FIFTY, WHETHER HE IS ACQUAINTED WITH SUBJECT AND HAS EVER VISITED WEST POINT. OBTAIN COMPLETE BACKGROUND AND DESCRIPTION OF [soldier's name]. EXPEDITE."

Ten days later, the FBI located the former Rosemarie Vogel. The woman, now married and living in Chicago, was understandably shaken about having a visit from the FBI. Her nervousness, however, soon changed to indignation. Not only had she no knowledge whatsoever of any Richard Cox but also she had never even been in Lichtenfels. Her father, moreover, who had worked as an army paymaster, had never been a schoolmaster. Clearly they had the wrong person.

The FBI, being thorough, nevertheless checked on Rosemarie's husband, who worked for the Harrison Sheet Metal Company in Chicago. Pay records showed he could not have been at West Point on the dates in question.

The following month, March of 1951, *True Detective* magazine ran a feature story on the mysterious disappearance of Richard Cox. The article included a few pictures of Cox plus several other photos relative to the investigation.

A *True Detective* subscriber, as might be expected, was the type of person who not only enjoyed reading about mysteries but also liked to play amateur sleuth. Almost immediately, the CID and FBI were deluged with tips concerning the identity of "George" and the location of Cox. Typical was a letter from a *True Detective* reader in

Jackson, Mississippi, who said he had been approached on the street by a man begging money for food who claimed to be from Mobile, Alabama. The description of the individual, he said, fit very much the description of Cox in the magazine. Unfortunately, he could furnish no information as to the person's subsequent whereabouts.

Another letter came from a Canadian man, R. L. Weaver, who wrote:

> I am not an informer, but . . . this picture of the missing Cadet Richard C. Cox looks very much like a U.S. soldier or marine I saw on the dance pavilion at Sunnyside, Toronto, Ontario, last August 1950, although it might not have been him this guy was in some kind of a uniform of the US forces. I spoke to him and asked him how the army was coming along and he turned and beat it. He was acting very queer and I told some of the people around me that I thought then he must be A.W.O.L. . . . the description fits the guy to a tee. I saw the guy there about a week later he was standing directly behind me. When I looked around and saw him I asked some of the guys around me what kind of a uniform he was wearing and he must of heard me because he just seemed to vanish when he heard me asking about the uniform. This is all I can say. Your man Cox might be working or roaming the streets right here in Toronto.

The FBI knew how unlikely it would be for Cox, last seen wearing a full-dress coat and long, caped overcoat, to still be traveling in a conspicuous cadet uniform. Nevertheless, through their liaison with the Royal Canadian Mounted Police, they arranged to talk to Weaver.

By mid-March, the snow was staring to melt in the mountains north of West Point. On March 20, near the town of Mountainville, a telephone company employee was checking lines leading to Camp Moodna, a busy spot in the summer but customarily abandoned throughout the fall and winter. A grayish-blue object, half-hidden by the snow, caught his eye. No telling how long it had lain there. He picked it up, saw it was some form of visored cap. On either side of the cap, securing the chin strap, were small brass buttons; on the front was what appeared to be a shield with insignia. He rubbed away the snow and dirt and read the lettering on one of the buttons: "CADET, U.S.M.A."

The lineman, like nearly everyone else in the Hudson Valley, had read about the missing cadet and knew this might be significant.

He went to the police station in the nearby town of Cornwall on Hudson and showed the cap to Police Chief Herb Odell. He and the chief then returned to the area, and the lineman pointed to the exact spot he'd found the cap. The two then looked around, but saw nothing else of interest.

The next day, Chief Odell gave the cap to the FBI, saying he thought this was the type of hat Cox had worn on the day he disappeared. From New York, a message went to FBI Director Hoover in Washington: "URGENT. RICHARD C. COX, C EIGHT ONE THREE TWO—FUGITIVE DESERTER. WEATHERBEATEN CAP OF TYPE WORN BY CADETS AT USMA, WEST POINT, NY, FOUND BY TELEPHONE LINE MAN, MARCH TWENTY LAST, IN VICINITY OF ROUTE THREE TWO, MOODNA RIVER, MOUNTAINVILLE, NY. CAP OBTAINED AND FORWARDED TO LAB FOR EXAM. PRELIMINARY SEARCH OF AREA UNPRODUCTIVE BUT IMPEDED BY SNOW. MORE THOROUGH SEARCH OF AREA WILL BE MADE AS SOON AS AREA CLEARS. BUREAU WILL BE ADVISED."

A few days later, an FBI team, led by Special Agent J. W. O'Beirne, had Odell lead them to where the cap was found. They weren't able to enter the buildings at Camp Moodna, which were locked and boarded up. The search was also limited by the nearby Moodna River, which was at flood stage. They *were* able, however, to make a careful search of the immediate vicinity, but with negative results.

The cap, meanwhile, as noted in the telegram, had gone to the FBI Laboratory in Washington, along with a request that it be given a microscopic inspection for the presence of hair and examined for identification marks. They also asked the lab, if possible, to estimate how long the cap had been exposed to the elements.

In Washington, over the next few days, FBI scientists found human head hair inside the cap, light brown to brown in color, and from a Caucasian. The cap was measured as size $6\frac{3}{4}$, although prolonged exposure had caused it to shrink, so they couldn't be positive as to whether that was the original size. However, their interest went up a notch when they learned, from records at the Academy, that Cox's cap size was also $6\frac{3}{4}$.

A call was made to Mrs. Cox in Mansfield. Did she, by chance, still have any hats belonging to Dick? She did: two uniform caps from his time as an enlisted man, which she gave to an FBI agent, who forwarded them to the Washington laboratory for comparison purposes.

The lab workers went over these new caps, which they labeled Q11 and Q12. Carefully and painstakingly, they extracted a few hairs, presumably from the head of the missing cadet. The hairs were then compared microscopically with hairs from the cap found near Mountainville, known as Q1.

After all this, the laboratory's report wasn't much more than a frustrating maybe: "The human head hairs removed from the cap, specimen Q1, have started to decompose from exposure to the elements and are, therefore, unsuitable for comparative purposes with the hairs removed from specimens Q11 and Q12. It was noted, however, that there were some general similarities between the hairs in specimen Q1 and those in Q11 and Q12."

On April 10, three weeks after the cap discovery, a woman phoned the Newburgh, New York, Police Department. She had been out walking near her home, she said, when she noticed a bulging gray bag, lying on the ground near the South Junior High School. Protruding from the bag was the arm of a cadet uniform. Police hurried to the scene and retrieved what turned out to be an old Hercules Cement Company sack. It contained a West Point cadet's short coat and two pairs of cadet trousers, all of which were badly damaged from moths and exposure to the weather.

The police went into the school and asked a teacher if he knew anything about the bag lying in the schoolyard. Yes, he said, his pupils had told him they had found some uniforms when they were playing near an old shack. He called for one of the boys, who, a bit nervous but still enjoying all the attention, said that he and several others had found the uniforms and the bag in the rear of the old Wilson Cement Company on Monument Street. They had stuffed the uniforms in the bag, he said, and had tried to sell them to a junkman. Because they were wet, though, the junkman wouldn't buy them. He and the others had then returned to the schoolyard and had dropped the bag where the officers found it.

The police went to the rear of 67 Monument Street, which turned out to be a group of old sheds once used by the Wilson Cement Company and later by a wood and coal dealer. After a while, they finally found the man responsible for all the excitement. He was a former worker in the Cadet Mess Hall, who, while working in the mess, had been given old, worn-out uniforms by various cadets. He had brought them home and given them to his nephews to wear on Halloween and similar occasions. Eventually, he said, the uniforms had been discarded and thrown into one of the old sheds along with other refuse. That seemed to settle it. Once again, a promising lead had come to a dead end.

Major General Irving, the incoming Academy superintendent, looked forward to his new assignment. He was on his last tour of duty before retirement, and this job would permit him not only to make a final contribution to the Military Academy and the U.S. Army but also to do so in a pleasant and predictable environment. Little did he realize that he was about to encounter the worst scandal in Academy history.

For some time, a system had been in place whereby members of the football team received special academic coaching from fellow cadets. It was understandable; a football player, while adhering to the same grueling schedule as any other cadet, was also putting in long hours on the practice field. The tutoring was a way of compensating and helping him to cope with the Academy's demanding academic program.

Under the system then in existence, members of the two cadet regiments often took the same exam on different days. Cadet tutors, therefore, frequently knew the questions to be asked on certain tests, and they began relaying this information, first in the form of hints and then by giving the answers outright. This was a clear violation of the honor system that was such an integral part of cadet life. The code said a cadet would not lie, cheat, or steal, or tolerate those who do. Finally, someone told the authorities what was happening. Before it was over, ninety cadets were found to be involved, most of them football players.

A special board was convened to examine the situation, and, based on its recommendation, all ninety were discharged. At the Pentagon, former superintendent Max Taylor concurred. Taylor, like other graduates, knew that the Corps of Cadets, to whom the honor system was sacred, would never be willing to accept any of the ninety back into the Corps.

On June 5, General of the Army George C. Marshall gave the graduation address to the Class of 1951. Among those receiving diplomas were John Samotis, the man who had seen Dick Cox talking to "George" near the east sally port; future astronaut Buzz Aldrin, and future army chief of staff Ed Meyer.

At Annapolis that week, one of the graduates was James Patrick Kelley, Cox's boyhood friend from Mansfield and subject of the "see

Kelly" entry on Cox's desk calendar, which had created a temporary stir. The Annapolis yearbook, after referring to Jim's fine sense of humor, which "brightened many days for those around him," said Kelley hoped to join the "Tailhook" navy after graduation, meaning his sights were set on becoming a navy aviator.

News of the West Point cribbing scandal was released to the press soon after graduation. Public reaction was one of shock and disbelief, indicating just how high was the pedestal on which the American people had placed the Academy. Half of those being discharged were members of Cox's Class of '52. Some of his classmates began to speculate: Was it possible that Cox had known of the cheating? If so, had he threatened to blow the whistle, and might someone have done away with him to keep him quiet? During the investigation, it turned out, Cox's name had indeed come up. Supposedly a group of football players, confronting one of the informants, had seemed to threaten bodily harm, whereupon the cadet had speculated that this might be what had happened to Cox.

An FBI bulletin, sent from New York to Washington on June 6 concerning "Richard C. Cox, Fugitive Deserter," contained the following:

> WIDESPREAD VIOLATIONS OF HONOR SYSTEM HAVE BEEN UNCOVERED AT USMA AND THREATS IN WHICH NAME OF COX WAS MENTIONED HAVE BEEN MADE AGAINST CADET SUSPECTED OF DISCLOSING SAME. . . . CADETS PRESENT AT TIME ALLEGED THREATS WERE MADE INTERVIEWED AND DENY ANY KNOWLEDGE OF SUBJ. THEY ATTRIBUTE MENTION OF NAME OF COX TO [name deleted] WHO DISCLOSED VIOLATIONS AND IS QUOTED AS ASKING, "IS THAT WHAT HAPPENED TO COX?" INTERVIEW OF ADDITIONAL CADETS INVOLVED AND ASSOCIATES OF COX FAILED TO UNCOVER INFO AS TO SUBJECT'S WHEREABOUTS OR TO REFLECT THAT SUBJ WAS INVOLVED IN VIOLATION OF HONOR SYSTEM.

Alternatively, of course, there was always the chance that Cox himself might have been involved with the cheating. As a proud person, which he was known to be, could he have left the Academy to avoid the shame of dismissal? They might never know, but it was something to ponder.

By the summer of 1951, the failure to find Cox had become an embarrassment to the army and to the FBI. The FBI men in particular, prodded on by their director—Mr. Hoover did *not* like to be embarrassed—reviewed what they had learned from past missing person searches.

In America, of course, someone seeking a new identity has certain advantages. He or she can travel long distances without being fingerprinted, using a passport, or crossing international borders, and even the uninitiated can often secure false papers.

The FBI's expert tracers, however, had advantages of their own, based on experience. Of the many reasons for running away, the FBI knew they generally were related either to money or to sex. For men, homosexuality was many times a factor; for women, it was frequently an emotional problem involving a husband or a lover. The tracers also knew that the fugitive, in three out of five cases, continued to use the same first name; even with a different name, the person would probably use the same set of initials. For a last name, the fugitive often relied on something familiar, such as a mother's maiden name, the name of a street he lived on, a hometown, or the name of a close friend.

Too much reliance, of course, couldn't be placed on behavioral patterns. In fact, the tracer might jump to a false conclusion. That had happened in February, when a Mrs. Claire Colvin was arrested in Cranston, Rhode Island, on charges of driving a station wagon used in connection with numerous thefts. (Earlier, Minnie Cox had suggested that Dick, if choosing an alias, might use her family name, and his own middle name, of "Colvin.")

It wasn't much of a stretch, in view of the name "Colvin," to couple auburn-haired Claire Colvin and her station wagon with an unsubstantiated rumor that Dick Cox had been seen in a station wagon with a red-headed girl. Upon further investigation, however, the FBI found that Claire Colvin, age twenty-nine, who at the time of her arrest had let her hair return to its natural dark color, was married to thirty-three-year-old Edward Colvin, a former athlete at Rhode Island State. Claire Colvin, when questioned, knew nothing at all of Richard Cox.

Fugitives, the FBI had found, also followed a pattern as to destination. Almost always they tried to lose themselves in a large city such as New York, Chicago, or Los Angeles. Also, wanting to put distance between themselves and their roots, they tended to go as far away as possible. Men from the Northeast, for example, frequently headed for one of the southwestern states. Finally, and ironically, experienced tracers knew that fugitives often ran toward that which they were trying to escape. A man deserting an unhappy marriage who wed again was likely to choose someone resembling the wife he just left; the former garage mechanic was apt to end up working in a different city, but in yet another garage. The FBI, of course, had no experience with fugitive West Pointers, but they thought it possible that an ex-cadet would wind up in another structured, service-oriented environment.

All in all, the FBI agents realized that their best bet was continued digging into Cox's background—questioning friends, family members, and army acquaintances—until they knew as much as possible about Dick Cox's family, personality, habits, likes, and dislikes. What kind of food did he prefer? What were his hobbies? His preferences in sports, in movies, in books, in politics? It was time-consuming, tedious, and usually boring work, but there was always the chance that some telltale clue would turn up when least expected.

Agents now decided, in addition to questioning men from one of Cox's units, to expand their investigation to include members of the basketball team he had played on in Germany. The Commanding General, European Command, was asked to "furnish names of members of the unit basketball team during the period 1946–1947, at which time Cox was a member of this team. Also, determine the game schedule that this basketball team played throughout the US Zone of Germany. The name of cities in the US Zone of Germany in which this team played during the mentioned period is also desired."

During the summer of 1951, a woman told the Cincinnati FBI office that on July 6, 1951, she had traveled on a Greyhound bus from Grand Rapids to Flint, Michigan. On the bus, she said, she had talked to a young man greatly resembling the newspaper photo of Richard Cox. She described him as shabbily dressed in an ordinary suit, twenty-two years of age, and of average height. He told her he was being "pushed by the government" and was traveling around, not staying in any one place. She interpreted "pushed by the government" to mean that he was being sought by federal officials. She said the man got off the bus just outside Flint. Local authorities were asked to be on the lookout for such a man, but it wasn't much to go on.

Later that month, a soldier who had read about the case and had known Cox in Germany said he had an idea about the name "Alice," which Cox had shouted while half-asleep. While Cox was stationed in Schweinfurt, he said, there had been a missing payroll of some three thousand dollars. Although, from what he remembered, the mystery had never been solved, one of the men under suspicion was a friend of Cox named "Ellis." Wasn't it possible, he asked, that what Cox really said that night was: "Who's down there? Is that you, Ellis?" And, if Ellis was "George," might Cox have known something that Ellis perceived as a threat, enough to provide a motive for murder? It didn't seem likely, but then again, who could say?

The investigation proceeded, albeit slowly, and suddenly it was the fall of 1951 and Cox's classmates had become first-classmen, or seniors. Soon all of those who knew Cox the best would be graduated and scattered throughout the world, many of them to Korea. Murray Kaplan decided to make use of Cox's former roommates while they were still available. Kaplan, of course, had heard rumors about Cox being sighted in Greenwich Village. He had also seen a report by CID investigator Steger that said:

> On 23 August, 1951, Confidential Informer "99," a known homosexual, who is very cooperative with this office, . . . was shown a group of photographs of which some of Cox were included. . . . Informer "99" examined the photographs and picked out Cox's photos. Informer "99" stated that he had seen Cox approximately four times in the NYC area in the winter of 1950 and early 1951. Informer "99" believed he had seen Cox in one or two of the known homosexual bars in the city. Informer "99" advised his associate, Informer "98," was with him at the time he saw Cox.

Steger's report said he next showed the group of photos to Informer "98," who picked out the ones of Cox and also confirmed the sightings by him and "99." Cautiously, however, Steger recommended that the informers' stories "be considered merely as investigative leads. Nothing in this report is to be construed to reflect that Cox is a homosexual, as the information from the aforementioned sources is uncorroborated."

Despite the uncertainties, Murray Kaplan felt the report justified further surveillance. Accordingly, on the evening of September 18, Kaplan, together with an FBI agent plus Welch and Urschel, drove into New York and headed for the Village. They would take a stroll and visit places where Cox was said to have been sighted. If anyone could make a positive identification, surely the roommates could.

The foursome, trying to appear casual but highly conspicuous nevertheless, visited various nightclubs, including the Riviera Cocktail Lounge, the Terrace Cafe, the Cork Club, the New Verdi Bar, and the Blue Parrot Cafe. During the evening, some of the men they saw were paired off with other men; those unattached appeared to be on the prowl, "cruising" in search of a partner. Several wore makeup; a few were in "drag." The two cadets kept scanning faces but saw nothing of their ex-roommate. In a way, they may have felt relieved. For Deane Welch and Joe Urschel, it had been, to say the least, a novel experience.

The Army football team that year, devastated by the loss of so many players in the cribbing scandal, was a far cry from the proud championship squads of the recent past. The team won only two games, and in Philadelphia, the usual midway site of the Army-Navy game, the season ended on December 1 with an embarrassing 42-7 loss to Navy. One of those at the game was Betty Timmons, who, accompanied by Mrs. William McKee, had come east for the weekend.

The Cleveland FBI office had asked Timmons, who was now working as a switchboard operator at Mansfield City Hall, to contact the agent handling the Cox case if ever she visited New York. Perhaps there were questions with which she might help. Accordingly, she called the New York office, an appointment was made, and on Sunday evening, December 2, she was interviewed in her room at the Taft Hotel on Fifty-first Street at Seventh Avenue.

After the game, Betty told the agent, she had attended a party in New York at the Empire Hotel. Most of those at the party were West Point cadets, including Deane Welch and Joe Urschel. She had discussed Cox's disappearance with them, but all had agreed it was still as baffling as ever.

After careful questioning, the agent, realizing she had nothing new to tell him, ended the interview and thanked her for her cooperation.

Two days later, on Tuesday, December 4, a man checked into the Sloane House YMCA on West Thirty-fourth Street, stayed overnight, and checked out the next day. On his registration card, he had given the name Robert R. Cox, an address in Binghamton,

New York, and a birthdate of July 25, 1928—*the same birthdate as Richard Cox!*

The registration card, turned over to the FBI and marked exhibit Qc13, was sent to the lab in Washington for a handwriting comparison. The lab report read: "A definite conclusion could not be reached whether any of the questioned handwriting or handprinting on Qc 13 was prepared by RICHARD COLVIN COX . . . or ROBERT R. COX . . . because of handwriting variations which cannot be explained on the basis of the available handwriting or because the handwriting was not comparable with the handprinting." It was another frustrating "maybe." (Although the file does not show any checking of the Binghamton address, presumably this was done with negative results.)

Whenever America is at war, West Point is no stranger to sorrow. Beginning with the summer of 1950, Korean casualty lists revealed the names of many recent graduates. In late 1951, however, a different kind of tragedy struck the Corps of Cadets.

On December 18, as cadets prepared for Christmas leave, the "unofficial" section of the *Cadet Daily Bulletin* had this notice: "Any Cadets desiring transportation to San Francisco via military aircraft, who have not already done so, contact Cadet Glasbrenner, Company C-2, prior to 2215 tonight."

Military pilots, by regulation, are required to log a certain number of flying hours each month to retain their proficiency. Evidently Karl Glasbrenner, an enterprising first classman, had found a pilot willing to arrange his schedule to provide "space available" free rides for cadets going to California over Christmas. It was no problem finding cadets eager to take advantage of the offer; for those unable to afford a commercial airline ticket, it might in fact be the only way they could get home for the holidays.

On December 30, Glasbrenner's group, appreciative about having spent Christmas at home, arrived at Hamilton Air Force Base, near Bakersfield, and loaded up for the return flight east. The pilot, Major L. G. Carlson, having received clearance from the Hamilton tower, took off at 9:10 A.M. His flight plan showed a first leg that would take them to Goodfellow Air Force Base in Texas.

Shortly after three that afternoon, they were in cloudy skies above Arizona, when the pilot, apparently having problems, radioed that he planned to make an emergency landing at nearby Willis Air Force

Base. He never made it. At 3:40 P.M., the plane crashed into the southwestern slope of Armer Peak, about sixty-five miles northeast of Phoenix. All aboard were killed: pilots, crew members, two transient military "hitchhikers," and eighteen cadets. Eight of the cadets, including Karl Glasbrenner, were former classmates of Dick Cox. It almost seemed as though a dark shadow was hovering over the class of '52.

The following spring, on April 5, Cadets Duane Hogan and Jim Peterson, on leave in New York City, were walking down Thirteenth Street when they were approached by a rather seedy-looking man. He was between fifty and sixty years of age, wearing a black hat, black overcoat, string tie, and white shirt, all considerably soiled. They later recorded, more or less verbatim, what happened next:

"Are you boys from West Point?"

"Yes, we are."

"Uh, are you still looking for this Cox?"

"What do you mean?"

"Well, wasn't there a piece in the paper a while back that they're still looking for him? Well, he's down around this neighborhood."

"Oh? Is that right?"

"Yeah. You look down around Twelfth Street between Fourth and [unintelligible]."

"On Twelfth between Fourth and where?" The stranger, looking over his shoulder, suddenly appeared quite agitated. The cadets, following his glance, saw a second man, standing near the curb. He was about six-foot-one, wearing a tan overcoat, and appeared to be between forty and forty-five years of age.

The first man, drawing close to Peterson, said, "Between Twelfth and . . ." Then, without finishing, he turned abruptly and hurried away. The two cadets, after walking on for a block, crossed to the other side of the street and looked back. Both men had disappeared.

Peterson, in his account of the incident, wrote: "The stranger who stopped us was not at all well off, presenting an appearance more like that of a bum. For instance, the black tie he was wearing was about to fall apart. Furthermore, when he spotted the second stranger standing so close and apparently eavesdropping on the conversation, his facial expression was one of fear, as his eyes grew large and he became nervous."

The cadets' statements, after being seen by the Commandant of Cadets, were turned over to the investigators. Later that week, CID

agent R. L. Rast conducted a surveillance of the area pointed out
by the nervous, shabby stranger. The neighborhood contained fac-
tories, small shops, one hotel, three rooming houses, and two private residences. Rast even talked to the local mail carrier, who knew
of no one resembling Cox. At the end of the week, a disappointed
Rast had nothing to show for his efforts.

David Myron Westervelt had been interviewed several times,
had taken a polygraph test, and had even offered a plausible alibi
for the night of Cox's disappearance. Nevertheless, the CID and
FBI still had some lingering doubts about him, perhaps because
Maresca and Samotis, although unable to make a positive identification, had said he was the "same type of person" as Cox's
visitor "George."

In April of '52, the CID decided to question Westervelt one more
time. Agent Rast, along with Lieutenant Joe Lawlor of the
Bergenfield, New Jersey, Police Department, went to Westervelt's
last known address, only to find he had moved. They checked with
the telephone company, which said Westervelt, when applying for
phone service, had said he was employed by Consolidated Film
Industries of Fort Lee, New Jersey.

In Fort Lee, M. P. Brown, Consolidated Film's personnel director, said Westervelt had resigned the previous month, saying he was
going to work for the U.S. Treasury Department as an "enforcer"
and would be working out of the Newark office. Brown said he
would call Westervelt and have him contact the CID to arrange an
appointment.

Westervelt got in touch with the CID office the next day, and
a meeting was arranged for 7:30 that same evening. When
Westervelt arrived, he was met by CID agent Rast and a New
York FBI agent from the Foley Square office. They went over
familiar ground, and, as before, Westervelt testified that he had
served with Cox in the Constabulary Squadron in Coburg and
that Cox had been a clerk-typist in the intelligence office. When
asked about names used by Cox (Richard, Harry, Dick),
Westervelt said he was only called Cox. Then, looking at photos,
he used the name "Dick." However, when they called him on
this, he denied having said "Dick."

The squadron, he said, had been disbanded in July 1947, and he
and Cox had then been sent to other assignments. His wife, Alicia,

he said, did not know Cox, since he had not met her until after he left Coburg. Westervelt said he had been in combat during the Battle of the Bulge and had received the Purple Heart for having frostbitten feet. Next, the agents had him examine some photos and he identified two men, not yet interviewed, who had been in Coburg with Cox: James Duffy, of the Bronx, and Halstead (Hal) Falch, from Brooklyn.

On April 14, 1952, just as interest in Cox seemed to be dying down, a major feature story appeared in *Life,* at the time probably the most popular magazine in America. It was titled "THE MYSTERY OF THE MISSING CADET: A young West Pointer goes out to dinner—and joins the small company of the permanently vanished."

The six-page article, after discussing past missing person cases, reviewed what was known about Cox and the events leading up to his disappearance. Accompanying the piece were several pictures, including a copy of the CID circular with Cox's photo and vital statistics.

In a way, the CID and FBI investigators welcomed the new widespread publicity, which promised thousands more people would be on the lookout for Dick Cox. Still, agents also knew it would mean a huge number of false leads, each of which would have to be run down. If they had any doubts about amateur sleuths springing into action, the agents only had to read the article's concluding paragraphs. The writer, quite deliberately, had made them as provocative as possible:

> The various investigative agencies concerned with the disappearance of Richard Cox hold to certain opinions, although admittedly with little evidence on which to base them. The CID for example thinks Cox disappeared voluntarily and is living in disguise somewhere. Some West Pointers who aided in the search are convinced he is dead. The FBI hints that it thinks he is alive but will not say why.
>
> The explanation of the case of the missing cadet must fit the known facts as well as others that may not be known. Hidden among the tangle of clues and (very likely) false clues presented in this article, there may lie a pattern, perhaps so clear that it is staring everyone in the face, which contains the answer.

As the agents had predicted, several dozen letters came pouring in, to the FBI, the CID, and the editorial offices of *Life*. In a memo attached to one letter written to the army, an investigator wrote: "Here is another of what I consider strictly crackpot letters from Chicago. If this goes on I'll probably be writing them myself soon."

Chapter 6

An Abundance of Theories

The U.S. Military Academy had been founded in 1802, so it was appropriate, 150 years later, for 1952 graduates to call themselves the "sesquicentennial class." The press, however, gave them a more colorful name. That spring the *New York Sunday News* printed an article, headed "The Hard Luck Gang," which read in part:

> Never in the 150-year history of the academy has a class been hit by adversity so often and so tragically. The class of '52 has been like a magnet for hard luck. It has dogged their heels from the classroom to the athletic field. It has even sought them out during Christmas vacation.
>
> Hard hit by tragedy and scandal, the class of '52, which numbered 701 men when they entered the gates of West Point back in 1948, has shrunk to a mere 530.
>
> The biggest disasters to overtake the class were the plane crash in Phoenix last December and the cribbing scandal of last Summer. . . .
>
> And there were many other incidents involving individual members of the class. Most notable of these was the disappearance of Cadet Richard Colvin Cox of Mansfield, Ohio. Cox vanished from the military reservation without trace on January 14, 1950. He has never been found. Investigating officials are of the opinion that Cox was murdered.

The article also told of Cadets Joseph Carabetta and James Cain. Carabetta had died a few weeks earlier while playing handball in the cadet gymnasium. Cain, star halfback on the football team, had seen the end of a brilliant gridiron career when, in a freak accident, he broke his ankle during a track meet in Madison Square Garden.

"While this gang has no intention of uncrossing their fingers," the story concluded, "the feeling among them is that nothing much more can happen between now and the 100 days left to graduation. That is, unless you consider the officers' bars they will receive that day. The bars only mean one thing—a one-way ticket to Korea."

By nature, of course, young people are ever optimistic, and so it was with the new lieutenants of USMA '52, who despite all adversities, were looking to the future rather than the past. Nevertheless, Company B-2's write-up in the *Howitzer* yearbook had a sentence that seemed to recall Dick Cox: "Many dear friends departed early will be remembered as the years increase one by one."

Among those anticipating the future were Cox's former roommates. Deane Welch, selecting the Corps of Engineers, would eventually join a Combat Engineer Battalion in Korea. Joe Urschel, who had opted for the Air Force, would head for flight school along with classmate Ed White, a future astronaut.

Also to be graduated was Dick Shea, Cox's cross-country teammate, who to no one's surprise was named the class's outstanding athlete. With a sense of pride, Shea would put on the infantry's crossed-rifle insignia. After infantry branch training, he, too, would be heading for Korea.

Periodically, of course, members of the class still wondered about Dick Cox. Joe Urschel, for example, when asked his opinion, said, "It's very, very confusing. You can go in so many directions, but not very far in any of them."

Urschel still felt that if Cox were alive, he would have tried to contact his family. In other words, he must have been murdered by his visitor "George." But Dick, a good athlete, was hard and fit; it would have been difficult for "George" to overpower him, especially since Cox would have been on his guard against someone he considered an unsavory character. Even if Cox *were* murdered, though, what had happened to the body? After all that searching, it was highly improbable—almost impossible, in fact—that it could have been buried on the West Point reservation. By the same token, all the draining and dredging had eliminated the possibility that the body had been dropped into Lusk Reservoir or one of the reservation ponds.

Then, could Cox's body have been dumped into the Hudson? That, too, was unlikely. For one thing, the Hudson's banks weren't readily accessible, and even if the killer somehow had managed to drag or carry his victim to the river's edge without being seen, in his agitated state, fearful of discovery, "George" would hardly have taken time to weight the body to keep it from surfacing downriver.

No, if Cox had been murdered, his killer must have smuggled the body off the reservation, perhaps in the trunk of his car. Even then, however, disposing of the corpse would have been a major problem, and the odds were that by this time it would have been discovered.

That left, then, the alternative—that Cox had left voluntarily. Supporting that theory was the cryptic last paragraph in the *Life* article. From the way it read, both the CID and the FBI must have hinted to the writer (off the record, presumably) that they had evidence of Cox being alive.

One possibility, of course, although a faint one, was that Cox and his visitor had gotten into an argument that resulted in "George," rather than Cox, being the victim. Perhaps they had fought over something that had happened in Germany. Maybe it was "George" that Cox had testified against in a court-martial case. Or perhaps "George" had tried to blackmail Cox, threatening to ruin his career by revealing something from the past. Homosexuality? Black market activities? Some border incident, even the selling of secrets acquired while Dick was working in an intelligence unit? Or could Cox have had an affair with a German fräulein? Thinking the unthinkable, might Cox, rather than his visitor, have made a girl pregnant and then killed her?

If Cox, rather than "George," had indeed been the killer, could he have changed into the other's clothes, hidden the body in the trunk, and then driven the car off the post as he went into hiding? Somehow, though, Urschel couldn't conceive of Dick as a murderer, and in his mind he dismissed such thoughts.

Well, what *did* he know for sure? As a start, Urschel was quite positive that Dick had no intention of running away when he left for dinner that night. So what could have changed his mind? Was it something to do with sex? That FBI man had dropped hints about homosexuality the time he and Welch went into Greenwich Village looking for Cox on that unusual "reconnaissance patrol." Despite what anyone said, however, neither he nor Welch believed their roommate was homosexual. They'd often heard of his involvement with girls in Newburgh, and the last time they saw Dick, right after he came back from Christmas leave, all he could talk about was how much he missed Betty Timmons and how he and Betty looked forward to getting married. According to Dick, in fact, they had almost eloped when he was home over Christmas.

If not sex, then, what about honor? Could Dick have been involved in the cribbing scandal? Did he run away to avoid the shame of dismissal? That, too, seemed impossible. If Dick had been guilty of anything like that, his roommates surely would have suspected something. Joe Urschel came back to his original thought—truly you *could* go in many directions, but not very far in any one.

Finally, Urschel wondered if Dick might have violated his honor in some other way. There was, for example, that alleged erasure in the Company B-2 departure book.

In May 1952, a month before graduation, a CID agent, reviewing every scrap of evidence for what seemed the umpteenth time, had noticed a suspicious smudge on Cox's departure book entry of January 7, 1950, the time he supposedly went to dinner with "George." This was the evening, the agent remembered, that Cox came back to his room and fell asleep, apparently having had too much to drink.

On May 16, the page in question was sent to the army's Criminal Investigation Laboratory at Camp Gordon, Georgia, with a request "that an examination be made to ascertain whether or not any erasure has been made in the area encircled in red pencil on the page indicated in subject Departure Book. If it is determined that an erasure has been made thereon, request original markings be determined." Three days later they had an answer:

> 1. An examination of the figures "1823" encircled in red crayon opposite the name, R. C. Cox in Departure Book #B-2, Exhibit "A," fails to reveal any indication of an erasure. However, the figure "8" is superimposed on another digit which is written with an indelible type pencil and which has the contours and characteristics of the figure "9." It is, therefore, the opinion of the examiner that the original figures appearing in the questioned area were probably "1923."
>
> 2. Further examination of the questioned area indicates that two different types of writing instruments were utilized to prepare the figures "1823." Figures "1," "2" and "3" appear to have been accomplished by use of an indelible type pencil. Figure "8" was prepared by use of an ordinary lead pencil.

The report was signed both by Military Police Corps Captain Joseph J. Corr, Jr., "Document Examiner," and by Major D. R. Dingeman, "Chief of Laboratory."

After sifting through the rather bureaucratic jargon, the investigating agent had his answer. Dick Cox that evening had signed in initially at 1923 (7:23 P.M.). At some later time, he had then changed the entry, rather clumsily, to make it read 1823 (6:23 P.M.), an hour earlier.

Normally, this change would have seemed unimportant. After talking to cadets familiar with the honor code, however, and giving it a little thought, the agent realized it could be significant. On January 7, Cox had signed out for Dining Privileges, in effect giving his word that he would be having dinner with his visitor at the Thayer Hotel.

But what had happened that night? They knew he had left Grant Hall around 5:45, returned to his room, changed uniforms, and been back in barracks around seven. Obviously he had not had time for dinner at the Thayer. Moreover, from Urschel's testimony, they knew Cox had come upstairs, with a towel wrapped around his middle, shortly after seven.

Putting it all together, it appeared Cox had signed in at 7:23, perhaps on his way upstairs after showering. (Cadet showers, called the "sinks," were in the basement.) Still groggy from the alcohol he said "George" had forced on him, he may not have realized until later that he had committed an inadvertent honor violation. Based on his signing out for dinner at the Thayer, he had stated that he was properly excused from the 6:30 cadet supper formation. By allowing someone to report him "accounted for," he had in effect told a lie. Presumably it was an unintentional offense, but under the honor code he was obliged to report himself. Instead of doing so, however, he apparently had altered the book to make it appear he'd been back in time for supper formation. He even may have done the alteration a day or so later; a different pencil had been used to change the numbers. In other words, to escape relatively minor demerits for an unintentional infraction, he may have committed a serious, deliberate offense, which, if detected, could warrant dismissal from the Corps. All this was conjecture, of course, but for once they seemed to have something tangible.

Throughout the spring of '52, the CID, the FBI, and the editorial office of *Life* continued to receive letters with wide-ranging, imaginative suggestions about Cox and his visitor. Many said they suspected a homosexual angle to the case; among them, several even named people they thought might be "George." Typical was a let-

ter from a former Coast Guardsman, liberally sprinkled with enthu-
siastic punctuation:

Dear Sirs:

. . . I would like to tell you about some incidents that occurred during my stay in the service while stationed on Staten
Island.
The article refers to a man named George—and I have reference to a man of the same name!! This may not have any
bearing on the case whatsoever but I thought it worth telling!!
This man was known to be a Homosexual character—!! I believe he lived on Staten Island—and I know he rode the fer-
ries quite often because he used to always talk to all the service men I knew!! I myself never met the man—but had
answered the phone several times when he called to talk to one
of the guys he had met!! If I couldn't find the one he asked
for—he'd say—"tell him 'George' called—an old friend"!
If your missing cadet was ever stationed around Governors
Island—there would be a likely chance this George I refer to
could have met up with him—!! There were several fellows that
went out with him—he had a car—and that is about all I
know—!! . . . As I remember—this George was a pretty persuasive person on the phone—always asking whoever answered the phone to come on out and have a drink—and take
a ride!! . . .
If anything should come of this—I'd rather my name not
mentioned.

A different theory came from a woman who claimed to be a
mystery writer. She hypothesized that Cox, rather than being a victim, was actually the murderer of his friend "George." Cox, she
believed, had "planted" the story about "George" having murdered
a pregnant girlfriend to make him sound evil and worthy of being
killed. Why else, she asked, would a West Pointer described as "reserved" reveal these horrible facts about someone he had greeted
as a friend?
Another letter came from a Poughkeepsie man who used to work
as a waiter in the cadet mess hall. He was writing to West Point,
he said, to be of assistance. Following this, an agent met with him,
talked to him, and realized the man had nothing to offer. Later the
man came to West Point in person, demanding to know why he

hadn't heard anything further. Without comment, the officer he called upon wrote in his report: "In the course of his conversation he showed me a discharge paper from the Veterans Administration Hospital at Perry Point, Maryland. He also stated that he had a silver plate in his head, the result of a blow on the head with a rifle butt." The man was thanked for his interest.

One of the most unusual suggestions came from a woman in Oyster Bay, New York. She enclosed a newspaper photo of Wally Cox, television's popular, mild-mannered "Mister Peepers." If you looked at the eyes, she said, you could see that Wally and Richard Cox were the same man. She concluded by asking: "Am I in for a reward, if by chance I have helped to solve the mystery?"

Even more unusual, and a bit chilling, was a "psychic" theory that was come upon almost by chance. It began when an FBI agent called at the Irvington, New Jersey, home of a former cadet who had known Cox. The young man's mother, after giving the agent her son's present address, asked if this had something to do with the missing cadet. When told that it did, she appeared very nervous and seemed to have something on her mind. Finally, almost reluctantly, she told her story.

Around 1939 or 1940, she said, she had a dream about a young soldier stationed in Hawaii named Malcolm Trudo, the brother of one of her son's friends. In her dream, she saw Trudo, on a motorcycle, crashing into a cement abutment. She then saw him at a hospital, crying for his mother. Next day she asked her son to contact his friend and see if his brother was in some kind of trouble or had been hurt. About a week later, she said, her son came home from school and said that Malcolm Trudo's parents had received word that their son had been killed in Hawaii as a result of a motorcycle accident and had died in the hospital.

Only once since then, she said, had she had a similar experience. The second dream had taken place in early January 1950. In this dream, she saw an unknown individual call at the cadet dormitory, asking to see a certain cadet. The visitor, whom she remembered as having a reddish complexion and being thirty to thirty-five years old, didn't wait for the cadet to come meet him, but instead headed to the football field. Apparently there was a prearranged meeting, for the cadet appeared at the field, wearing a long overcoat. They both then entered a car, which she described as an old-model gray sedan, and drove through the gate leading to Camp Buckner. The cadet was hunched down to avoid being seen by the guard at the gate. Before getting to Buckner, the stranger pulled the car off the road, and the two men walked up a path to a garage-type shed, which she described as unpainted, having windows, and with no adjacent buildings.

Inside the shed, she said, the two began arguing—she didn't know what it was about—and the cadet began insisting he had to return to West Point before check-in time. At the height of the argument, the stranger, from behind, looped over the cadet's neck what appeared to be a leather thong and, with it, strangled him to death. At this point, she said, she awoke in a cold sweat.

Next day, she asked her husband to take her to West Point, but he had only laughed at her, saying the officers at the Academy would only smile and call her story ridiculous. She didn't think anything more about the dream until her son called her from New York City the first part of February and said a West Point cadet was missing. She then told him of her dream, saying she was sure it was Cox she had seen. Several times, she said, she had come to the Newark FBI office, but each time she had backed out before contacting anyone.

The agent, who had noticed her nervous state earlier, now saw that the woman, after telling her story, appeared to be entirely different and more relaxed. Although the agent didn't believe in dreams, he nevertheless recorded her story in detail. When they interviewed the woman's son, he said he remembered his mother telling him of the dream shortly after Cox disappeared and he vouched for the earlier dream incident. Also, he thought there were some abandoned construction shacks on the road to Camp Buckner, one of which might fit the description in his mother's dream.

The ex-cadet son said his mother should be taken seriously. She hadn't been ill in any way, and during the war she had held a supervisory position in the Veterans Administration. (The FBI later verified this.) Although the woman offered to accompany the FBI to West Point in an effort to identify the shack, the records do not show whether this was ever done. In any event, it appears nothing came of this bizarre episode.

Tirelessly, agents continued to pursue all leads. Analyzing one batch of forty-one letters received by *Life* magazine, they noted that thirty-five of them contained suppositions as to the reason for Cox's disappearance and subsequent murder by "George," five letters intimated that Cox was homosexual, and one said that "George" must have been perverted.

In addition to letters, the people at *Life* also received telephone messages. One call came from a man who refused to identify himself, but who said he had read the Cox article in the magazine and that Cox was living in Vails Gate, New York, under the name of "Banks." Following up on this, CID agent R. L. Rast visited the tiny Vails Gate community, about twenty-one miles north of West Point. There was a general store, two bars and restaurants, a radio repair shop, barbershop, filling station, and a few scattered homes. It was a place where everyone knew his neighbor—and an unlikely site for someone trying to hide.

At the general store, which doubled as a post office, Rast talked to postmaster H. L. Phillips, who said only one family named "Banks" received mail at Vails Gate. Phillips, who had lived there all his life, couldn't recall ever seeing anyone resembling Cox. Rast then talked to Ellen Grammis, who lived across the road from the Banks family. The family, she said, consisted only of a husband (in his late forties), a wife, and a twenty-one-year-old daughter. No one resembling Cox had ever been seen around the Banks home. Rast then talked to Mrs. Banks, a pleasant woman who knew of no other family named Banks in the vicinity. At day's end, Rast had concluded that the anonymous tipster was either an unbalanced crank or someone trying to make trouble. Back at the office, working with the telephone company, he tried to find out who had placed the call, but without success.

For more than two years, Minnie Cox, brooding constantly about her missing son, had mood swings alternating between hope and despair. When talking to interviewers, she sometimes said she was sure Richard was dead. At other times she would declare, almost wistfully, that Dick must have amnesia, and when he recovered, she knew he'd return home. Often Minnie Cox received letters from strangers. Some were merely messages of sympathy; others offered new theories or even alleged a sighting. By this time, having discovered how many irrational people there were in the world, she mostly turned over such letters to the army or the FBI without comment. Then, in late May 1952, Minnie Cox called the FBI in a state of excitement. She had just received a letter, dated May 21, from a woman in Owosso, Michigan. This one, she said, appeared to be the real thing.

Mrs. Cox, Sorry to open a wound, but I have reason to believe your son, Richard, missing since January of 1950, is in the vicinity of Bennington, Michigan. . . . In April of 1950 I met a young man who gave his name as Johnny Powers. He was between 22 and 25 years old. Blue eyes, brown growing-out crew cut, weight about 165 or so and about five feet eleven inches tall. He was a nice looking boy. He was quite muscular looking.

I went with him for two or three months and he wanted me to marry him, but I met another fellow and married him in March, 1951. However, I do see this fellow that calls himself Johnny Powers every so often and he visits us once in a while. I have more reason to believe this is not his name, as when he first told me it he said it was Dick, then after he said Dick was just a nickname.

He has a buddy with him by the name of George Vasseur. . . . They said something about being army buddies in 1947 or 1948. Someplace around there anyway. They were quite close. This George has kind of a New Yorker way of talking. If possible I will try to get a picture of the boys or just the one I believe to be Richard Cox. My mother-in-law remembered reading something about a missing cadet and she said he fitted Johnny's description enough to be twins. If the description does fit, please notify me and I will do what I can to find out just who he is and will try to get a picture.

After signing her name, she added: "P.S. I would not have written this letter if I wasn't pretty sure they're one and the same boy. I'm sorry, but if he is all right and I have reason to believe he is, I'm sure you want to know."

Soon a team of agents was on the scene, questioning the young woman, who gave further details about Powers, saying she had seen him on an almost daily basis the first six months of 1950. She still saw him around occasionally, she said, and sometimes he insisted on following her, her husband, and her parents. It turned out, however, that neither her husband nor her parents had ever actually seen him. The agents, by this time suspicious, continued the interrogation with more pointed questions. The answers didn't seem to add up.

Talking to the young woman's sisters, ages fourteen and fifteen, they found that both of them had heard a great deal about Powers from their sister, but neither of them had ever seen him. The fifteen-year-old said she didn't believe there was such a person. The mother-in-law, in turn, said she knew nothing about a missing cadet and had never suggested Powers and the cadet might be the same person.

Further stories about Powers, including tales of threatening phone calls, told to the FBI or to others, proved wildly imaginative and unsubstantiated. Local townships were visited, and although police departments, credit bureaus, and many citizens were interviewed, no record could be found of either a Johnny Powers or a George Vasseur. Moreover, no one ever had seen either of them, nor when shown Richard Cox's photo, did anyone say he looked familiar.

In Owosso, Police Chief Ted Rice said that the woman's testimony couldn't be trusted. In the past, she had on several occasions passed worthless checks, but her father had made restitution and she had never been prosecuted. The chief was convinced that Johnny Powers was a figment of her imagination. That seemed to wrap it up. The FBI and CID concluded that this had been another wild goose chase. Johnny Powers and George Vasseur did not exist. Then why had they been concocted? The reason, hidden deep within one young woman's troubled psyche, might never be known.

Finally, on June 3, 1952, it was time for USMA '52's long-awaited graduation. After an address by Secretary of the Air Force Thomas Finletter, and appropriate remarks from the superintendent, General Irving, 527 new second lieutenants stepped forth to receive their diplomas. When each name had been called, each diploma awarded, and the last man had returned to his seat, the joyful noise erupted in its time-honored traditional sequence. The First Captain dismissed the class, the graduates yelled and threw their caps high in the air, and smiling spectators—friends, families, sweethearts—applauded with gusto, many with tears in their eyes, tears mostly of joy, but tears also prompted by thoughts of the war raging in Korea and its ominous possibilities for the young men of USMA '52.

Meanwhile, tips about Cox continued to come in at the rate of nearly three a day. One report said a man resembling Cox was working at Miami University in Ohio; another message said a man of Cox's description was a frequent user of the pool at the Hotel St. George in Brooklyn. Then a soldier at Camp Kilmer, on his way overseas, said he had seen Cox, more than once, at the bus depot in Atlanta, Georgia. That report, like all others, was run down, and the bus station was placed under surveillance. Results were negative in every instance.

One interesting report came from a soldier who in 1947 had been stationed in Kitzingen, Germany. It concerned a man he knew there only as "Red." He couldn't recall the last name, but he said that "Red" was a former ranger whose military specialty was that of hangman. According to the soldier, "Red" often spoke of his hangings of German soldiers, civilians, and a German woman he had made pregnant. He said that "Red" was later transferred into Cox's unit, the Twenty-seventh Constabulary Squadron. The soldier had seen the article about Cox in *Life,* and the investigators wondered if the well-meaning details about "Red" were from actual memory or from the article's description of "George."

In December of 1952, a report was received that an unkempt, heavily bearded man resembling Cox had been seen at two public libraries in Atlanta, Georgia. The physical description seemed to fit: age twenty-four to twenty-five, medium height, weight 160 to 165, blue eyes, brown uncut hair.

At Atlanta's main library on Carnegie Way, he was seen making notes from technical books in a manner indicating he was well-educated and proficient at note taking. The caller said his mother had seen the same individual at one of the branch libraries, asking for New York newspapers, then looking through them rapidly as though he was searching for something. Both he and his mother had seen the Cox article in *Life,* and both felt the bearded stranger resembled Cox.

In Mansfield by this time, Betty Timmons, Dick Cox's former fiancée, had resigned herself to the fact that Dick was probably dead. At least she had long since given up on ever hearing from him. On Christmas Day 1952, Betty Timmons was married in Mansfield to a man named William Broad. The Cox family understood her decision and accepted it. After all, they said, Betty had her own life to lead.

In the spring of 1953, S. L. A. "Slam" Marshall, writer and military historian, arrived in Korea. Many considered Marshall to be the foremost expert on the behavior of soldiers in combat. Among other attributes, he was an excellent listener and a perceptive interviewer. As he talked to line officers, Marshall was told that American morale had deteriorated, and because of the rotation system, the troops lacked both drive and guts. Then came Pork Chop Hill. In that battle, Marshall wrote, Americans "outgamed" the Red Chinese, and a principal factor was the command presence of their young officers. One such officer was Cox's classmate and cross-country teammate, twenty-six-year-old Dick Shea.

On the night of July 6, 1953, when his unit was attacked by a greatly superior force, Shea led a counterattack, and in the bitter fighting that ensued, he personally managed to kill two enemy soldiers with his trench knife. Throughout the night, he fought side by side with his men, constantly moving among the troops and urging them to hold firm. At dawn, the enemy launched still another fierce attack. Although his unit by this time had suffered heavy casualties, Shea rallied a group of twenty men and charged the enemy. Despite being wounded, he refused evacuation and continued to press the attack. When the assaulting element was pinned down by heavy machine-gun fire, Shea personally rushed the emplacement. Firing his carbine and lobbing grenades with deadly accuracy, he neutralized the weapon and killed three more of the enemy. The fighting raged on, throughout the day of July 7 and into the following morning. On July 8, the enemy came again in overwhelming force, determined to overrun the position. Despite additional wounds, Dick Shea launched still another counterattack and was last seen in close hand-to-hand combat with the enemy.

Dick Shea was awarded a posthumous Congressional Medal of Honor. The heroic Shea would always be remembered, by fellow cadets, by those he led in battle, and by a grateful nation. As a fitting tribute, West Point's track stadium was later named Shea Stadium in his honor.

Ironically, the Korean truce was signed on July 27, less than three weeks after Shea's death, when the Chinese and North Koreans decided they could gain very little by prolonging the war. Many felt the American determination shown on Pork Chop Hill was a significant factor in causing the enemy to reach that conclusion.

Before long, tragedy struck down still another of Dick Cox's friends. This time it was Jim Kelley, his boyhood pal from Mansfield. Following his 1951 graduation from the U.S. Naval Academy at Annapolis, Kelley, just as he had wished, joined the "Tailhook navy" and entered flight school. By the fall of 1953, he wore the golden wings of a naval aviator and was a member of VF 21 at the Oceana Naval Air Station near Virginia Beach, Virginia.

On a chilly November morning, Lt. (j.g.) James Kelley, USN, took off from Oceana in his Cougar jet. Although Jim wasn't superstitious by nature, he probably noted that it was Friday the thirteenth. Some fifteen miles away, near Great Bridge, Virginia, horrified observers saw the plane suddenly slam into the ground; Kelley was killed instantly.

In April of 1954, five months after Kelley's death, CID investigator John Steger received a tip concerning the Pine Tree Inn in West
Hurley, New York, a village about fifty miles north of West Point,
near Kingston. According to the source, the inn's owner, John J.
Collins, had left West Hurley in early 1950 under circumstances that
neighbors thought "unusual." Many of the neighbors said a person
resembling Dick Cox had somehow been associated with Collins.
Reading between the lines, it appeared that some of the people in
West Hurley resented Collins, perhaps because of the tavern he ran.

By this time the Collins family was living in their new home on
Long Island. Mrs. Collins, interviewed by Agent Steger, said that she
and her husband had sold the tavern at West Hurley as a result of
poor business, poor health on the part of her husband, and because
of the unneighborly attitude of local residents.

What about the report of their association with someone resembling Dick Cox? Mrs. Collins, no doubt with a smile, showed Steger
several photographs of her son, who had visited them in West
Hurley several times while he was serving in the U.S. Army.

Steger noted the marked resemblance between the younger
Collins and Richard Cox. "This resemblance," Steger wrote in his
report," may have led neighbors to the mistaken belief that he was
COX."

By late 1954, the FBI and CID investigators knew a good bit about
Richard Cox, and they had more to work with than during their first
round of interviews. Accordingly, they decided to go over the same
ground again, talking to soldiers who were with Cox in Germany,
either in the Constabulary or as fellow members of the unit basketball team, talking also to men who had known him at the Stewart
Field Prep School, and, last, talking to former cadets, who by this
time were scattered worldwide.

The problem, of course, was that Cox by now could be anyplace
in the world. Despite the reports, they thought it unlikely that he
would still be in the New York area. Perhaps, in fact, like many
New York runaways, he could have headed for the American Southwest. Suggesting this was a provocative letter to Mrs. Cox from a
woman in San Diego, California:

Dear Madam or persons concerned,

The following is perhaps a coincident but maybe not. In
early Sept. '54 I went to Tiajuana, Mexico, to get a hair permanent . . . two young men entered one in a way answering Mr.

Cox's description asked for a permanent and his hair dyed black. I remember his hair as brown and slightly wavy. Operator said his hair was too short for a permanent but could take a black hair dye—which was done for him. The tall young man spoke border Spanish but the short lad about 26 or 27 years old rattled off short lines in German and very poor dialect. I asked this slim tall fellow why the awful hair dye when the natural light brown sort of wavy hair was so becoming. He answered (U.S.) if he is to stay in Mexico he must have black hair. . . . The stout lad with dyed hair was most charming in manner and physical structure seemed military. . . . They seemed uneasy and anxious for hair job to be done. . . . The short fellow said good morning to me in a most pleasant manner, like a gentle man . . . had rather a muddy complexion but the walk of a soldier. . . . I wonder could it have been Mr. Cox.

This above is the God's honest truth and I am writing it because I am so puzzled at the dyed hair and excellent behavior of the young man.

After signing the letter "Wondering Lady," she enclosed a card from the Tijuana beauty shop, noting that the operator there spoke little English, and added, rather touchingly: "Don't give up someday some how we will know all the answers. The short man I wonder about had a very nice way to an elder person was your boy like that?"

In Tijuana, CID agent Ross Milton talked to Rosario and Yolanda Morales, owners of the beauty shop. They said they did not remember the incident in question or anyone resembling Cox. Obviously they did not want to get involved. When questioned further, they said they had no idea who "Wondering Lady," the letter writer, might have been.

After much searching, the FBI had finally found Rosemary Vogel, the girl to whom Cox had written that "undeliverable" letter.

In Maineck, Germany, Frau Sophie Vogel, Rosemary's mother, told a CID agent that Rosemary had married Army Sergeant William Padgett in November of 1953 and six months later, in April 1954, left Germany to join her husband at Fort Meade, Maryland. Frau Vogel lent the agent a picture taken at the wedding, showing not only the bride and groom, but also the best man, whom she identified as American Sergeant Edward McCurry. McCurry, the agent thought, looked a lot like the photos he'd seen of Richard Cox.

In America, CID investigators given this information wondered if Cox might have returned to Germany under the name of McCurry. Further investigation, however, including a fingerprint comparison with the help of the FBI, showed that McCurry, who was now living in upstate New York, was definitely not Cox.

On August 6, 1954, at Fort Meade, Maryland, Rosemary Padgett, née Vogel, at first said she had no recollection of Dick Cox and had no idea why he might have written to her. This was understandable; Cox, in fact, had begun that letter by asking if Rosemary remembered him, and evidently she did not. She did remember Cox's friend Bud Groner, however, and when shown a photo of Cox and Groner, taken together, she vaguely recalled Cox. As for helping the investigation, however, she had no information whatsoever.

Still another Cox article was to appear, one that would cause a remarkable witness to come forward. *Coronet,* a popular magazine resembling *Reader's Digest* in size and content, had in its November 1954 issue a story by Jerome Edelberg:

> After five years and a world-wide manhunt
> the Army still seeks to solve . . .
> ## THE MYSTERY
> ## OF THE
> ## WEST POINT CADET

Edelberg summarized the known facts in the case, added a bit of conjecture, and even included a new theory: "Some believe he was smuggled out of West Point and perhaps out of the country— that he may now be held captive behind the Iron Curtain. Although at no time was he stationed near the border of Iron Curtain countries, he could easily have made junkets there on military passes."

Edelberg ended by quoting a CID spokesman: "'In view of the fact that the man hasn't turned up and that we have no evidence to prove he is deceased,' the CID says, 'we must hold to the belief that he is alive. Therefore we will search for him until we arrive at a solution of his disappearance.'"

The *Mansfield News Journal* took note of the article in a November 6, 1954, story headed "SAYS MOVIES SEEK STORY OF CADET COX":

> The strange disappearance of Mansfielder Richard C. Cox nearly five years ago from West Point is being retold again— this time in the current issue of Coronet magazine.

The story of events leading up to and following Cox's disappearance is repeated in an article entitled "The Mystery of the West Point Cadet" written by Jerome Edelberg.

Yesterday, New York Columnist Dorothy Kilgallen said that two film studios are bidding for the screen rights to Edelberg's story of Cox's disappearance.

Whether or not this mystery, which has fanned into a worldwide hunt by U.S. Army authorities will ever be solved, is a mystery in itself.

The case of the Mansfield youth who signed out in the register of the Military Academy Jan. 14, 1950, and never returned, has received widespread publicity in nearly every metropolitan newspaper in the United States, and many of the largely-circulated magazines.

Evidently Edelberg and the studios never reached an agreement about turning the Cox story into a movie. His article, nevertheless, would have important repercussions. The statement about Cox not being stationed near the Iron Curtain was disputed immediately by Master Sergeant Richard Ellis, who wrote the CID from California to say he didn't know Cox personally but that he had run with him at a track meet in Germany in 1947. "He and Dick Shea," Ellis wrote, "both were runners from the Constabulary as I was. . . . In the article I read that Cox was in the 27th Constab. Sqdn. in Lichtenfels, Germany. The Edelberg write-up states, 'at no time was he stationed near the border of Iron Curtain countries.' These two statements are opposing each other. I was stationed in similar nearby border towns of Weiden and Coburg, and know that Lichtenfels isn't too far from the Czech border."

Sergeant Ellis was right, and proximity to the border would add fuel to the "Soviet prisoner" theory that later developed. For now, though, the CID and FBI were focusing on the most sensational bit of testimony yet received.

In November 1954, the FBI office in Newark received a phone call from the U.S. Coast Guard Receiving Center at Cape May. The Center's security and personnel officer said one of his men had told him that he had been reading the article on Cox in *Coronet*. The coast guardsman, named Shotwell, had formerly been in the army and had attended the West Point Preparatory School at Stewart Field, although he had later failed the entrance exam. At the prep school, Shotwell had known Cox personally. The two, in fact, had often spent time together socially, and on one occasion Cox had had dinner at the home of Shotwell's uncle.

So what was the point of the call? Shotwell, the officer said, *had spoken to Cox in Washington, D.C., in 1952, two years after his disappearance.* The officer agreed to make Shotwell available for interview.

Chapter 7

The Greyhound Post
Restaurant

L ike an electric current, the news surged rapidly through the FBI
and CID communities. Since January 1950, thoroughly and pa-
tiently, fighting monotony, weariness, and frustration, agents had
pursued hundreds of leads, even those that seemed far-fetched
or ridiculous. Making it worse over those many months was the
thought it might all be a useless spinning of wheels—that Cox
might be long dead, his body swaying with the tide on the bottom of New York Harbor or crumbling to dust in some lonely
upstate grave.

So now—was it possible? Did they finally have a valid sighting, an eyewitness account, not from some crank, but from someone who actually *knew* Richard Cox? They were eager to talk to
Shotwell, and when he arrived at the FBI office, special agents
were ready with their questions.

First, of course, they had to establish that Ernest Shotwell knew
Cox well enough that he was not mistaken. To begin, they asked
the young coast guardsman to summarize his own service background. He had been an Army Air Corps medic, he said, a sergeant,
and after receiving an appointment to the Military Academy, he had
reported to the Stewart Field Prep School in September of 1947. A
few months later he met Cox, who arrived at Stewart in early 1948.
At the prep school, they were in the same student company, although in different platoons; Shotwell in the first platoon, Cox in
the third.

Shotwell said he and Dick Cox had attended the same classes at Stewart, all geared toward preparing for the West Point entrance examinations. During their free time, they often socialized, sometimes going together into New York City on weekends. Once, he remembered, they had stayed at the Flanders Hotel, around West Forty-seventh Street. On another occasion, he and Cox had had dinner at the home of Shotwell's uncle. Then, in June 1948, they had taken the entrance exams. While Cox had passed, Shotwell had failed the physical aptitude portion of the test and consequently was unable to enter the Academy. He had left the prep school on July 1, 1948, and, after being discharged from the army, had reenlisted in the Coast Guard. He did not see Cox again until that meeting in Washington.

What could he tell them about that? Well, he was in Washington, D.C., the first weekend of March 1952, and had stopped at the Greyhound Post Restaurant, where he formerly worked, to see some of his old friends. While sitting at the counter having a cup of coffee, he looked around the room and observed Cox sitting at a table near the rear window.

Shotwell said he got up and went over to Cox, calling him by name. "Cox . . . you are Dick Cox."

"Yes, how are you?"

"Fine. Say, what are you doing here? Why aren't you at West Point?"

"I resigned from the Academy last year."

"What are you doing now?" Shotwell asked, and as he best recalled, Cox said he was going to work in Germany for himself. He also said he was currently working for himself but did not say what type of work he was doing or what he contemplated doing in Germany.

Shotwell thought Cox, who seemed uncomfortable, was acting surprisingly cold toward a friend he hadn't seen in years. The rest of the conversation, he said, was "small talk—about the weather and things like that." Five minutes later, Cox got up and left. He was lightly dressed, and in view of the chilly weather, Shotwell surmised that Cox must be living close by.

That was about it. Only in November of 1954, more than two and a half years later, when Shotwell saw the article in *Coronet*, did he realize Cox was still considered missing. At that point he had contacted the authorities.

At the restaurant, agents showed a photo of Cox to Murlin Kuykendall, the cashier. She said a man resembling the picture occasionally had breakfast there, usually between 8:30 and 9 A.M. A morning surveillance was established at the restaurant. Although by this time the CID files on Cox were officially closed, it was decided to continue the surveillance indefinitely.

Shortly thereafter, on January 16, 1955, a story in the *New York Sunday News* reviewed the Cox case, noting the fifth anniversary of Cox's disappearance.

Fortunately or unfortunately, as the case might be, Minnie Cox was about to receive one more anonymous letter. Someone tore out the clipping from the *Sunday News*, circled the name "George," and wrote a note to the effect that she should have the authorities contact "ex-Marine Constr. George Tice, once of Middletown and Ellenville, N.Y." This lead, however, like so many others before it, turned out to be worthless.

Agents checked on Tice family members in both Middletown and Ellenville. The only George Tice in Middletown was a sixty-seven-year-old army veteran of World War I. In Ellenville, where there were several Tices, only one was named George. At age fifty-four, this George Tice could hardly be the youthful "George" of the Cox case. However, since he had once served in the Marines, he was evidently the one referred to by the anonymous tipster.

In Washington, it was decided to publicize the sighting at the Greyhound restaurant, presumably in the hope that someone who knew Cox would come forward.

"Search for Missing Cadet Revived Here," read a February headline in the *Washington News*. The article, by reporter Stan Felder, began:

> Richard Colvin Cox, 22-year-old cadet who vanished from West Point five years ago—one of the most baffling disappearances in recent history—is believed to be alive and possibly in Washington, The News learned today.
>
> Military authorities distributed pictures of the missing cadet to Washington police and other law enforcement agencies last week and asked them to keep a sharp lookout for him "because he may be in the area right now."
>
> Army investigators said they received "highly important information" just last month from a "former service buddy" of Cox which led them once again to press the search.
>
> The man, whose name officers refuse to disclose, told investigators he saw and spoke to Cox, now 26 years old, at the

Greyhound bus station at 11th Street and New York Ave. NW, nearly three years ago.

He said later he didn't think anything about meeting at the time as he didn't know Cox had been reported missing.

Last month, he said, he saw a story about Cox in a pocket magazine and put "two and two together."

On January 31, 1955, forty-six-year-old Theodore Miller called the FBI in San Francisco to say he not only knew Richard Cox but also had traveled with him around the country in December 1950. It was a long, rambling tale, beginning when Miller met a man named Mike Bey in a San Francisco bar. The two had struck up a friendship and decided to travel east together. Along the way, they had pawned various items and sold Miller's used car to cover traveling expenses and liquor.

When they reached Mobile, Alabama, Miller said, Bey made a long-distance call to Jersey City to a girl named Gail Shea, a nightclub entertainer, asking her for money. Bey showed him her picture, Miller said, adding, "She was a real looker."

Soon after this, Bey had confided in him that his real name was Otis Brumfield and had showed him a seaman's identification card with his photo and the name "Brumfield." Later, though, the man said that "Brumfield" was an alias, as was "Bey."

From Mobile, they had traveled to Atlanta, and from there to Charleston, South Carolina, where they parted company. On his way back to California, Miller said, he saw a newspaper article with Cox's picture, and he recognized his recent companion. The article had mentioned something about Cox having been seen near an Atlanta bus station, and this would have been about the time Miller and Bey were in Atlanta. At this point, Miller said, he placed a collect call to Mrs. Rupert Cox in Ohio, but the call was refused.

Agents found no listing for either Bey or Brumfield among merchant marine or Coast Guard records. Perhaps, they thought, they could find him through his lady friend. There was no Gail Shea in the Jersey City phone directory, but they found a listing for a Gail *Shay*. Then, through the New York City Police Department, they learned that the Gail Shay from Jersey City (real name Kiminis) was working as a dancer at the Famous Door Club on West Fifty-second Street.

At the Famous Door, a CID agent, along with Detective Casey of the NYPD, saw Shay, after completing her performance, standing at the bar with a man bearing a striking resemblance to Cox and conversing, according to the agent, "in a manner that indicated strong attachment."

With Casey's help, the agent questioned Shay and her companion separately. When shown photos of Cox, Shay agreed that this was the man who was with her at the bar, her "date" for the evening, but that his name was not Cox.

The man, when questioned, displayed identification that indicated he was employed by the Power and Light Company of Poughkeepsie, New York. He was asked to show his right arm, and though he was puzzled by the request, he did so willingly. There was no scar. Once more a balloon had burst—the subject was merely a Richard Cox look-alike.

Back with Shay, agents again turned their attention to Brumfield. She had known, she said, a man named *Bromfeld*, but she had since married and hadn't seen Bromfeld for over two years. In a later interview, she showed them pictures of Bromfeld, but said there was little resemblance to Cox. Bromfeld, for instance, was over six feet tall, which ruled him out as a Cox possibility.

Further record checks, coincidentally, showed that a man named "Brumfield" had once been in the Twenty-seventh Constabulary, Cox's unit overseas. He was Master Sergeant Jack W. Brumfield, presently assigned to the Northwestern Military Academy in Wisconsin as an ROTC instructor. A CID agent, following up on this, interviewed Sergeant Brumfield at the Wisconsin school and learned that almost all Brumfield's time in Germany had been spent with another Constabulary unit; he had been in the Twenty-seventh for only a few days. Brumfield had not known Cox personally; shown his picture, he could not recall him.

In Hattiesburg, Mississippi, where Miller was reinterviewed, he told basically the same story. Once more he claimed that Cox was his traveling companion in December 1950, and he again identified a photo of Cox as being the likeness of Bey/Brumfield. A military policeman doing the interview noted that Miller was a known alcoholic with a very poor reputation in Hattiesburg: he was described as a hobo, bum, tramp, and worse. The MP ended his report by saying that Miller's "reliability can be judged accordingly."

Finally, it was decided that the alcoholic Miller had been wasting everyone's time, to include CID agents, military policemen, and Master Sergeant Jack Brumfield, who by this time was no doubt wondering, "How did *I* get involved in all this?"

Back in the nation's capital, meanwhile, although the stakeouts at the bus depot hadn't yielded anything, the articles in the Washington papers, as might have been expected, had resulted in several tips and alleged sightings.

On March 22, 1955, a Julie Hackett, of Arlington, Virginia, said that about six months earlier she saw a man resembling Cox board a bus as it was passing through Georgetown. She further stated that George Edward Birch of Arlington answered the description of "George," the last person known to have been with Cox, and that Birch bragged about doing bodily harm to Germans and was alleged to have lost a child by a German girl.

Boardinghouses, bars, restaurants, dry cleaners, and hotels were checked in a thirty-five-square-block area near where the alleged Cox got on the bus. Results were negative. Also, an FBI check on George Birch found no evidence that he could be the "George" of the Cox case.

As a result of the same newspaper article, Ridgeley Belt of Washington notified the provost marshal of the Military District of Washington that a man resembling Cox was living at 1111 Thirteenth Street, N.W., and working at the Safeway store in that neighborhood. The Safeway clerk turned out to be a James E. Weaver, who did indeed have a strong resemblance to Cox. When agents saw the prominent birthmark near Weaver's right eye, however, they realized he could not be Richard Cox.

If anyone doubted the CID's tenacity, they would only have had to follow the trail initiated by a call about this time from Carl Wetzel of Washington. After seeing the newspaper article, Wetzel told the army he saw a man resembling Cox on a Trailways bus between New York City and Washington. Wetzel, who had left the bus in Washington, believed the alleged Cox had continued on to North Carolina.

Trailway records indicated that the bus Wetzel referred to had been driven by an Alvin McGowan. McGowan, shown photographs of Cox, was unable to help. However, he said his leg of the trip had ended in Washington; the next driver, from the Richmond Division of Trailways, was Willis Hardiman, who had the run from Washington to Richmond.

Hardiman, interviewed in Richmond, was likewise unable to help. In Richmond, however, he had been relieved by R. H. Heres of Trailways' Raleigh Division, who drove the bus from Richmond to Raleigh, North Carolina. Finally, in Raleigh, Heres was interviewed and shown pictures of Cox. He remembered the bus trip, but said he did not specifically remember anyone like Cox on that particular run. He felt sure, however, that he *had* seen a person resembling Cox; unfortunately, he couldn't say where or when.

Sadly, the summary report concluded: "To date, this investigation has disclosed no additional evidence which would indicate that COX is in the Washington, D.C., area."

In January 1955, John H. Noble had stepped out of a plane at New York's Idlewild Airport with an incredible story. Noble, an American citizen living in Germany, had been seized by the Russians in 1945 and held prisoner for nine and a half years, four of them as a slave laborer in the prison camp at Vorkuta, north of the Arctic Circle.

From April 3 to April 7, 1955, the *New York Times* ran a series of articles in which Noble told of his ordeal. It was a gripping, heart-wrenching tale of cruelty, misery, and injustice, compounded by Noble's revelation that other captive Americans had been in the Soviet gulag.

In the April 5 installment, Nobel wrote: "I was known as the 'Amerikanitz.' I was the only American prisoner in Camp Number 3. After I was there a while, though, I heard about other Americans in Vorkuta." Noble mentioned five names. *One of the names was* "*Cox.*"

Those following the Cox story came to full alert. Some recalled the earlier theory, that Cox, while in an intelligence unit in Germany, somehow had become involved with the Soviets. Could he have been kidnapped, spirited out of the country, and later shipped to Vorkuta? Was Cox, even now, a forgotten slave laborer in the Soviet Union, suffering unspeakable torment hour after hour, day after endless day?

Shortly after his arrival in the States, Noble had been interviewed at length by various agencies of the U.S. government. Now, on April 22, 1955, with the name "Cox" having come to light, he was interviewed again, this time by the FBI. Noble told the agents that the Cox mentioned in the article was a *Homer* Cox, who had been taken prisoner by the Russians in 1945. He was released over a year previously, had returned to his native Oklahoma City, and had since died.

Noble said that Homer Cox was well known to the U.S. State Department, and a different person from Richard Cox. When shown a number of photos of Richard Cox, Noble said he had never seen the man.

A CID investigator, scanning the report on Ernest Shotwell, thought the name sounded familiar. Soon he remembered why. In the CID files was a report from the FBI's New York field office, a memo stating that Shotwell, on July 26, 1951, had contacted an FBI agent in Danville, Virginia, in response to a newspaper article requesting information about Richard Cox. In his Danville statement, Shotwell had said he had known Cox in 1948 at the Stewart Field Preparatory School. Then, apparently wanting to be helpful, he had furnished certain personal information about Cox. The agent who talked to him, however, had noted that all this information could have been obtained from *Pretirona*, the prep school yearbook that Shotwell had in his possession.

This was troubling. If Shotwell knew in 1951 that Cox was missing, why did he not report the 1952 meeting right then and there? And why did it take the *Coronet* article, some two and a half years later, to make him come forward? In short, was Shotwell's story to be trusted?

A message was sent to Texas, near Shotwell's current Coast Guard duty station:

> Request that SHOTWELL be reinterviewed and a written statement obtained if possible to determine the reason for the discrepancies in his statements. . . . It should be noted that SHOTWELL stated he had no knowledge that Cox was missing until November 1954, and yet he volunteered information to the FBI on the Cox case in 1951. Request further, an exploration in interview of SHOTWELL'S reason for not stating the full facts, in order to determine whether he knows more than he has so far revealed, or whether he has been consistently and successfully lying.

Ernest Shotwell was interviewed once again, this time at Freeport, Texas, where his ship, the Coast Guard cutter *Dione*, was berthed. When questioned about the discrepancy, he admitted knowing in 1951 that Cox was missing but said that when he saw him in 1952, he just assumed Cox had returned to the Academy and resigned prior to that chance meeting. Shotwell, still most cooperative, unhesitatingly agreed to write out a statement, one he would sign and swear to. When he did so, he told the same story, beginning with his attendance, along with Cox, at the Stewart Field Prep School.

During this time, I knew Cox fairly well, however, not a close friend. He appeared to be a good soldier, and neat in appearance. At no time did [he] appear to be homosexual, and made no advance to me, or anyone, that I can recollect.

I saw Cox in 1952, around Feb. or March, in the Greyhound Bus Depot, Post Restaurant, Washington D.C., for about 5 minutes.

I went over to speak to him, and called him by name. He appeared startled and not overly joyful at seeing a friend. At that time he said "I resigned from the Academy last year and am going to work in Germany." When I talked to him he appeared to be in a hurry, and left the restaurant through the street entrance. His personal appearance was not in keeping with a West Point Cadet and [he was] clothed light for the weather. I have not seen him since 1952 or know of his present whereabouts.

The statement, signed "Ernest J. Shotwell, Jr.," was witnessed by Agents John F. McCauley and James L. Beasley. Next, Shotwell was asked if he would be willing to take a lie detector test. He would.

Shotwell passed the polygraph examination with flying colors. The test showed no attempt at evasion; indications were that Ernest Shotwell was telling the truth. Meanwhile, despite the obvious invasion of privacy, a search had been made of Shotwell's locker and other personal effects aboard the *Dione*, but nothing was found to indicate Shotwell knew anything more than what he had already testified.

Suddenly, on August 5, 1955, further background information on Richard Cox came from an unexpected source. Joseph Vaux, a military policeman, told the CID that he was investigating John Anderson (not his real name), an instructor at the Stewart Field Preparatory School since 1947. Before coming to Stewart, Anderson had been a public school teacher in New Rochelle, New York. The present investigation, Vaux said, stemmed from a report accusing Anderson of homosexual activities during the time he was teaching in the New Rochelle school system.

The CID, although leaving the current Anderson investigation to Vaux, still wanted to talk to the man. He had been at Stewart

Field while Cox was there, and in view of his alleged homosexual tendencies and the similar stories about Cox, they felt he might provide useful information.

Anderson, fully cooperative, was interviewed at length by the CID. Recalling the period when Cox was at the prep school, Anderson said it was his custom at the time to conduct conversation groups in his office at Stewart Field for the benefit of the cadet candidates. Each year, he said, certain students would attend and enter into the discussions. He would guide most of the conversations, he said, and would answer any questions the boys would have.

When asked the nature of these "conversations," Anderson admitted that most of the discussions pertained to sex. He would speak at length on the topic, he said, since he considered himself an expert on the technical aspects of the subject and capable of explaining many theories of sexual relationships. It was his personal belief, he said, which he could back with authoritative references, that there was nothing abnormal about homosexual activity. He believed it a man's duty to determine if he was heterosexual or homosexual and to live according to his decision. He tried, therefore, Anderson said, to aid the young men at the prep school who attended his conversation meetings to reach their decision.

In their report, the investigators made no comment on their reaction to Anderson, nor did they say what they thought about an older man in a position of authority trying to influence the sexual orientation of young students. Similarly, they did not say what they suspected about Anderson's motives.

The investigators asked Anderson if he remembered Richard Cox. Yes, Anderson said, he remembered him very well, and in the spring of 1948, Cox was a regular attendee at the conversation meetings. Cox, he said, never participated in the discussions, but always sat a little apart from the group and merely listened.

Anderson described Cox as a "swell guy," well liked by all, but never too close to anyone. Why was it, Anderson was asked, that he seemed to remember so much about Cox?

"It was the eyes," Anderson said. "I would never forget him because his eyes seemed to express a certain sadness derived from having been hurt deeply in an emotional way at some time in the past." He couldn't say why he felt this, because he and Cox never became friendly. He had often hoped that Cox would confide in him, he said; he felt they could have developed a great friendship, but Cox never did.

Anderson's personal opinion was that Cox was a homosexual who, through some combination of circumstances, had met with foul play. He had no specific reason for saying Cox was homosexual, but based his belief on years of experience in judging men's characters, particularly men inclined toward homosexuality. He was inclined, however, to feel that if Cox wanted to leave West Point to run away with a homosexual friend, he would have left in an orderly fashion after submitting his resignation.

Finally, Anderson said that for several years he looked for Cox every time he entered a bar, and he admitted that the bars he was in the habit of visiting were ones where known homosexuals would congregate.

Putting all this together, and even weighing Anderson's so-called expert opinion, agents felt they still had no proof that Richard Cox had been actively homosexual. At the very least, however, it seemed that Cox had been fascinated with the question of his own sexual identity, whether it was heterosexual, homosexual, or a combination of both.

Wickenburg is a quiet town in the middle of Arizona, about fifty miles northwest of Phoenix. When dawn broke on November 3, 1955, the morning promised to be peaceful and uneventful, much like other Wickenburg mornings. Mary Pollay, following her usual routine and unaware that something dramatic was about to occur, left home shortly after seven.

Mary and her husband owned the Pollay Electric Store in Wickenburg, and on this particular morning, it was Mary's turn to open up the shop. She arrived at the store around a quarter to eight, and as she unlocked the front door, she noticed something on the floor, just inside the door.

It was a small white envelope, smudged with what appeared to be bloodstains. Picking it up, she read: "Very important must get to this place. Police West Point Military Academy." Startled, she opened the envelope and read the handwritten note inside:

"About Richard C. Cox (Dick) 3rd Class US Military Academy. It has been over five years, but I know where he is, but it will cost a life to fine him, my life. You see he is my husban. If you know what a Red dove means you won't under any way try to contact me. Please. He needs help so do I badly."

The note was signed "Alice Loraine," under which she had written *"Alles kaput,"* German for "all is lost." Off to one side were the words "Betty forgive him"; at the bottom of the sheet, as a kind of postscript, was an unfinished phrase: "If one would know I am writing my life would not be worth a . . ."

On the back of the envelope, adding to the weirdness, was written: "I am wearing silver bracelet. Have wore for many years." There was a drawing of a bracelet plus a crude diagram, apparently showing a pattern of stones on the bracelet's face.

The letter appeared to have been written by someone who had been reading too many mystery stories, and it was hard to take such a note seriously. However, Mary Pollay was taking no chances. She promptly gave the letter to Richard Savage, the Wickenburg chief of police, who in turn contacted the FBI office in Phoenix and then, as the writer had requested, sent it on to West Point.

Neither Mrs. Pollay nor Chief Savage recognized the handwriting on the letter, nor did either of them have any idea as to who could have written it.

During the next several weeks, CID agent Sidney Stark spent time in Wickenburg, talking to local residents and taking a statement from Mary Pollay. In her statement, she described finding the letter, then added: "I do not believe that the letter had been written just before I found it as it was soiled and appeared to have been carried by someone for quite some time. Other than that I know of nothing else that would be of help."

On January 10, 1956, Sidney Stark was forced to conclude, in the words of his report, that while Chief Savage "would continue to maintain a search . . . identification of the writer of the letter, found on 3 November 1955 at the Pollay Electric Company, Wickenburg, Arizona, could not be determined."

Throughout 1955 and 1956, CID agents continued to interview and take sworn statements from former cadets who had known Cox, primarily men who had been in the same cadet company or who had been with him on the track or cross-country team. Although nearly every one of them had been interviewed back in 1950, when Cox first disappeared, there was still a hope that some new bit of information might emerge. However, by this time memories were getting hazy, and even witnesses trying to be scrupulously honest found themselves confusing what they knew for a fact from personal experience with what they had picked up over the years from rumors and hearsay.

At Fort Sill, Oklahoma, for example, on May 5, 1956, Tom Strider, Cox's former cadet squad leader, now a captain, told military police investigator Byron Roberts:

> Stories of Dick and theories of his disappearance ran in five directions: 1. "George" had murdered him. 2. Dick had gone home to his girl friend. 3. His roommate Welch had fallen for his girl friend and "did him in" to stand first in line for her. 4. He had developed amnesia either with or without "George" beating him up, and finally, 5. He was tired of school and just left.
>
> I am sure that the story of "George" has been repeated time and again and with more accuracy than I am able to recall at this time, however this is what I "learned" from his two roommates . . . in Germany, he had testified at a trial as a witness for the prosecution against another EM (enlisted man) named "George." The trial, I believe, was for murder . . . when "George" called that Saturday, Dick had expressed a sense of dread to his two roommates but had dressed to go to the Thayer for supper with him. . . . If the story of "George" is true, I have always wondered why the records of courts-martial never tracked down "George." I cannot conceive of Dick Cox fabricating the story, and I did not hear the story from him.

Strider was being frank and honest, but, as might be expected from testimony blurred by the passage of time, he was incorrect in the details. Whoever had mentioned Cox's alleged trial testimony, it had not been Cox's roommates, and neither of them had said anything about Cox having a "sense of dread."

Others, however, said they had heard Cox's "testimony" story firsthand. In Ansbach, Germany, for example, Robert Wells, who had been at Stewart Field with Cox, said on April 5, 1955: "I did not personally associate with Cox, only in a group. As far as I know he seemed like a nice guy and was a fairly good athlete. One time in a bull session Cox said he was glad to get out of Berlin, because he was a witness in a rape case, and the subject threatened to get him. Not knowing Cox as a personal friend, I do not know if he was homosexually inclined."

Among those interviewed was Cox's former roommate Deane Welch. On May 17, 1955, at Fort Carson, Colorado, where he was assigned to Company A of the Thirty-second Engineer Battalion, Welch said he had visited Cox's family in Ohio on several occasions, but neither he nor they had any new information.

The other roommate, Joe Urschel, was reinterviewed on July 8, 1955, while he was a member of the 3505 Pilot Training Group at Greenville Air Force Base in Mississippi. The questioner was Military Police Captain Dennis Sibert.

"My best theory," said Urschel, "is that Cox is dead, more likely through foul play. I would not discount the possibility, however, that he could have met with an accident."

"Why do you believe that Cox is dead?" asked Sibert.

"I don't believe that Cox could stand to have his mother suffer so much, and well, just knowing him as I did, I can't believe that he is still alive. . . . If Cox *was* possibly still alive, I am sure he could be back in Germany since he always talked about Germany and the good times he had there."

"Do you believe that Cox had homosexual tendencies?"

"I don't see how that could be possible. Knowing Cox as intimately as I did, I would have gotten some indication. He just couldn't have been the type."

Also interviewed from the Class of '52 was Edward Higgins White II, a member of the Twenty-second Fighter Day Squadron at Bitburg Air Base in Germany. White, who would soon join NASA as a member of the astronaut program, had been listed as a cross-country teammate of Cox, but on July 2, 1956, he told an interviewer that was an error.

"I was a member of the track team during all four years," White said, "which may account for my being listed somewhere as a cross-country man. During the fall of 1949 I played soccer which is played during the same period as cross-country. I did not know Richard C. Cox well at all; we exchanged greetings occasionally but I do not recall ever having had an extended conversation with him."

Throughout 1956, FBI and CID agents continued to locate, interview, and take statements from every conceivable source, but with little to show as a result. Typical of these sessions was one held August 22, 1956, with First Lieutenant Edgar McClung at Fort Polk, Louisiana. His statement read:

> I, 1st Lt Edgar B. McClung, was a member of the Class of 1952 at the United States Military Academy at the time of the disappearance of Cadet Cox, and was a classmate of Cox. Cox and I were members of the Cross country team. We were not close friends, and the only contact I ever had with him was as a member of this team. We had casual

conversations on many occasions but I cannot recall any of the topics of these conversations or any remarks that were made. . . . Our classes were not at the same times and I seldom ran into him except at cross country meets or practices. . . . To the best of my knowledge he got along well in his studies, was well liked and was a good athlete. After his disappearance I heard rumors about what may have happened to him, such as his being kidnapped for unknown reasons, his disappearance for financial hardship or other personal difficulties, but to my knowledge none of these reasons were substantiated. I had no knowledge of any homosexual tendencies or communistic leanings or connections on his part. Any direct knowledge or ideas I now hold have been formulated as a result of articles I have read in newspapers or as a result of conversations with other friends of mine who have had no direct knowledge of the case.

Statements like this, or ones close to it, were repeated hundreds of times. Meanwhile, of course, random letters, allegedly with information about Cox, continued to arrive with some regularity. Of these, one prolific source was the country's penal system, where prisoners with time on their hands became most ingenious, offering to provide "valuable" information in exchange for some small favor such as a positive parole board recommendation. Lurid, foundationless "tips" about Cox came from a variety of institutions, including the Federal Prison at Leavenworth, Kansas; the Kansas State Penitentiary at Lansing; the Massachusetts Correctional Institute at Bridgewater; the Princess Anne Jail in Virginia Beach, Virginia; and the Tioga County Jail in Wellsboro, Pennsylvania. One prisoner wrote of a friend named George who had confessed to killing Cox and who had showed him Cox's cadet overcoat, complete with its gray and red trim. Since the color red was no part of any cadet uniform, the writer had overplayed his hand, apparently as a result of an overabundant "creativity."

In July 1956, FBI Director J. Edgar Hoover wrote to Cox's mother in Mansfield "regarding Richard C. Cox, whom you reported missing in January of 1950."

"At this time," said the letter, "we are checking our files and will appreciate your letting us know whether the location of the above person is still desired by you. If so, the notice will, of course, be continued in file."

Understandably, Minnie Cox asked the FBI to continue the search. In her reply to Director Hoover, she wrote: "As you note, seven years will have elapsed Jan. 14, 1957 since my son disappeared. The State of Ohio states that at that time he will be declared legally dead. Please keep file open. Thank you!"

As it happened, there would be some advantage to having Cox declared legally dead. When he first entered the service in 1946, he had taken out a small life insurance policy on himself with the Pioneer American Insurance Company of Houston, Texas, listing his mother and his sisters as beneficiaries. After he disappeared, his mother had paid the premiums to keep the policy active, so this policy, as well as his government National Service policy, were still in effect.

On January 25, 1957, Congressman J. Harry McGregor made reference to Cox's life insurance as he contacted FBI Director J. Edgar Hoover. Referring to the Cox case, McGregor wrote:

> I am sure your files will show my interest in the case since the boy was an appointee of mine to the United States Military Academy at West Point, N.Y. On January 14, 1950, he disappeared from the Academy without a trace.
>
> Because of the seven year time lapse with no trace of the boy, we are attempting to do everything proper and within the laws to see his widowed mother, who is the beneficiary, receives the face amount due on his National Service Life Insurance Policy, as well as any accumulated dividends.

Early in 1957, as a result of all this, Richard Colvin Cox was declared legally dead. In due course the face amounts of both policies were paid to his mother. Generously, however, she kept none of the money for herself, but instead divided it among her children.

Following this, in June 1957, the Army Criminal Investigation Division decided it had done all it could in the case of Richard Cox. A final report summary said:

> Over seven years have passed since COX disappeared from the United States Military Academy. During that period, an extensive and thorough search by both military and civil law enforcement agencies has proved futile in determining the whereabouts of COX and the circumstances surrounding his

disappearance. Available information indicates that COX has been continuously absent from the United States Military Academy, and his home in Mansfield, Ohio, during the past seven years. In addition, COX has been unheard from by his family, associates or those with whom he might normally have corresponded or contacted. All investigative leads have been exhausted; therefore, this investigation is being closed in the files of this office. In the event any additional information pertinent to this investigation is received, a supplemental report will be submitted.

A complete file on this case, to include a copy of all progress reports, the final report, and other pertinent correspondence, has been forwarded to the United States Army Military Police Repository for Criminal Investigation Reports, Fort Gordon, Georgia, for file and will thus be available in the event it is needed at a future date.

The file, several inches thick, contained a wealth of backup data, including various reports by individual CID agents, names of witnesses, and sworn statements from more than two hundred people who had been seen by investigators during their fruitless search. Understandably, army officials believed they finally were justified in putting the Cox mystery behind them, and they doubtless believed they had heard the last of Richard Colvin Cox, the missing West Point cadet.

They were wrong.

Cadet Richard C. Cox in his West Point uniform. Cox vanished suddenly on January 14, 1950. His disappearance stumped investigators for nearly half a century. *USMA Library, Special Collections*

The Cox family home in Mansfield, Ohio. Investigators thought that Cox would probably try to contact his mother, Minnie, who was particularly close to her youngest son. *Marshall Jacobs*

This 1947 snapshot shows Cox (leaning against Jeep) with his best friend Joseph "Bud" Groner (behind the wheel) and Rosemary Vogel in Coburg, Germany, where Cox and Groner served together in the army. With few leads about Cox's disappearance, the FBI put Groner under surveillance, expecting that Cox would contact him and to make sure Groner wasn't "George," a prime suspect in the disappearance. Authorities also searched for Vogel, a German citizen to whom Cox had written just days before he vanished. *Marshall Jacobs Research Files*

Photo of Richard Cox prior to entering West Point. *USMA Library, Special Collections*

Cox, in his plebe year, from his class photo in the 1949 *Howitzer,* West Point's yearbook. *Howitzer*

In the summer of 1949, Cox was a student company commander at West Point's Camp Buckner, where plebes undergo military training between their plebe (freshman) and yearling (sophomore) years. *USMA Library, Special Collections*

Cox relaxes during the busy and arduous summer training at Camp Buckner. *USMA Library, Special Collections*

Deane Welch, one of Cox's roommates. For a time, Welch was under suspicion in Cox's disappearance and kept under surveillance by the FBI. *USMA Library, Special Collections*

Cox's roommates, Joe Urschel (above) and Welch (below), in their 1952 *Howitzer* pictures. Authorities had received several reports alleging that the missing cadet had been involved in homosexual activities and conjectured that he could have dropped out of West Point for this reason. FBI agents even dragged Urschel and Welch, who emphatically denied any knowledge about Cox's suspected bisexuality, to several gay bars in New York City, hoping they might be able to spot Cox. *Howitzer*

Cadets from West Point's class of 1949 celebrate graduation by throwing their caps high in the air. As these cadets were about to begin their military careers, Cox was just finishing his first year at the Academy. He would have graduated in 1952. *USMA Archives*

The last known photo of Richard Cox, taken in fun on January 7, 1950, by his roommate Deane Welch as he dozed at his desk. A drunken Cox had just returned from a visit with the mysterious "George," a man Cox said he knew in Germany. Authorities suspected this man may have known what happened to Cox—and some speculated that he may have even kidnapped or killed the young cadet. *USMA Library*

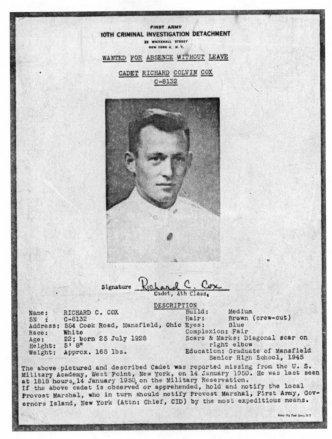

After Cox disappeared, the FBI and the Army's Criminal Investigation Detachment tracked down hundreds of leads, all to no avail. In February 1950, the army officially declared Cox AWOL and widely distributed this wanted poster. *Army CID files*

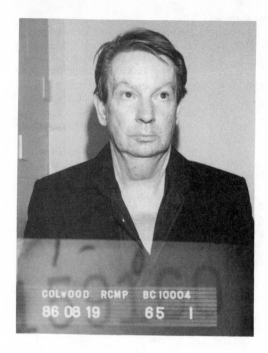

A mug shot of Robert Frisbee, who murdered his wealthy companion Muriel Barnett aboard a cruise ship off the coast of Canada. Independent investigator Marshall Jacobs thought Frisbee might be "George," Cox's visitor. *Royal Canadian Mounted Police*

COLWOOD RCMP BC 10004
86 08 19 65 1

An artist's depiction of Cox as he might look today. *Marshall Jacobs*

Part Two

Chapter 8

Marshall Jacobs

The West Point visitor, a slender, neatly dressed civilian in his late fifties, walked slowly along Thayer Road past the cadet barracks. He paused and looked around uncertainly, causing a cadet to stop and ask if he could help.

"Yes," said the visitor, "can you tell me which of those buildings is Washington Hall?"

"Yes sir, it's the one over there."

The visitor thanked the cadet and then, on an impulse, said, "Tell me, have you been here very long?"

The cadet smiled. "Yes, sir, I sure have, nearly four years. I'm a first-classman."

"Well, I was wondering," said the other, "have you ever heard about a cadet who mysteriously disappeared?"

The answer came almost reflexively. "Oh, you must mean Dick Cox."

"Yes, that's the one."

"Y'know, when cadets start swapping stories about West Point legends, his name often comes up. Tell me, sir, do you know much about him?"

"Yes, quite a bit," said the visitor, thinking to himself that the cadet had asked the right man. By this time, Marshall Jacobs was undoubtedly the country's leading authority on the case of Richard Colvin Cox.

He had been a ballplayer in the Boston Red Sox and St. Louis Cardinals farm systems, a left-handed pitcher with good control and a wicked curveball. After baseball came a teaching career spanning more than thirty-five years. Then, in 1985, Marshall Jacobs was nearing retirement and looking for a new challenge.

125

He had been a good husband, a good father, a respected member of the community. Although life was comfortable, recent years had brought a great deal of routine and not enough adventure. Well, he had an answer for that—upon his retirement he would become an amateur sleuth and set out to solve a thirty-five-year-old mystery, the greatest mystery, in fact, in West Point history.

It would be a time-consuming effort, Jacobs knew, even a costly one, but it would probably be intriguing, and in a way it was fitting that his project would focus on West Point. His fascination with the Military Academy had begun a long time ago.

Marshall Jacobs celebrated his tenth birthday in October 1936. He would always remember that autumn, for it marked his first visit to the famed U.S. Military Academy and his first contact with West Point cadets.

Earlier that year, the Jacobs family had moved to Newburgh, a city on the Hudson just north of West Point. In 1936, Newburgh was a warm, slow-moving, friendly community, and for young Jacobs, who had spent his early life in Jersey City, it seemed almost pastoral. Across the street from his home was a grassy, tree-lined park, with playgrounds and a swimming pool, where he and his friends would gather to swim, play ball, or just talk. And when they talked, it was mostly about sports.

Sometimes, as a special treat, he would be taken down Storm King Highway to West Point, perhaps to watch cadets drilling on the Plain. In the fall, of course, from three to five each afternoon, the main attraction was football practice, held on the far corner of the Plain near Trophy Point. With admiring eyes, he and other area youngsters would watch the scrimmaging and select their own particular heroes. It was a happy time.

In 1939, the Jacobs family returned to Jersey City, where Marshall entered Henry Snyder High School and became a pitcher on the school baseball team. At this stage of his life, he was consumed by a desire to become a professional ballplayer, and on the side, using an assumed name to preserve his amateur eligibility, he pitched for a semi-pro team known as the "Jersey Dodgers." Their uniforms, of which they were inordinately proud, were hand-me-downs worn the previous season by "Dem Bums," the major league Dodgers from Brooklyn.

In 1944, during World War II, Jacobs at age seventeen left high school and joined the navy, with his dad's support and approval and a reluctant blessing from his worried mother. By mid-1945, he was a crew member on an LST (Landing Ship, Tank), a ship scheduled to head for the Panama Canal and the Pacific in preparation for the invasion of Japan. With war's end, however, the trip was canceled, and early in 1946, eager to begin his professional baseball career, Jacobs received his honorable discharge from the navy. Within weeks he signed a contract to play for the Lenoir, North Carolina, Red Sox.

It was a far cry from the major leagues, and starting pay was only $125 a month, but for Marshall Jacobs, playing professional baseball was a boyhood dream come true.

Jacobs was a mainstay of the Lenoir pitching staff that summer, helping them to become league champions. Then, at season's end, he hustled back to Jersey City to finish his high school senior year and receive his diploma. The following spring, as he returned to baseball, Jacobs learned the Lenoir team's contracts had been bought by the St. Louis Cardinals. He joined the Winston-Salem Cardinals, did well, was promoted to the next-higher level of the Cardinal farm system, and joined the Cardinal team in Lynchburg, Virginia.

That season, unfortunately, he began to have arm problems and a local doctor discovered bone chips in the left elbow. Even after surgery was performed to remove the chips, his pitching just wasn't the same. His southpaw curveball, long his major weapon, had lost much of its bite. Finally, he was forced to admit that the arm was never going to recover fully. As a promising member of the St. Louis farm system, he had visualized himself one day pitching for the major league Cardinals. It was not to be. Reluctantly, Jacobs abandoned his dreams of playing in "The Show."

With baseball now behind him, education became doubly important, and Jacobs entered Bergen Junior College in Teaneck, New Jersey. The following year he transferred to Duquesne University in Pittsburgh. In January 1950, while he was at Duquesne, Jacobs saw a newspaper story about a cadet missing from West Point. It was a strange tale, and because of his past interest in the Military Academy, he read everything he could find about the case. Even after the press lost interest and the stories faded away, he remembered the missing cadet and wondered what had happened. Maybe someday he'd try to find out.

Following his sophomore year at Duquesne, Jacobs, seeking warmer climes, transferred to the University of Miami in Coral Gables, Florida. One Sunday afternoon, early in his senior year, he

was with some friends on a beach in Miami when he was introduced to Lois Sakrais, a petite, vivacious blonde. According to the
girl making the introduction, Lois swam professionally in a water
ballet.

Later that week, Jacobs summoned his courage and asked the attractive Miss Sakrais to go out with him. Today, with a smile, Lois
Jacobs says, "After that, I never dated another boy." They were
married on April 6, 1952, the spring following Jacobs's graduation.
By that time he was teaching in the Dade County school system,
and in the years that followed, he taught both social studies and
history in a fulfilling career spanning more than three decades. Then,
in 1985, as his retirement time approached, Lois asked what he was
going to do.

"Well," he said, "I've a project in mind, actually it's a form of
research. I'm going to find out what happened to Richard Cox."

"Who?"

"Richard Cox—he was a cadet at West Point who disappeared
back in 1950."

"Never heard of him." Normally Lois and Marshall confided in
each other, but this was the first time he had ever mentioned what
he called his "research project." Lois was startled, even a bit
amused, but if that was what he wanted. . . .

Jacobs had been teaching history for more than thirty years, always relying on what someone else had recorded. Now, perhaps,
if he could research and eventually solve a thirty-five-year-old
mystery, he could make his own small contribution to the historical record.

Marshall and Lois mentioned this new project to a couple with
whom they often socialized. To their amazement, the woman, a
good friend, said she was originally from Mansfield, Ohio. Moreover, she had been in Dick Cox's high school graduation class and
knew the Cox family. It was a remarkable coincidence; maybe it was
a good sign.

Jacobs began by visiting the main branch of the Miami Public
Library, a large, modern facility with outstanding research capa-
bilities. The staff was friendly, cooperative, and eager to help, and
with their assistance he obtained a wealth of material. There were
newspaper clippings from wide-ranging sources, all the way from
the *New York Times* to Cox's hometown paper, the *Mansfield News
Journal*; magazine articles included those from *Life*, *Coronet*, and
Redbook. The librarians even came up with a number of books on

West Point for Jacobs to study. Painstakingly, he read every item, and, where appropriate, he made a copy for his files. As might be expected, there was much repetition, and many of the stories were mere rehashes of what had appeared elsewhere. The most thorough reporting, in his opinion, appeared in a series of pieces in the *Mansfield News Journal*, written in 1982 by reporter Jim Underwood.

Underwood had done an excellent job of summarizing the case, and his stories included previously classified information obtained from both the FBI and the CID. It was apparent that Underwood had also conducted a number of in-depth, face-to-face interviews. Over the years, many theories and scenarios had been advanced. In his articles, Underwood touched all the bases. In sum, however, like the FBI and CID investigators, reporter Underwood was forced to leave the story dangling; he had ended his series not with answers, but with a number of provocative questions.

Jacobs, who realized he would be going over the same ground, meeting some of the same people, and sifting the same evidence, knew he owed much to Underwood's efforts. He recognized, of course, that he, unlike Underwood, was not an experienced interviewer or investigator. Still, he felt he could build on the work that had gone before, including Underwood's, and perhaps start a new line of research. At least he was going to try. As a teacher, he had prided himself on being thorough. He'd give this new avocation the same maximum effort.

At this point, Jacobs felt he knew all that had been made public, enough at least to get started. It was time to commence digging, and West Point, he felt, was the logical place to begin.

Jacobs wrote to the Military Academy, mentioned his desire to research the Cox case, and gave the date he proposed to arrive. The question, of course, was how the Academy would react to someone resurrecting an ancient mystery, a mystery the authorities might feel was better left forgotten. He was pleased by the prompt reply, saying in effect that he would be more than welcome to visit the West Point library and avail himself of its facilities.

Lois came with him on that first visit, perhaps out of curiosity, perhaps to give moral support. In any event, by this time she had become more than a little interested herself. They drove north from New York City along the scenic Hudson Valley, passed through the town of Highland Falls and came to the Academy's main gate. A military policeman waved them through. At the library, Marshall and Lois were greeted politely and ushered to the top-floor archives area. There, already spread out for him on a large oak table, were all the Academy's files on Richard Cox.

Jacobs happily got to work. On this and subsequent visits, two people in particular, the late Kenneth Rapp, and archivist Suzanne Christoff, went out of their way to be helpful. The head librarian, Eric Weiss, was also highly cooperative, and on a later visit Weiss asked Jacobs, when he completed his research, to consider donating his materials to the special collections branch of the West Point library. Jacobs agreed to do so, and, as a historian, he was more than pleased when Weiss said, "I want you to know that, a hundred years from now, when you're long gone, people here at the Academy will be going through your files and reviewing your research."

Now that he had seen the newspapers, the magazines, and the archival material at West Point, the next step was to ask the FBI, citing the Freedom of Information Act, for a copy of the Bureau's files on Richard Cox. After several delays and follow-up phone calls, during which he was reminded more than once of the considerable copying expense that would be entailed, Jacobs received the files— more than fifteen hundred pages of them.

There were frustrations right from the start. As soon as he looked at the documents, he realized that a great deal of material had been deleted. Individual names of both agents and witnesses were blacked out, and frequently a whole paragraph or even an entire page was deleted, with the initials "i.p."—meaning invasion of privacy—inserted by way of explanation. At this late date, Marshall wondere why it was necessary to be so secretive. Whenever a complete page was omitted, a notation was made to that effect. Eventually, Jacobs counted some 165 missing pages.

To this point, Jacobs's efforts had been confined to reading and studying inanimate words on paper. After many weeks of this, he felt it was high time to begin working with *people*. When he was at the Academy, he had obtained a copy of a 1952 *Howitzer*, the class yearbook, as well as the Alumni Association's *Register of Graduates*, an annual publication organized by graduating class, with an address and a brief biographical sketch for each alumnus. Dick Cox, Jacobs noted, was not forgotten. Following the 1952 class roster was the entry: "Richard Colvin Cox: Mysteriously disappeared 14 Jan 50, Cadet a-21."

Jacobs, after reading the files, knew there were several people he'd want to interview. For starters, what about one of the roommates? Through the *Register* he located ex-roommate Joe Urschel and found he was living in the Key Largo area.

"Another good sign," thought Jacobs. "He's a fellow Floridian. Let's begin with him."

He phoned Urschel and made an appointment to get together the following Saturday. The drive from Miami down to the Keys took about an hour, and as he drove, the schoolteacher-turned-detective, a bit nervous, wondered how he'd be received.

Jacobs arrived at the Urschel home and introduced himself. Joe Urschel, wearing shorts, loafers, and a colorful sport shirt, was short and stocky, with a ruddy complexion and an athletic appearance. He had an open, friendly, and casual manner but still retained the military bearing Jacobs had seen in other West Pointers.

Urschel introduced Jacobs to his daughter and his wife, Marti. Everyone was smilingly cordial, and soon Joe and Marshall were on a first-name basis. Urschel obviously was interested in Jacob's project. At the same time, he was curious about his motives and surprised that anyone was concerned with the case after so many years. Nevertheless, he said he would be happy to answer any questions and to help where he could.

Urschel and Jacobs withdrew to a bright, sunlit den, furnished attractively in a typical South Florida decor. Urschel, after fulfilling his service commitment, had resigned from the Air Force in 1956. It appeared he had been successful in civilian life, since he mentioned rather off-handedly that he owned his own business, one from which he was semiretired. Urschel said he and his family were just renting the Key Largo place, and they planned to move soon to a permanent Florida location.

Jacobs had prepared a list of questions. With Urschel's consent, he turned on his tape recorder. The former cadet's answers were thoughtful, carefully framed, and often preceded by long pauses or by the phrase "to the best of my knowledge."

Jacobs, in his somewhat formal, schoolteacher manner, asked, "What was Dick Cox's attitude on the night of January seventh, 1950, when he returned to room 1943, Old North Barracks, apparently having been drinking?"

"I can't answer that, " Urschel said. "It happened so long ago that by this time I can't remember what I honestly know, instead of what I read or what somebody told me."

Jacobs nodded his understanding. "Let's try again. It has always puzzled me, as I read your statements in the files, that you and

Deane Welch didn't ask more questions about Dick Cox's visitor. Wouldn't it be natural to say, 'Hey Dick, who's this guy George? Where's he from? What's he doing here at the Point visiting you? Who's this girl Alice?' If he were *my* roommate, I would have asked those questions."

"You have to understand my relationship with Dick Cox," said Urschel. "Dick was not the type of guy you questioned. You never asked him for help on a problem. He was older than I was, and although we were roommates, we were not what you would call close friends. He never went around with my friends; I never went around with his.

"However, don't get me wrong. He was a good roommate, and we never had any problems. As for his visitor, I do remember Dick saying the man was a friend of his from Germany, a real 'weirdo.'"

"My research confirms what you say. Cox wasn't the type of man who answered questions or confided readily in someone."

"Right. Deane and I had that kind of relationship, but Dick was another person."

Jacobs paused. Then, in a quiet, serious tone, he asked: "Was there ever any suspicion of homosexuality?"

"Never. We were roommates for nearly two years, and there was never any action, or reaction on his part, that would be indicative of that."

"Did Dick Cox ever reveal to you any doubts about marrying Betty Timmons?"

"None whatsoever."

Jacobs, again referring to his list of prepared questions, mentioned something he had seen in one of the Underwood articles in the Mansfield newspaper: "Albert Allen, Cox's brother-in-law, heard a rumor that a body had been discovered in one of the tunnels which run under the barracks area, and that the Academy had covered up the story."

"Somewhere I heard that rumor," Urschel said. "I can't remember where. Along those lines, Deane and I had one of the old rooms, with a fireplace, and at one point people even searched the chimney to see if a body could have been stuffed up it."

"Could the Academy have covered it up if a body had been found?"

"Perhaps they could have—but they wouldn't."

"Next question. Could Cox have been involved in the honor code scandal which broke the following year?"

"No, he didn't mix with football players. I've never even thought of any connection."

"Well, other than football, could he have left the Academy because of some other minor honor code violation?"

"No violation is minor," Urschel said. "You either broke the code or you didn't break the code."

Urschel, to whom the cadet honor system was still sacred, realized it would be unusual if Jacobs—or any outsider for that matter—fully understood the subtleties of the code. He continued to explain: "A cadet does not lie, cheat, or steal. I guess that's obvious. What may not be so obvious is the difference between violating regulations and violating honor. A man may break regulations by sneaking off the post for a clandestine date or a drink and, if he can, return unscathed. No one would be 'honor-bound' to report him for simply leaving the post without authorization. But if the cadet who sneaked off post lied by signing in the departure book that he was going to the Thayer for dinner, he would have violated the code and his roommate or anyone else who knew about it would be obligated to report him."

"I understand," Jacobs said. "Now, could Dick Cox have violated the code the evening he met with George?"

"I don't know," Urschel said. "But if he did break the code for some reason, he was such a proud person that I don't think he could have taken being drummed out for an honor violation. Knowing his character at that time, I'd say he would have left voluntarily on his own."

Jacobs, changing the subject, asked: "When you and Deane Welch discussed the case, were you generally in agreement?"

"Yes. I think we both felt that something bad must have happened to Dick, otherwise he would have tried to contact his family."

"Are you familiar with the names 'Joseph Groner' or 'William K. Hill'?" (Hill's was a name Jacobs had seen in one of the Underwood articles.)

"No, neither one rings a bell."

"Did you hear any rumors, or did Cox ever indicate to you, that he thought of leaving the Academy?"

"Never." Understandably, some of Urschel's answers had seemed vague or uncertain. This time, however, he sounded quite positive. Clearly he had no doubts about Dick Cox's state of mind when he last saw him. Even if Cox had left voluntarily, Urschel was sure he had *not* planned to leave in advance.

Jacobs thanked Urschel for both his time and his hospitality. Urschel, in turn, said he'd be willing to talk again if it would help.

Jacobs returned home, once more took out his files, and began to arrange and catalogue them. The pages had to be sorted and resorted; few of them were in any kind of systematic order. On an impulse, he again called the FBI and mentioned the 165 missing pages.

"I'd sure like to see those pages," he said. "When do you think they might be declassified?"

"Not in your lifetime," said the voice on the phone. The answer seemed needlessly abrupt, even rude. What, he wondered, was so special about the Cox file?

After talking to Urschel about all the people who had questioned him, Jacobs realized that the army Criminal Investigation Division had been at least as involved as the FBI, maybe more so. Urschel had said that in July of '55, more than five years after Cox's disappearance, he was stationed at an air base in Mississippi when two agents, one an MP captain, had arrived to question him at length in a hot downtown hotel room. The questioning—which to Urschel seemed more like a "grilling"—had made him, despite his complete innocence, feel very uncomfortable.

Jacobs wrote to the Pentagon and asked for a copy of the CID files on the Cox case. In time, he was told that the request had been forwarded to Fort Gordon, Georgia, where the files had been sent for storage. While he waited for them, he resumed his interviews. The next person on his list was Joe "Bud" Groner. After checking his notes, he called the last known location for Groner and talked to someone who knew him. It turned out that Groner, like Urschel, was now living in Florida. Jacobs found him listed in the Daytona phone book, made the call, and arranged an appointment.

The drive from Miami to Daytona took about four and a half hours. As he drove, Jacobs thought of the task he had set for himself. It was now 1985, thirty-five years since Cox's disappearance. Was it far too late, he mused, ever to learn the real facts? So much time had passed, and so many things had occurred in the intervening years, not only to the nation, but to those who had known Richard Cox.

Jim Kelley was dead in a plane crash. Dick Shea had been killed on Pork Chop Hill. Ed White, first American to walk in space, had later perished when fire broke out in a command module during a test program.

Fortunately, though, all stories did not end tragically. Tom Ayers, Cox's classmate and best friend at Stewart Field, was now a three-star general. Mike Collins, another classmate, had made history as he circled the moon while Neil Armstrong and Buzz Aldrin took that "first small step for man." Others who had known Cox had gone on to interesting, often distinguished careers, both military and civil. By now they were scattered throughout the world, but he would meet as many of them as he could.

Was there a chance, Jacobs wondered, that Dick Cox, wherever he was, was also making some sort of contribution? From what people said of him, it didn't seem impossible.

Jacobs arrived at Daytona, checked in at the Holiday Inn, and called the Groner home. "Come on ahead," said Groner, "I'm anxious to hear about your project. But I can't believe that someone is still trying to find Dick Cox!"

Jacobs, following Groner's directions, found the house quite easily. It was a ranch-style, two-bedroom place, in a well-groomed, upper-middle-class neighborhood. Groner came to the door, smiled, invited Jacobs to enter, and introduced him to his wife, Elaine. They were an attractive couple. Bud Groner, tall, neatly dressed in a sport shirt and slacks, with a round, somewhat lined face, had a low-pitched, pleasant voice: despite living in Florida, his accent was still that of a Northerner.

"Please," he said, "call me 'Bud.' And after you've come all this way, Elaine and I insist that you stay for dinner. I think I was Dick Cox's closest friend, and I'm glad someone is still trying to unravel the mystery." It was a good beginning. Bud Groner, warm and friendly, was more than willing to talk about Cox. By the same token, he said he had spent a good bit of time talking to Mansfield reporter Jim Underwood when Underwood was doing research for that twelve-part series.

Jacobs started by summarizing what he'd learned from the files. Much of the information Groner already knew; other things, such as the fact that at one point Groner's phone had been tapped, came as a surprise.

"Why do you suppose," Jacobs asked, "that the FBI felt you knew more than you were telling?"

"Oh, I just think they were stumped in their investigation, and after all, I knew Cox."

Jacobs took out his list of prepared questions. "How did you first hear that Cox was missing?"

"I'm not sure. Maybe the CID called and said they'd like to make an appointment."

"When you were in Germany, was Dick Cox involved in black market activities?"

"No, not at all."

"If Cox was in an office which handled intelligence information, why wasn't he given a security clearance? According to the Pentagon, he never had any G-2 clearance."

"I think," Groner said, "that when he first went into the intelligence office he was just a little clerk, shuffling papers, and probably didn't need it. Then, as he moved up, when Westervelt was his boss, Westervelt probably overlooked it or just didn't require it."

"Westervelt?" Jacobs was startled. By this time he considered himself pretty much of an expert on the Cox case. He had to admit, however, that this name was unfamiliar.

Groner was shocked. "He's the key to the whole case, Marshall. I'm convinced that Westervelt was 'George'! Underwood, when he was here, showed me the FBI and CID file on Westervelt, and there's nothing about him that doesn't fit. Little things, like his bragging, his swagger, his being a sharp dresser. Even the way he talked—'Hey fella, you got a Dick Cox in your company?'—I can just hear him saying it."

"But why would Westervelt have gone to West Point to see Cox?"

"I'm not sure, but personally, I always thought Westervelt might have been trying to recruit Cox for some government agency like the CIA. That's what I told Underwood when he was here."

That seemed awfully far-fetched. Nevertheless, Jacobs decided that eventually he'd try to learn more about Westervelt. Then he returned to his questions. "I believe, Bud, that you visited Cox's home after Dick was reported missing. . ."

"Yes. Another guy and I flew together to Mansfield. He dropped me off, then he went on to Akron and picked me up on the way back."

"Did you meet Betty Timmons at that time?"

"I did. Betty was very distraught and had no opinion as to what happened. Minnie Cox, incidentally, I thought was a very nice person. Kind. Not at all like Dick painted her. His sister Carolyn Colby was also a fine person. She thought sure that Dick was dead, said she felt he had 'gotten in with the wrong crowd.' I'm not sure what she meant by that."

"Bud, is it possible that Cox was homosexual or bisexual without your knowledge?"

"No, not while I was with him."

"Could anything of importance have happened between the time you were separated from Cox and his return to the States in January of 1948?"

"Not likely."

"Well, were you so close to Cox that he would contact you if he were still alive?"

"Oh, I was close enough, and if he had needed some help along the line, I probably would have given it to him. He could have come in my station for gas, and even if I was being watched, he could have said, 'Meet me tonight at so-and-so' and I'd have done it. But— no contact at all, so I had to keep thinking it had to be foul play. Somehow, though, I feel optimistic; I think he may *still* be alive. And if he is, the only reason not to get in touch would be government regulations or some other restriction."

"Let me refer to the letter Cox wrote to Rosemary Vogel, the one that was returned as 'undeliverable.' Why did Cox ask her, more than once, about the Russians?"

"Well, we were stationed near the border, and the Vogels, who lived close to the border, were very concerned about the Russians, as we all were. It was probably just natural to ask her about them."

"Do you still correspond with Rosemary Vogel Padgett?"

"Yes, or she calls here occasionally."

"What about the Shotwell sighting in Washington—had you heard of that?"

"I heard of it, but I never met the man."

"Finally, do you think the FBI and CID searches were extensive enough? Did one surpass the other?"

"I think the FBI did a more thorough job, and now, knowing what I do, I think some of it may have been suppressed by the CIA because a certain person worked for them."

"Do you mean Westervelt?"

"Absolutely. David Myron Westervelt. I think he's the key."

It had been a good interview, and Jacobs decided to give it a rest, at least for the moment. He, Bud, and Elaine enjoyed each other's company at dinner and became better acquainted. They assured him he'd be welcome anytime. Jacobs appreciated that, and he said he'd probably be back, especially after he went through the CID files, learned more about David Westervelt, and possibly developed a few more questions.

Maybe Groner had put him on the right track, but only time would tell.

A few days later, back in Miami, Jacobs received the army CID files, more than two thousand pages, many of which had originally been classified. Eagerly, he began to go through them.

Comparing the FBI and CID material, he often found reports of the same incident. Soon he had a pleasant surprise; frequently, a name that had been deleted by the FBI would be listed in the clear in the corresponding CID document.

It became something of a game, almost a contest, between Jacobs and the bureaucratic "classifiers," the clerks who blacked out names and deleted pages. Because the CID usually determined there was no need to conceal a particular witness's name, he could use the CID material in effect to break through the FBI's protective shield. Whenever, through a process of deduction, he identified someone whose name had been lined out elsewhere, he felt like a true sleuth and gave himself a pat on the back.

Well, he now had all the files, at least all that he was likely to get. Also, he had begun the interview process. Now, before going any further, he should review the bidding. What material did he have, and which of it was important?

As might be expected, most of the CID and FBI material related to the years 1950 to 1957, the time from Cox's disappearance until he was declared legally dead. First, of course, there was the cadet testimony from January 1950: roommates Welch and Urschel relating what Cox had told them about his visitor; charge of quarters Peter Hains and the phone call from "George;" sightings of "George" by Cadets Samotis and Maresca.

Then came the documents relating to the activity once Cox was found missing. Here were the statements from Cadet Louis Bryan, who made the initial report, and from Major Henry Harmeling, the officer in charge that evening.

Reading further, Jacobs was impressed by the actions of the West Point authorities. From day one, there'd been hands-on involvement at all levels, beginning with General Moore, the Academy superintendent, and Colonel Harkins, the Commandant of Cadets. In the newspaper accounts, he had read of the searches of buildings and grounds. Now, in the files, he saw just how exhaustive those searches had been. He also began to realize how much effort had been put forth by the New York City Police Department, the New York State Police, even by the Park Rangers at Bear Mountain.

From the CID files, Jacobs read of the initial work by Murray Kaplan and Joe Cavanaugh, both at West Point and in Mansfield. It must have been frustrating, he thought, to have done so much, worked so carefully and painstakingly, and yet to have come up empty.

Jacobs then began reviewing the accounts of the many alleged sightings, tips, and possible clues. He made notes on the most interesting items. From the early phase of the investigation, he wrote down:

- "See Kelly" note on desk calendar
- Letter to Rosemary Vogel, asks about Russian situation
- Letters from Cox to mother and Betty; expresses dislike of cadet life
- Money, watch, and civilian clothing left behind

Jacobs also made notes on later events. Some of the supposed sightings, such as the one at the gas station in Mt. Gilead, Ohio, had been tracked down and proven false; he didn't worry about those. A few of the tips and sightings, however, were still unresolved. He jotted down:

- Stories about Greenwich Village
- Court-martial testimony. Happen as Cox said? Someone seek revenge?
- Theory relating disappearance to cribbing scandal
- New York City sightings (along with female companion) at Sloane House and Little Hofbrau Restaurant
- Alleged sightings in Boston, Philadelphia, Atlanta, and elsewhere, many involving bus ride or bus station. Could Cox be hopping from place to place by bus?
- Cadet cap found near Mountainville
- Psychic's weird "dream story"
- Stories from Southwest such as "hair dye" incident in Tijuana and "wife" letter left in Wickenburg, Arizona
- Shotwell account of chance 1952 meeting in Washington. Again a bus station.

There might be much of value in the various reports between 1950 and 1957. For now, though, he'd accept only the Shotwell sighting as valid. Studying the files, Jacobs found many contradictions.

Some said Cox was an inveterate gambler; others said he gambled infrequently, and then only for small amounts. Some said Cox was outgoing, others saw him as a shy "loner." In addition, there was conflicting testimony about Cox's desire to remain at West Point, his drinking, sexuality, character, even his honesty.

Jacobs, thinking of the line from the popular TV show, muttered to himself, "Will the real Richard Cox please stand up!" Well, there were lots of things to learn, and lots of ways to go. He began planning his next moves.

Chapter 9

Strange Encounter

To most people, government records seem dry and tedious; to Marshall Jacobs, they were fascinating. He especially enjoyed the ingenious stories of Cox "sightings." Even when they were patently false, they were great fun to read.

There was, for instance, the tale spun in February 1958 in New Orleans by a man the U.S. marshal was holding for a violation of Section 2312, Title 18, of the U.S. Code—that is, transporting a stolen vehicle across state lines. While in custody, the man told the marshal that he was acquainted with Richard Cox, a cadet who had deserted the U.S. Military Academy some years ago. They first met, he said, at a party in Hollywood, California, in either 1952 or 1953.

That wasn't all. He again met Cox in November 1957 and had been traveling with him throughout the western states until a few days ago, when Cox took a plane for Mexico City, where he had been living.

The FBI, known to be interested in the Cox case, was notified of this development, and two agents arrived to continue the interrogation. One FBI man, R. J. Abbaticchio, skeptical from the start, thought the man was lying but didn't want to overlook the possibility that this might be the mysterious "George." Abbaticchio suggested the two might have met earlier than 1952, perhaps prior to the time Cox left the Academy.

At that point, with no further prompting, the story shifted. Actually, the man said, he had met Cox in New York City while Cox was a cadet. The weather was very cold, so it must have been midwinter. He then saw Cox several times in New York during the next two months.

How many times? Oh, about six times, he said, and once or twice he had gone to West Point to meet Cox. On one occasion, after calling Cox at the Academy, he had met him for dinner at a hotel at West Point. Had he stayed overnight at the hotel? No, but he thought he might have been registered.

He always called Cox by the name "Dick," he said, and Cox knew him as "George." The agents looked meaningfully at each other and told the man to continue. Once, he said, he picked up Cox at West Point, and they went into New York City together. He had left the cadet, who was then in full dress uniform, on an unrecalled street in New York at 1:30 or 2:00 the next morning. He said that was the last time he saw Cox in New York.

Two or three months after this, he said, Cox contacted him at his home in Fort Worth, Texas. He then took Cox to El Paso and across the border to Juarez, Mexico, in an effort to get him back to Mexico City, since the ex-cadet did not have enough money himself to get back to where he'd been living. Subsequently, he said, Cox had left Mexico City, and from 1953 to 1958, had lived and worked either in Phoenix, Arizona, or in California. Cox came to Hollywood in late 1957, he said, but was now back in Mexico.

The part about frequent meetings in New York was obviously false, but much of the story seemed plausible. Information bulletins were sent to FBI offices around the country. In Los Angeles, which the man in custody called home, agents located his current wife, a woman he had lived with for only three days. Her husband, she said, was a pathological liar, one who constantly made up stories about himself. Further checking revealed that the husband, diagnosed as psychotic, was receiving a 55 percent disability pension from the Veterans Administration for psychoneurosis.

The FBI decided the man was lying, embellishing things he had learned from a magazine or newspaper. Even if he *had* met Cox at some point, agents knew the statute of limitations had run out on the charge of desertion, and some time back the army had withdrawn its request for Bureau assistance. To be on the safe side, however, an FBI memo dated February 19, 1958, said that "information he furnished concerning Cox should be given local army authorities for their information and any action they may deem appropriate."

Day after day, Marshall Jacobs pored over the FBI and CID files, sorting and cataloguing. Methodically, he placed colored tabs on items relating to key people. Perhaps, he mused, if he did a good job of organizing the data, some new pattern would start to emerge, even a pattern that would point him in the right direction.

At this point he considered only a single Cox sighting to be valid—the one by Ernest Shotwell in 1952 at the Greyhound Post Restaurant in Washington. Following up on this, he learned Shotwell's current address and phoned him at his home in Millis, Massachusetts.

The phone call was something of a disappointment. Shotwell, suspicious of the caller's motives, was understandably reluctant to talk to a complete stranger about an event so far in the past. Jacobs persisted, however, and asked a number of direct questions. Shotwell added little to what Jacobs already knew from the files but nevertheless confirmed that he had met and talked to his former friend in 1952, well after Cox's disappearance from West Point. He had no doubt that the man he met was indeed Richard Cox.

Suddenly, in the FBI files from 1960, Jacob found reports of what appeared to be *another* valid sighting, one in which a person admitted to being Richard Cox. It was odd. While the chance 1952 meeting with Ernest Shotwell had received a good bit of contemporary press coverage, this other appearance had *not* been publicized. Apparently the first public mention of this second sighting came only in 1982, some twenty-two years after the event, as part of Jim Underwood's series in the *Mansfield News Journal*.

According to the files, on May 16, 1960, a known FBI informant was at the Sho-Bar tavern in Melbourne, Florida, having a drink, perhaps talking to the bartender, and waiting to meet someone. The files were silent about the informant's real name, so Jacobs decided to call him "John." In the past, John had frequently provided information to the FBI and had always proven reliable. He was, in fact, currently working a case for the Bureau.

At the bar, a few seats away, sat an attractive young woman. John sidled over, introduced himself, and struck up a conversation. The woman said her name was Allie and that she was from the Key West area. From the start, Allie made it clear she wasn't there to be picked up. She was, rather, waiting for her date and another man to join her.

Allie's friends arrived, and John introduced himself. As they shook hands, one of the men said his name was Walsh. The other gave his name as R. C. Mansfield. It was unusual, John thought, for someone to introduce himself by giving only initials. It was a small matter, however, and when Allie used the name Richard when talking to Mansfield, John did the same.

Walsh left, but Mansfield remained, and he, John, and Allie had several drinks together. Tongues loosened, the conversation became more unguarded, and soon John and Richard were reminiscing about time spent in the service. John said he was a former U.S. Marine, and damned proud of it.

"You should have been in a good outfit," Mansfield joshed. Personally, he had served in Germany and had been in "the finest unit in the army." He did not say what unit that was, but it was obvious he preferred the army to the marines.

This was too much for John, the proud ex-marine, who proceeded to ask, half-jokingly, "If you liked the army so well, why don't you go back in it?"

"I can't," Mansfield answered. At first he didn't say what he meant by this, but after a pause, he added, as much to himself as to anyone else, that as far as the army and his mother were concerned, he was a dead man. He had been considered dead, in fact, for more than eight years.

John decided that Mansfield must be wanted for something. Perhaps, he thought, this would be of interest to his contacts in the FBI. He began paying closer attention to Richard, even prodding him with an occasional question.

The drinks and the conversation continued, and finally Richard blurted out that his true name wasn't Mansfield, it was Cox. He didn't say anything more about his mother or where she was, nor did he say anything further about his personal life, except for mentioning that he liked scuba diving and had done some of it with diving clubs in Miami and Key West.

John, when he later reported the conversation, said he thought that Cox/Mansfield either owned a boat himself or had worked on a boat, but he couldn't recall why he had that impression.

At some point during the evening, Cox mentioned Fidel Castro, saying that Castro's time in office was limited. Expressing what John assumed was a personal opinion, Cox said that much pressure was being put on Castro and before long the Cuban people would be getting rid of him.

Later in the evening, Cox mentioned certain individuals in Melbourne and asked if John knew them. John said he did, and Cox asked if he would introduce him to them. John agreed to do so. From the way his new acquaintance asked about these people and apparently stood ready to meet with them at any time, John had the impression he must be staying nearby.

Meanwhile, Walsh had returned. He did not say where he had been while he was away from the Sho-Bar. (John thought Walsh's return was sometime *after* Cox had revealed his true identity.) Walsh, Cox, and Allie all left together. John described Walsh as being white and about forty years of age.

Four days later, on May 20, John met Cox in Melbourne, as prearranged, and introduced him to the people about whom he had inquired.

On May 24, John set up a meeting with his FBI contact, an agent from the Miami office. In the past, John's information had always proven to be reliable, and as he told of this chance encounter with an alleged fugitive deserter, he was taken seriously. The agent asked questions, wrote down what John had to say, and urged him to pursue the matter. The FBI would be especially interested, the agent said, in finding out Cox's present location.

The Miami agent next asked about the people Cox wanted to meet. Who were they? John hesitated. Since no federal violation had occurred, he said, their names and addresses would mean nothing to the FBI. Therefore, he didn't want to reveal their identity. Evidently the kind of people John associated with wouldn't appreciate being brought to the attention of the authorities. John agreed, nevertheless, to try finding out what they had learned about Cox.

The agent phoned his boss and reported the conversation. Soon a telegram, marked URGENT, was on its way from the Special Agent in Charge, Miami Office, to J. Edgar Hoover's office in Washington. It included a request that the information be forwarded to New York. Despite the passage of time, the FBI's New York office still retained primary responsibility for the Cox investigation.

> TO: DIRECTOR, FBI AND SAC, NEW YORK
> NEW YORK VIA WASHINGTON
> FROM: SAC, MIAMI
>
> RICHARD COLVIN COX . . . DESERTER DASH MISSING PERSON . . . [Informant] ADVISED MAY TWENTY FOUR, LAST, HAS NOT SEEN SUBJECT SINCE APPROXIMATELY MAY TWENTY, LAST, IN MELBOURNE, FLA., AND NOT PRESENTLY AWARE OF EMPLOYMENT OR RESIDENCE ADDRESS OF COX. [Informant] PRESENTLY MAKING INQUIRIES IN MELBOURNE AND ORLANDO, FLA., AREAS

REGARDING LOCATION OF COX AND WILL ADVISE MI-
AMI ON DAILY BASIS OF RESULTS OF INQUIRY.

On May 27, 1960, when they next met, John had a disappointing
report for his FBI contact. He had been unable to locate Cox, either
in Orlando or in Melbourne, and unfortunately had no way of
knowing where Cox might now be.

What about the people Cox wanted to meet, the ones John had
introduced him to? They weren't able to help, John said, except for
saying that they thought Cox was somewhere on the lower east
coast of Florida. They couldn't (or wouldn't) give any more definite location than that, nor did they know anything about Cox's
present employment. As a matter of fact, they weren't even sure he
was still in Florida. Once again, and for the same reason, John refused to name these other people; plainly these folks wanted nothing to do with the "Feds."

The Army CID office in Orlando was brought into the picture,
and for the next few weeks, CID and FBI agents made inquiries in
the area and asked their informants to be on the lookout for anyone fitting Cox's description. They also staked out the Sho-Bar. Once
again, however, Cox, if indeed that's who it was, had faded into
the shadows.

Marshall Jacobs, reading the reports, wondered if the stranger at the
bar had really been Cox. He was inclined to think it was. This wasn't
like the earlier sightings, ones generally prompted by stories like those
in *Life* and *Coronet*. By 1960, the Cox disappearance was old hat; the
press had long since lost interest, and few people even remembered
the name. It seemed unlikely, in the absence of any recent publicity,
that someone would concoct such a tale out of thin air, particularly
an informant who valued his reputation for reliability.

Certainly the details made sense: using "Mansfield," Cox's hometown, as an alias; saying he was "dead" as far as his mother was
concerned; mentioning service in Germany in one of the army's top
outfits (presumably meaning the Constabulary); and finally coming
out and openly admitting his name was Cox.

These were all details someone might have learned from a newspaper story, of course, even though no such story had appeared for
years. Then again, the mention of scuba diving was new, and
neither the informant nor "Mansfield" would have known that
Richard Cox had been a remarkably strong swimmer, the type of
person who would enjoy scuba diving.

Jacobs thought it a shame the FBI hadn't done more to pursue the matter, even if it meant pressuring their informant to name his publicity-shy acquaintances. By that time, the army had withdrawn its request for FBI assistance, however, and local agents may well have thought they had enough to do without worrying about some stale case from New York. If the army didn't care, why should they?

Finally, in reviewing the Melbourne documents, Jacobs thought it significant that the stranger at the bar had said Castro wouldn't be around much longer, and had made the statement some eleven months before the ill-fated Bay of Pigs. Could Richard Cox, wherever he was and whatever he was doing, have had some inside information about the upcoming operation?

Early on, Jacobs had decided that roommates Welch and Urschel, plus best friend Bud Groner, were the ones who could tell him the most about Richard Cox. He had met with Urschel and Groner; now he turned his attention to Deane Welch.

The *West Point Register* showed Welch to be living in Lawrenceville, New Jersey. Jacobs called information, found the number, and placed the call. When Welch answered, Jacobs introduced himself and explained his interest in Cox.

Deane Welch, although surprised, was both receptive and friendly. He answered a few basic questions and then said he'd be willing to get together if Jacobs came to New Jersey.

One afternoon a few weeks later, Jacobs checked into a motel in Princeton. He called Welch, received directions to an apartment complex in Lawrenceville, and made an appointment for a personal interview. At midmorning the next day, he was at Welch's door.

Deane Welch, who still spoke with a trace of a New England accent, was a likable, smiling host and a good conversationalist. He was sincerely interested in Jacob's research and seemed impressed by how much he'd already learned about the case, including one item that came as a shock. The files, said Jacobs, showed that at one point Welch was not only under suspicion himself but also kept under personal surveillance for a considerable length of time.

Prompted by Jacobs, Welch gave a brief sketch of his own activities during the past few years. Upon graduation from the Academy, he had been commissioned in the Corps of Engineers and had served overseas in both Germany and Korea, the latter in 1953, with a combat engineer battalion during the Korean War. He had received a master's degree from Iowa State, and in 1964, by which time he'd been promoted to major, he had resigned from the army to enter private life. He had been married but was now divorced. Presently he was working for E. R. Squibb and Company.

Then they turned to the Cox mystery. Welch spoke of the many times he had been interviewed, by both the CID and the FBI, and of the day he and Joe Urschel had been taken to New York for a tour of gay bars. One of the agents he remembered, and liked, was Fred Wilt of the FBI. For some reason, though, some of the other agents seemed to suspect that both he and Urschel knew more than they were telling. Laughing, he mentioned the time he met an FBI man working undercover at Little Creek, Virginia, and found to his surprise that the agent knew who he was.

Welch remembered quite clearly the events of January 14, 1950, the day Cox disappeared. He recalled Dick's idea about the two of them slipping out to Newburgh that evening. They had never acted on it; in hindsight, maybe it would have been better if they had. He also remembered returning with Cox from the basketball game that Saturday, and Dick's excusing himself to go check on his grades.

Somewhat wistfully, Welch said he also remembered the last time he'd seen his roommate, about an hour later. He had a vivid mental image of Dick Cox, standing in front of the mirror and buttoning his long gray overcoat. Welch also remembered the previous Saturday, January seventh, when Dick had liquor on his breath and ran into the hallway, shouting something incoherent about "Alice."

Jacobs repeated the question he had posed to Urschel. Why hadn't Welch asked more questions about Cox's visitor—who was he, what was his name, what was he doing at West Point? Welch's answer was similar to Urschel's. Not only did cadets tend to respect each other's privacy but also Cox was the kind of guy who just didn't like to answer questions.

Welch then added another reason: Because of the honor code, he said, you sometimes had the feeling that "what you didn't know wouldn't hurt you." For example, if Cox, the night he was drinking, had gone off limits and violated his honor, Welch didn't want to know about it: had he known, he would have been obliged to report it.

Over the years, Welch admitted, he really hadn't thought much about Cox. Someday, however, he surely would like to find out what had happened to him. Jacobs mentioned various scenarios that had been advanced by reporters and others, many of which assumed that Cox had left West Point voluntarily. Well, said

Welch, if Cox *did* leave willingly, he'd truly like to think he did so under honorable circumstances.

Jacobs's next call was to John Samotis, West Point '51, the man who had seen Cox talking to "George" near the sally port on the day he disappeared. Again referring to the *West Point Register*, Jacobs found that Samotis had retired from the Air Force in 1979 as a full colonel and was now living and working in South Carolina.

Over the phone, Samotis—saying, "Call me Sammy"—was very friendly and receptive. He was interested in Jacobs's project and said he had a good memory of the events preceding Cox's disappearance. Samotis, saying he'd like to help, gave Jacobs an open invitation to visit him anytime at his place on the shores of Lake Murray in Columbia, South Carolina.

Jacobs accepted the invitation, and some time later he arrived at Samotis's home. They began by going over the events preceding Cox's disappearance, particularly Samotis's sighting of "George." That evening, he said, he was returning from an Army-Rutgers basketball game and heading for his room on the first floor of Old North Barracks. Although it was about 5 P.M., it was still light enough to be able to distinguish people clearly. As he passed through the sally port entrance to the cadet area, he saw Cox talking to a male civilian. The man, although probably less than six feet, was definitely taller than Cox's five-foot-eight. The visitor had dark hair and was wearing a trench coat with turned-up collar.

Samotis recalled being brought to New York, along with Mauro Maresca, to observe a man who was taking a polygraph. He didn't know, until Jacobs told him, that the suspect he saw was David Westervelt. In any case, neither he nor Maresca, the other man who'd seen "George," had been able to make a positive identification.

Samotis said that Maresca was now deceased. He, like Samotis, had gone into the Air Force after graduation and had risen to full colonel, but in 1975 he had died at Bolling Air Force Base, near Washington, while still on active duty.

Overall, Samotis said, Cox was a good student, although he had some difficulty with Russian, and in fact Samotis had been tutoring him in that subject. Sammy Samotis went on to say that he was always impressed with Richard Cox and felt he would have made a good officer. Despite what Jacobs said, it was hard for him to believe that Cox might have been bisexual.

Jacobs and Samotis talked a bit about West Point, and, like most "old grads," he felt the plebe system might not be as tough as it was in his day. On the whole, however, he felt the Military Academy had not lowered its standards, which were as high as ever.

Deane Welch had mentioned the name of FBI agent Fred Wilt. It took a bit of doing, but Jacobs finally located him through the Retired FBI Agents' Association. Wilt's background, he found, encompassed more than law enforcement. In his earlier days, he had been an outstanding track star at Indiana University, holding NCAA records at 3,000, 5,000 and 10,000 meters. He had also been a member of the U.S. Olympic team in 1948 and 1952. Fred Wilt had retired from the FBI in May 1977 and was currently women's track coach at Purdue University in Lafayette, Indiana.

Wilt obviously knew nothing about Jacobs, and at first he was reluctant to talk. Marshall tried breaking the ice by mentioning a high school friend of his, Andy Stanfield, who had been an Olympic teammate of Wilt's in 1952. After that, Wilt became much more relaxed and open.

Jacobs asked if Wilt recalled the case of the missing West Point cadet. He certainly did, Wilt said. After all, he had worked that case for a full year. They had tried every angle; once they even listened to a fortune teller. Marshall asked if Wilt recalled the time Welch and Urschel had been taken to certain bars in Greenwich Village. Yes, Wilt said, he had been one of the agents accompanying them. There had, of course, been no sign of Cox, but even after that, he said, the Bureau had continued to stake out some of those same locations.

Wilt knew of the honor code scandal that broke in 1951 but didn't feel that had any connection with Cox. If Jacobs wanted his personal opinion, it was that Cox just got fed up with West Point. After a year on the case, with no physical sign of foul play or a body, his belief—you might even say his firm conviction—became that Richard Cox left West Point voluntarily to start a new life.

Bud Groner, when Marshall met with him, had suggested that Cox's visitor "George" was David Westervelt, the man who had been Cox's immediate supervisor in Coburg. He had also suggested that Westervelt was a recruiter for the Central Intelligence Agency. This seemed far-fetched to Jacobs, even when Groner pointed out that he himself had been approached. In early 1950, Groner said, the CIA was a brand new outfit, heavily recruiting ex-servicemen, at times even advertising for applicants in magazines.* He thought that Cox, who had worked in an intelligence unit in Germany, would have been a natural for the agency.

Jacobs, although dubious, still thought it might be good to talk to someone from the CIA. He saw a piece in the *Miami Herald* about an ex-CIA man named Frank Sturgis, a participant—did one say burglar?—in the Watergate break-in. (In 1993, Frank Sturgis died of lung cancer at age sixty-eight. Twenty years earlier, in 1973, he had gone to prison for a year as a result of his role in Watergate.)

Jacobs called, introduced himself, and set up a meeting. The following afternoon, Sturgis came to Jacobs's condominium in North Miami Beach. Frank Sturgis, hair combed straight back, with broad shoulders, large hands, and a solid muscular build, gave an impression of self-confidence and strength. He was friendly, didn't know whether he could help, but said he was willing to try.

They sat at Jacobs's dining room table and talked for more than two hours. Watergate was not mentioned. Jacobs carried most of the conversation, outlining what he'd learned about the Cox case. The ex-CIA man, a good listener, interrupted only to ask a question or to clarify a point. The well-traveled, streetwise Sturgis had never heard of the Cox mystery, and it seemed to intrigue him.

Jacobs outlined the circumstances surrounding Cox's disappearance. Then, for Sturgis's benefit, he reviewed Cox's background, beginning with his boyhood in Mansfield, his enlistment in the army, and his service in Germany in an intelligence unit.

Sturgis said he, too, had been in Germany. That would have been in '50 and '51, first in Berlin, then in Marburg and Darmstadt. He had worked with a lot of Top Secret material, he said, often typing up records of documents that were going to be destroyed.

"If Cox was working with intelligence material like that," Sturgis said, "I'm thinking, without knowing the full background, that possibly there's something there. . ."

"You mean he could have come across some information? Could have learned something classified through the work that he did?"

"Well, if he was in intelligence, he would have come across a lot of classified stuff, especially in Germany. West Germany was a hotbed of activity. It was like a war being fought between the in-

*"The Men Who Spy for America," an article in the *American Legion* magazine of March 1949, had as its final paragraph: "Legionnaires who consider themselves qualified for clandestine work abroad or for research work in America and who want to join the undercover fight to safeguard America, should write the Director, Central Intelligence Agency, Federal Works Building, Washington, D.C."

telligence services. Maybe he was tracked all the way back, and if he knew of something or was on to something . . .

"You said Cox didn't recognize the name 'George.' I'd assume it was a phony, and the man didn't want to tell anyone his right name. Have you spoken to the cadet who was on duty in Grant Hall?"

"No," Jacobs said. "That man, named Maresca, died several years ago. However, I've reviewed his testimony in the CID files, and I've also interviewed Cox's best friend from Germany, a fellow named Bud Groner. The two of them hung around together, they went out drinking together, they went out with German girls on dates together. When I interviewed Groner, he told me there was absolutely no doubt in his mind that Dick Cox left the Academy because he was recruited by the CIA."

Sturgis looked dubious, but Jacobs continued. "I asked Groner what he based the assumption on. He said that the CIA at that time was actively recruiting ex-servicemen who had been overseas, and he himself had been approached. Because of Groner's insistence, Westervelt was polygraphed, but it turned out inconclusive."

"Was this fellow Westervelt married?" Sturgis asked.

"Yes, he was married in Germany, to a Russian girl he met in a displaced persons' camp. Frank, is it possible that Westervelt went to West Point for the purpose of recruiting Cox?"

"I don't believe it. You know why? The agency, when they recruit, they have professors that work for them in different universities. They keep their eyes on good potential recruits—A students. Supposedly these professors have a side job, being associated with some big company, but secretly they're with the CIA, either as employees or on a contract basis. These selected students might be given a grant paying their tuition, and they'd sign a contract that they might be willing to go to work for whoever gave them that grant. As time passed, they'd be told about the CIA, and when they graduated, they'd be given a choice—to work for the CIA or for the other institution."

"But from what I've told you, Frank, isn't it plausible that Westervelt was CIA?"

"No, I don't think so. Oh, he may have been at one time, but even if he was a contract CIA man at times, he could also have been working for the Russians. Why? Because of greed. I've known of people who worked as double or even triple agents. Let me give you something from my experience. Here in the Miami area there are many international spies, and they're always looking for someone who's greedy. This place, I tell you, is loaded. It's worse than Casablanca. I have been in touch with a lot of them, and I know some of the communist elements, and let me tell you, I *hate* the communist elements. Believe me, greed is a terrible thing. You couldn't pay me enough to betray my country. You could offer me a hundred million dollars and I wouldn't do it. I hate the communists so much. But some people are greedy."

Sturgis continued. "From what you're telling me, it sounds as though this visitor—'George,' Westervelt, or whoever—set up this kid Cox so the communists could go ahead and grab him. Maybe he wasn't personally involved in killing the kid, but from what you've told me of his background, emasculating Germans, killing a pregnant girl, maybe he feared the kid from something he had told him. Maybe when they were drinking he told more than he wanted. Either Cox knew something he didn't want him to reveal or the guy was working for the Russian intelligence service and he set the kid up."

Jacobs rummaged through his files, then took out a sheet of paper. Citing the Freedom of Information Act, he told Sturgis, he'd made many requests of the CIA for the files on Richard Cox. At first he'd been told there were no such files. Then, after a lengthy delay, he'd been sent a "file" consisting, rather improbably, of but a single page. It was this page that he now handed to Sturgis.

The document, dated May 24, 1957, and originally classified Confidential, had been approved for release on January 25, 1983:

MEMORANDUM FOR THE RECORD

SUBJECT: American Prisoner at Vorkuta Camp, USSR

1. On 17 May 1957, [deleted] research analyst, at the direction of the Chief, [deleted], requested that certain information concerning an American Cox (fnu),* reported held in a prison camp in Vorkuta, USSR, be brought to the attention of appropriate officials in the Department of Army by [deleted].

2. [Deleted] reported that he attended a West Point Preparatory School and entered West Point Military Academy in 1948 with Richard Alvin [sic] Cox, Mansfield, Ohio. Cox mysteriously disappeared from West Point on 14 January 1950. He is still missing and there is no trace of his present whereabouts.

---

*Full name unknown.

3. According to [deleted], the American prisoner in Vorkuta Camp described in Air Intelligence Information Report ... 18 December 1956, would accurately fit the description of Richard Alvin [*sic*] Cox as he [deleted] knew him.

4. At the suggestion of Lt. Colonel M. F. Moucha, Assistant Chief of Staff, Intelligence, Department of the Army, this information was brought to the attention of the West Point Liaison Officer to the Deputy Chief of Staff for Military Operations, Lt. Colonel A. C. Hamblen, Jr. . . . Lt. Colonel Hamblen was permitted by the writer to make a verbatim extract of that information concerning Cox which appears in Paragraph 7.b., Page 10, of report cited above.

5. Lt. Colonel Hamblen advised that he would personally bring this report to the attention of the Commandant, U.S. Military Academy on his next trip to West Point in about ten days.

6. Lt. Colonel Hamblen expressed his appreciation for this information and extended his compliments to [deleted] for his alertness in bringing it to the attention of the Department of the Army.

A single page—it wasn't much. Still, as Jacobs commented, it was something. Before 1966, when the Freedom of Information Act was passed, he would have received nothing.

Jacobs waited for Sturgis to finish reading the document and then said, "It appears that someone resembling the missing cadet was seen in Vorkuta, a prison camp about fifty miles north of the Arctic Circle. That's the largest Soviet camp for political prisoners, with about eight thousand people incarcerated there.

"Let me give you one more bit of information, Frank. The last time I was at West Point, I talked to the head librarian, who told me about a freelance writer who went to West Point and spent quite a lot of time there. That writer told the librarian that he believed Cox had been abducted from West Point, taken to New York, and put on board a Polish ship, the *Batory*, which was then called a 'spy ship' because it brought Russian diplomats and agents back and forth between Europe and the U.S. Its regular route was between Gdynia, Poland; Southampton, England; and New York. You may remember Gerhard Eisler, the German communist indicted for spying. When Eisler jumped bail, he fled the country aboard the *Batory*, but was apprehended in Southampton before he could escape behind the Iron Curtain.

"Anyhow, I've checked. Cox disappeared on a Saturday, January fourteenth. The *Batory* sailed into New York Harbor the following Tuesday, the seventeenth, and left on the twentieth."

"I see here an international situation," Sturgis said, "and you're not going to get the complete truth, from the FBI, the CIA, or anyone else. As for Cox going with the CIA, forget it. I think it was abduction, and whether that was followed by his being killed or being recruited by the other side, who knows?"

Jacobs asked, "If Cox was abducted, does that substantiate this document about a man resembling Cox being seen in Vorkuta?"

"Well, you say he was seen in Washington and again in Florida, and if that was really Cox, it means he wasn't in Vorkuta, at least not then. I think they targeted him because of his bisexuality. If he was in Germany as a homosexual, there's a good possibility he was in contact then with the Russians. At West Point they could have worked on him, worked on the sex angle, offered him something, maybe brought up something from his past such as information he'd turned over when he was in an intelligence job. Remember, he was vulnerable because of his sexuality. He might have thought, 'They're going to destroy me anyhow, I might as well work for them.' Maybe they squeezed him, indoctrinated him, and turned him around. If he became an agent, either for the Poles or the Russians, Washington would have been a logical place to be."

"But why Cox?"

"Well, the guy must have had something they were interested in. They set him up first, abducted him, put the squeeze on, and turned him around. They couldn't have squeezed him while he was at West Point, because he would have told someone."

Frank Sturgis was a savvy veteran of intelligence work and knew its seamy underside. You had to respect his opinions. Jacobs, however, couldn't accept his conclusions. To Jacobs, despite all he'd learned, Dick Cox was still a puzzle, a young man of many faces. Nevertheless, Jacobs refused to believe that one of those faces could be that of a traitor.

Chapter 10

Mansfield, Ohio

On the afternoon of Saturday, May 14, 1966, a man rang the door-bell at 492 Topaz Avenue in Mansfield, Ohio. Moments later, Della Parkhurst, an attractive twenty-nine-year-old divorcée, answered the door. A story in the *Mansfield News Journal* told what happened next. Parkhurst, as she opened the door, was confronted by a young man in his late thirties, whom she later described as having "staring blue eyes which looked right through me."

"It was as though he was trying to recall something out of his past," she said.

The man asked where the Seaton residence was, saying that Mrs. Seaton was an old friend of his. Just then Della Parkhurst became distracted as two babies, hers and her sister's, started crying in the background.

The flustered young mother told the stranger Mrs. Seaton lived nearby, but she didn't know the specific address. However, she'd try looking it up in the phone book. She closed the door, then went back into the house to the phone. When she turned around, the man was standing in the middle of the living room.

"I think he stopped," she said, "when he saw my mother standing in the doorway of the bedroom.

"He wore a baseball cap and jacket and kept his hands in his trouser pockets all the time he talked to me. I don't recall ever seeing his hands.

"I was frightened even though my mother was in the house because he kept staring at me. He must have asked me five or six times if I had ever worked at Reed's department store. He said he used to go with a girl who worked there."

Parkhurst gave the man the Seatons' address, at which point he said, "I'm Dick Cox. I'm from Columbus." He mentioned something about West Third Street and a garage, and said Mrs. Seaton was an old friend of his. Following this, Parkhurst said, he asked what people in Mansfield did for excitement and invited her to go to dinner with him.

"He noticed I wasn't wearing rings," she said. "I told him I was divorced and that I didn't go with strange men."

The man then turned to leave. As he did so, he said, "I'll be back in Mansfield next Wednesday. If I don't find Mrs. Seaton home now, I'll stop back and see her and I'll stop here. Maybe you'll change your mind about going out to dinner with me."

Evidently Mrs. Seaton was not at home, for a bit later Della Parkhurst looked out the window and saw the man driving away in a long, blue, late-model car.

"I didn't get the license number," she said. "I guess I was just so relieved that he was gone. It was disturbing, the way he stared and the way he seemed to go off for a second or two."

Della Parkhurst called Mrs. Seaton a couple of days later and told her of the visitor. "At first the name didn't ring a bell," she said. "Then she called me back and said the only Dick Cox she knew in her lifetime was the Dick Cox of the Rupert Cox family who used to live near her on West Third Street." Although Richard Cox had been missing for more than sixteen years, Clara Seaton well remembered his mysterious disappearance.

Mrs. Seaton stayed home the following Wednesday, "hoping that the man would come back so I could be sure if it was Dick." However, the stranger did not return that day or on any of the days thereafter. Although Clara Seaton and Della Parkhurst told friends about the visitor who gave his name as Dick Cox, they decided not to tell Cox's mother about it, so as "to save her heartaches." They did, however, notify the FBI, which in turn relayed the information to the army's Criminal Investigation Division.

The story made the rounds in Mansfield. Even Dick's sister Nancy Allen, and her husband, Robert Allen, heard about it. They too, however, decided not to tell Dick's mother about the incident, feeling she had already suffered through too many disappointments. A month or so later, as it happened, Minnie Cox heard about the visitor from her beauty operator. The *Mansfield News Journal*, now free to break the story, ran a bold headline across the entire front page: "Lead Uncovered in Cox Case."

The story, by reporter Marguerite Miller, included statements from Minnie Cox, Della Parkhurst, and Clara Seaton, and began: "'Mrs. Seaton . . . West Third St. . . . garage.' These three words, spoken by a man who identified himself as 'Dick Cox' of Columbus . . . may be a fresh and best lead yet to the whereabouts of West Point Cadet Richard Colvin Cox, who disappeared more than 16 years ago."

The story quoted Minnie Cox as saying that her son Rupert had once kept a boat in Clara Seaton's garage and that no one except the Cox family and Clara Seaton would have known of the boat-garage connection. The story's final paragraph read: "His mother, a woman of strong religious faith, says the man who came to the Topaz Ave. home did 'not act as my son would have acted. But then, who knows what has happened to him? We want him back.'"

On June 29, 1966, the *News Journal* reported that military investigators were likely to reopen the Cox case. The story quoted Chief Warrant Officer Ray E. Bidwell, special agent in charge of the Columbus CID office, as saying that information on the man's appearance had been forwarded to CID headquarters at Fort Meade, Maryland.

"We're quite interested," Bidwell said. "We've probably followed up 1,500 leads in the Cox case to date, so far to no avail."

One of those reading the story was Joy Gaubatz of Mansfield, like Della Parkhurst a young divorcée. Gaubatz picked up the phone, called the Mansfield Sheriff's Department, and spoke to Detective Roger Hampton.

Joy Gaubatz, referring to the story in the *News Journal*, said she thought the sheriff should know about something similar that happened to her.

On a Saturday, she said, either in late April or early May, a man came to her door and asked, "Do you know where the Seatons live?"

Gaubatz told Hampton that she recognized the man because she had gone to school with him. She invited him in while she looked in the phone book for the address of persons named Seaton. The man was wearing khaki trousers, a hip-length jacket with orange lettering, and a baseball cap with the word "Coach" on it. This was identical to the way Della Parkhurst's visitor had been dressed, and the man's physical description also matched.

Gaubatz told Hampton that her visitor said he thought he knew her from somewhere and said perhaps they had run in the same social circles. Also, he asked if she used to work at Reed's department store.

Then she asked him, "Aren't you David ———?" (His last name was deleted in the newspaper story.)

The man said he was. Then he asked who she had been married to. "This took me back a little because it sounded like he knew I was divorced," she said.

Detective Hampton, now that he knew the stranger's name, began checking around. Soon he learned, from the man's brother, that the person who visited Gaubatz and Parkhurst was a schoolteacher, married and with a child. According to the brother, the man was presently on vacation in Canada. He showed Hampton two postcards he had received recently, the latest mailed a few days before from Victoria, British Columbia.

Hampton turned over his information to the military authorities investigating the Cox case and determined, when the man returned from vacation, to bring him in for questioning. Upon his return, the impostor not only denied everything but also arrogantly refused even to appear at the prosecutor's office. At this point, Hampton was advised by his bosses that impersonating someone who had been missing as long as Cox was not a criminal violation. Detective Hampton, both angry and frustrated, was forced to drop the case.

The headline in the *News Journal* said it all: "Lead Fizzles As Man Identified."

Marshall Jacobs smiled. He had come to Mansfield and was now sitting in the back room of the *Mansfield News Journal*, going through the paper's voluminous file on Richard Cox. While the 1966 impostor story was interesting, basically it was but another example of the weird characters and hoaxes that kept popping up in the course of his research.

Jacobs flipped through the file, found another Richard Cox story from 1966, this one dated October 16 and based on a poignant interview with Minnie Cox. "Cadet Cox's Mother Never Stops Hoping" was the heading, and in the story that followed, Minnie Cox said that from three to four hundred persons had written her during the past sixteen years; some wanted information, some were cranks, but most were simply people offering sympathy.

About five years earlier, she said, she received a letter from a woman in southern Illinois who was positive Dick Cox was living there. Her older son, Rupert, had gone to the town and sought out the man's home. When a small boy answered the door, Rupert's heart began beating rapidly, for the little boy closely resembled Dick at that age.

Then, she said, when a car appeared in the driveway, Rupert hurried to it, thinking the long search might be over. The boy's father, however, despite a resemblance, was definitely not Richard Cox. It was another in a long string of disappointments.

Minnie Cox said she was perturbed by reports that Richard had frequented nightclubs and had gotten in with fast company. "He was lively, but he was not that kind of boy," she said. She was a devout Christian Scientist, and she explained that over the years her religion had been of great value to her in keeping her hopes alive and helping her cope.

From the people at the *News Journal*, Jacobs obtained the current address of Jim Underwood, who had left Mansfield and was now working for a newspaper in Columbus. He then returned to his room at the Holiday Inn and began looking up names in the phone book; it was time to begin some long-anticipated interviews with the people of Mansfield.

Jacobs would have preferred to begin with Betty Timmons, Dick Cox's former fiancée, but that hadn't worked out. Some months earlier, using an indirect approach, he had tried to obtain an interview with Betty, who was now married and living in Ridgewood, New Jersey. His intermediary had been Doris Alverson Kersting, whose brother Warren had graduated from West Point in 1954, and who had known both Betty Timmons and Dick Cox in high school. Doris, who lived close to Ridgewood in the town of HoHoKus, said she'd talk to Betty and try to arrange a meeting between her and Jacobs. Some two weeks later, Doris called Jacobs and said Betty didn't want to talk to him. It had been disappointing, but in a way not unexpected. More than thirty years ago, Betty had talked at length to various investigators and reporters, and by this time she probably felt she had nothing more to add.

For Jacobs, now that he was in Mansfield, the logical place to start was with Cox family members who still lived locally, specifically, Dick's sisters, Nancy Cox Allen and Mary Cox Slabaugh. When he phoned, both women said they had heard of him. They seemed puzzled as to his motives and initially somewhat cool. However, they both were polite, and while they did not invite him to their homes, they agreed to meet with him the following day in the lobby of his hotel.

Around two the next afternoon, Mary and Nancy came to the Holiday Inn. Jacobs introduced himself, and he and the two sisters then withdrew to a corner of the lobby where they could talk undisturbed. As to his motives, he explained his natural curiosity as a researcher and also said that someday a book might be written about their brother's disappearance.

The Cox sisters, well-groomed and soft-spoken, wearing light-colored summer dresses, sat rather stiffly as they waited for Jacobs's questions. Bit by bit, as the conversation proceeded, they became more relaxed.

Neither sister had read the FBI and CID investigative files, but both felt the key to the mystery lay in Germany. Nancy suggested that Dick might have left West Point voluntarily, intending to return within a short period, but was prevented by "George" from doing so. By contrast, their mother was always convinced that Dick did *not* leave voluntarily. Mary and Nancy both found it difficult to believe that Dick could have left on his own and stayed away without contacting his family or friends, particularly his mother.

Jacobs asked about Betty Timmons. Betty, they said, was always well liked by the Cox family. Under normal circumstances, they felt she and Dick would have married.

Mary, the older sister, said she was thirteen when Dick was born and often took care of him as a child. When Jim Underwood interviewed her for his series, she had been surprised at the mention of homosexuality. "I guess the FBI didn't want us to know about that. In a way, I'm just as glad," she said.

She asked Jacobs what he'd seen in the files about this. He said there were "indications" of such behavior, but made a point of stressing the word "indications" and the fact of bisexuality rather than homosexuality. Both women said that any aspects of homosexuality would have been out of character for their brother as they remembered him.

The women described their family as being close-knit, held together after their father's death by their mother, the family disciplinarian, an admirable, strong-willed, dominant woman. Because Dick was the youngest, they thought that perhaps their mother tended to "baby" him too much. Dick, they said, was on good terms with all the family, but probably not as close to his brother, Rupert Jr., who was much older than Dick and who had died in 1981. Their brother Dick, they said, always tended to be close-mouthed and independent. Once, for example, on a family trip to New York, he went off to the movies and disappeared for three hours without telling anyone.

Jacobs asked who else they thought he should talk to. They mentioned their sister Carolyn, Nancy's twin, who was now living in Cleveland, and gave him her phone number. Carolyn's husband, Bill Colby, now deceased, had been a detective on the Mansfield police force and had later joined the FBI. The family always felt that Bill knew more about the episode than he was telling. Perhaps, if he confided in Carolyn, she might know more.

Mary and Nancy wished Jacobs well on his research and said they had no objection to someone writing a book on the case. They parted on good terms, and, as they left, they suggested that Jacobs, while he was in Mansfield, also talk to Bob Gandert, who had been one of Dick's closest friends.

Jacobs contacted several people who had known Dick Cox in his youth. There were high school friends Jean and James Voyik; Jean Hugo, who as a young girl had lived across the street from the Cox family; and Helmut Wiehms, who had worked alongside Dick Cox on summer jobs. In general, while the conversations were interesting, they mostly confirmed what Jacobs already knew. His most productive interview, as Cox's sisters had predicted, was the one with Bob Gandert.

On a Sunday afternoon, Bob Gandert, a cordial, neatly dressed man in his late fifties, came to Jacobs's room at the Holiday Inn. Jacobs turned on his tape recorder.

"Before you ask me any questions, " Gandert said, "let me tell you. I would never say anything disparaging about Dick, whether I knew anything or I didn't—I'm just too close to the family—right now, one lives two houses away from me, the other lives just around the corner."

"I understand," Jacobs said, "and if you don't want to answer something, just say 'No comment.' I might tell you, though, that I already know a good bit about Dick Cox. In some ways I know more about him than his family does. Dick, I feel, was intelligent enough, discreet enough, and tactful enough, to keep certain aspects of his personality to himself."

Gandert said he had been a good pal of Dick's, as had Jim Kelley, the Mansfield boy who, after graduating from Annapolis, had been killed in a plane crash. In 1946, Cox and Gandert had enlisted in the army and had gone together to Camp Atterbury, Indiana. After Atterbury, they had split up, Gandert going to Fort Bragg and Cox to Fort Knox. They did not see each other again until Cox, as a cadet, came home on Christmas leave in 1949, shortly before his disappearance. During that leave, he said, he and Dick were together nearly every day, and Dick gave no indication of any trouble or problem.

Asked to characterize the Cox family, Gandert said he remembered them as solid, middle-class people. They were not affluent, money was tight, and they all worked hard to make ends meet. Once, in high school, he asked his friend why he didn't go out for athletic teams, and Dick told him he didn't have time, he always had an after-school job such as delivering newspapers.

Even in the summers, he remembered Cox as always having a job. Once, working on a road crew, Dick fell and cut his arm badly on a scythe. He came home, streaming blood, and his mother, a Christian Science lay reader, began to "read over him." The cut became infected, and later a woman who lived next door brought him to a doctor. As a result of the accident, Dick ended up with a prominent scar.

Jacobs mentioned the conflicting stories he had heard about Cox. Some people, for example, said he was a heavy drinker; others said he couldn't handle alcohol.

"Well, I can tell you for sure that he couldn't handle it when I knew him. Maybe later on he became a drinker, but when I knew Dick, I'd see him get sick to his stomach and throw up after only one or two drinks."

Jacobs told Gandert some of the theories about Cox's disappearance, and Gandert said he agreed that the key to the mystery lay with something that happened in Germany. He also believed that Cox might have left the Academy that night under the influence of alcohol and then feared he would be kicked out and sent home in disgrace if he went back. However, he doubted that Dick on his own could have established a new identity, for which he would have needed, among other things, a Social Security card. Then again, he said, Cox had an independent, self-contained nature and was the type who might have been capable of leaving the Academy and starting a new life with no regrets.

Jacobs next talked to Carolyn Colby, the Cox sister who now lived in Cleveland. Somehow he felt that Mary and Nancy, sitting together when he interviewed them, might have inhibited each other; perhaps Carolyn, talking one on one, might be more forthcoming.

Carolyn was both friendly and cooperative. She already knew of Jacobs and had heard of his interview with her sisters Nancy and Mary. Yes, she said, her husband, Bill, who had died of a heart attack several years earlier, had indeed worked for the FBI in its

Cleveland bureau. Despite what her sisters seemed to have implied, she felt sure that Bill told her and the other family members everything he knew about Dick's disappearance. She remembered his saying the trail on Dick was cold and that there were no valid leads. Still, he always held out the possibility that Dick might still be alive, remarking how "hard it was to hide a body." Maybe, though, he just said that to ease her feelings and give her hope. As a general rule, of course, Bill was close-mouthed and never discussed the cases he was working on.

Carolyn confirmed that her brother Dick was not a drinker. Like her sisters, she said she couldn't imagine him as being homosexual. Jacobs asked if she thought Dick might have had negative feelings about West Point. If he did, she said, the family never gave him a chance to express them. Everyone was always very positive and supportive about his being at the Academy.

Knowing Dick's personality and character, Carolyn felt sure her brother did not simply walk away from West Point. If he were dissatisfied and unhappy, she thought he simply would have resigned and returned home.

Next stop for Marshall Jacobs was Columbus, where he met with Jim Underwood. Underwood, who had spent so much time on the Cox case as he developed his 1982 series for the *News Journal*, may have felt a certain kinship with Jacobs, perhaps the only person who knew as much about the Cox investigation as he did. Underwood and his wife, extremely cordial, invited Jacobs to have dinner with them and stay overnight in their home.

Underwood told Jacobs about the many weeks he had spent on the Cox assignment, describing the cross-country traveling he had done and the people he had interviewed. By the time it was completed, the twelve-part series had cost the *News Journal* more than eighteen thousand dollars, a considerable expense for a hometown paper. In Jacobs's opinion, Underwood seemed like a good researcher, a bulldog type who would have persisted until he had what he needed.

Generously, Underwood showed Jacobs his Cox files and lent him some of the memoranda. One item was of particular interest. It involved a 1982 meeting between Jim Underwood and two of Richard Cox's high school friends who were now judges, Robert Mangnan and Ralph Johns.

According to Underwood's notes, Mangnan remembered Cox as a decent sort of kid, a bright youngster, and one who was something of a prankster in school. Mostly, though, he remembered him with Betty Timmons. He recalled their walking to school together, often holding hands, and regarded by everyone as very close.

Ralph Johns also remembered Cox and agreed with Mangnan that Dick was a bit of a prankster, one who liked to play tricks on people, but without being malicious. Johns said he and another Mansfield man, William McKee, grew very interested in the Cox case and had frequent contacts with local FBI officials. He said McKee once threatened to get the FBI files on Cox and "solve this thing."

Johns also told Underwood that on one occasion, when discussing the Cox case with former FBI agent Vince Napoli, Napoli told him and McKee that the FBI had been within twenty-four hours of grabbing Cox, and he couldn't understand why the FBI would not let them pick him up or why they pulled them off the case. According to Underwood, Johns had speculated, perhaps based on Napoli's story, that Cox might have gone into some secret government agency such as the CIA.

Johns told Underwood that he mentioned Napoli's remark to another FBI agent. "I'll bet that son-of-a-bitch ran out and sent a teletype on that," he said, and he thought he might have gotten Napoli in trouble for repeating the remark. Napoli, in fact, later denied having said it.

Underwood didn't know if the "picking up" incident related to something he'd heard from Cox's sister Mary. Once, Mary said, Carolyn's husband, Bill, had gone to check out a story that Dick was in Kansas City or "someplace in Kansas."

"I remember him laughing, and wondering what he would say to him if it was Richard. He went there and the FBI had already been there and checked it out," she said.

In his *News Journal* articles, Underwood had touched on the subject of Cox's sexuality, but sensitive to the feelings of Cox's family and friends in Mansfield, he had handled the topic with great discretion. Underwood, like Jacobs, had seen the FBI and CID files, and as a good reporter, he had felt obliged to quote the statement that "two separate, unrelated witnesses have provided information that they had engaged in homosexual activity with Cox."

Immediately following that quote, however, Underwood had written: "The allegation of homosexual conduct is largely dismissed by all associates of Richard Cox." He had interviewed people, he wrote, who had known Cox in school, in the army, and at West Point, and none believed he was homosexual.

The article had gone on to quote Cox's army buddy Joseph Groner: "Believe me, I knew Richard Cox before we went to Germany, while we were in Germany, and after we got back from Germany. There's no way he was gay." It appeared that the statements by Groner and others had been enough to gloss over the issue. At least no one in Mansfield appeared to have been unduly upset by the reference.

Shortly after the Cox series appeared in the *News Journal*, and perhaps triggered by the mention of possible homosexuality, Underwood told Jacobs, he had learned something more about Cox's past. A Mansfield businessman, since deceased, told him about an event that had occurred in 1946. It was a secret the man had kept to himself for more than thirty-five years. In the summer of '46, he said, one of his employees had discovered a male fellow employee and Dick Cox having sex in the basement of his store.

The two young men had been brought to him, he said, and he had fired the employee on the spot. He had then threatened to tell Cox's mother what had happened. Young Cox, he said, was terrified by having been discovered and threatened to kill himself if his family ever learned of the incident. The store owner, out of respect for the family, particularly Mrs. Cox, never repeated the story. However, he told Underwood, he felt the Cox family must have known about Dick's sexual behavior. Underwood did not agree, nor did Jacobs.

After spending so much time on the case, Jim Underwood had developed some personal opinions. These he shared with Jacobs, while stressing they were *only* opinions and mostly unproven. There was a possibility, as Ralph Johns believed, that Cox had ended up working for some government agency such as the CIA. He thought it interesting that Vince Napoli had first said—and then denied— that the FBI could have picked up Cox and was told to back off.

Underwood believed that Dick Cox, before he disappeared, was struggling with himself concerning his own sexual identity. However, he felt Cox was smart enough to be able to conceal those conflicts from his friends. Even those who denied having any suspicion might have done so as a kind of defense mechanism. Betty Timmons might also have been aware of Dick's sexual problems. However, this was pure conjecture on Jim Underwood's part. Just as with Jacobs, she had refused to talk to Underwood.

Finally, Underwood was convinced that homosexuality had played a part in Cox's disappearance, but he couldn't say in what respect or to what degree. He also believed that if Cox had been killed, it happened immediately after he disappeared. If he was alive, which Underwood considered quite possible, he thought Cox might someday come forward. Today's social climate, far different from that of 1950, had increased that possibility.

Marshall Jacobs had some follow-up to do. Specifically, he wanted to know more about that story of the FBI being close to picking up Cox and then being told to forget it. It tied in to the theory that Cox had gone with some government agency such as the CIA.

Through the Retired FBI Agents' Association, Jacobs learned that Vince Napoli was now living in Jackson Springs, North Carolina. Jacobs reached him by phone, and as they began to talk, Napoli, while friendly, appeared reluctant to say much; he seemed to be someone who "didn't want to make waves." While he agreed to answer questions, it was obvious that Vince Napoli would choose his words carefully.

Napoli said he had been assigned to the FBI's Cleveland office in 1951 and had retired from the Bureau twenty years later, in 1971. He and Bill Colby, who was also with the FBI in Cleveland, had known each other. He was unaware, though, of any sighting of Cox in Kansas City or of Colby having gone there to check it out. Similarly, he said he could think of no reason for the FBI not to have apprehended Cox had they been in a position to do so. After all, he said, the Bureau would have benefited from grabbing him.

Napoli said he thought of the Cox case from time to time, and as a matter of fact it had come to mind just last week. Jacobs asked the direct question: Had Napoli ever known of the FBI being within twenty-four hours of seizing Cox? No, he had not, Napoli said, and he had never heard of their being told to back off. Was it possible, Jacobs asked, that Cox could have been associated with the CIA without the FBI knowing? Napoli agreed it might be possible.

Since Napoli's testimony contradicted that of Judge Ralph Johns, Jacobs obviously needed to hear what Johns had to say. He reached the judge by phone at his home in Mansfield. It soon became evident that the judge, as a good legal man, was every bit as interested in asking questions as in answering them.

Ralph Johns said he had graduated from high school in 1945, a year ahead of Cox, and the two had known each other only slightly. Overall, however, his recollection of Dick was highly positive, and he had long been interested in the case and curious about the reasons for Dick's disappearance.

The judge asked about the Cox family. Did they now assume that Dick was deceased? And what were Jacobs's conclusions about the case? And had Jacobs ever interviewed retired FBI man Vince Napoli?

Jacobs said he had, and he told Johns what Napoli had said. The judge stuck to his story, saying it happened over lunch when he, Napoli, and Bill McKee had been sitting together. There had been no mention of Kansas City, he said, but Napoli had told them that the FBI had been twenty-four hours behind Cox and were called off before they could pick him up. At no time had Napoli asked them to keep what he'd said to themselves.

Next day, he said, he had called Napoli's superior and questioned the statement. Ralph Johns said he assumed full responsibility for what happened next, and he feared that Napoli must have been severely reprimanded for talking out of turn. Nevertheless, Johns said, he was certain of what he'd heard that day. He had no explanation as to why the FBI might have been called off, unless, of course, there had been interference from some other federal agency. Jim Underwood, he said, was under the impression that the CIA had been involved in Cox's disappearance. (Interesting, Jacobs thought. Underwood had said it was the judge who had that idea.)

Johns had heard the rumors of homosexuality. However, from what he remembered of Dick Cox, he said he would have to disagree. Jacobs described some of the rather convincing evidence he had seen in the files, and the judge conceded he might be wrong. Perhaps, he said, the Dick Cox who disappeared from West Point had become a much different person from the young man he recalled from Mansfield.

As they concluded the conversation, Johns suggested that Jacobs might want to talk to Bill McKee, and gave him McKee's address in Lillington, North Carolina.

McKee, like Johns, was friendly, willing to talk, and interested in Jacobs's investigation. He was a year behind Cox in school, he said, graduating in 1947. He had known Cox only slightly, but had known Betty Timmons fairly well. His friend John Bishop, he said, a Mansfield football player, had dated Betty before Dick had.

Once, when Betty was flying to New York, she and McKee's wife had met on the plane. During that trip, he said, Betty had been interviewed still further by the FBI, and the meeting did not go well.

The agents were using a "good cop–bad cop" routine to question her, and according to McKee, Betty had lost her temper, telling them it was their job, not hers, to find Dick, and to stop bothering her. It didn't surprise him, he said, that Betty had refused to talk to either Underwood or Jacobs.

His gut feeling, McKee said, was that Dick Cox must be dead, for it seemed inconceivable that Cox could have left West Point voluntarily and stayed away from his family.

Jacobs asked about the luncheon conversation among McKee, Ralph Johns, and Vince Napoli, when Napoli said the FBI had been told to back off when it was close to finding Cox. McKee said he could *not* recall Napoli saying that, and he was therefore unable to corroborate what Johns had said.

Jacobs returned home, and in the weeks that followed, he continued to seek out persons who had known Richard Cox or who had been involved in the investigation. He especially wanted to meet Murray Kaplan and Joe Cavanaugh, the CID agents assigned to the case at the very beginning. He learned, however, that Kaplan had since died. That left Cavanaugh, the investigator who had traveled to Mansfield soon after Cox's disappearance.

Finding Cavanaugh was not easy. He had resigned from the army CID more than thirty years ago, gone into private industry, and by now would be fully retired. Most of those who had worked with him were either deceased or had long since lost touch. Eventually Jacobs got a break. Someone said he had heard that Cavanaugh had been in security work and might have been associated at one time with an atomic energy plant. Jacobs kept checking and finally found someone who said that Joe Cavanaugh now lived in Columbia, South Carolina. Jacobs found the phone number and placed a call.

Joe Cavanaugh, in poor health, said he'd be willing to talk on the phone and would even be willing to respond in writing to any of Jacobs's questions. However, because of his illness, he wouldn't be able to meet with Jacobs in person. Jacobs said, under the circumstances, that he appreciated Cavanaugh's willingness to talk with him by phone, and after they chatted a bit, he would mail Cavanaugh a list of written questions.

Unfortunately, Cavanaugh said, he couldn't find any of his records, files, or pictures from the Cox investigation. However, he remembered quite well his interviews with the people in Mansfield.

Cavanaugh agreed with Jacobs's assessment of Cox's mother, Minnie, saying he thought she was a good person, strong-willed, and possessed of a dominant personality. Toward Dick, her young-est, she probably had tended to be overprotective, which may have bothered Dick. Cavanaugh suspected, for instance, that Dick had resented his mother's efforts to secure him a congressional appoint-ment to West Point when he already had won an army appointment through his own efforts.

What about Betty Timmons? Cavanaugh said he had interviewed her at length, but that she had been unable to offer any substantial help to the investigation.

Cavanaugh, on the phone and later in answer to written ques-tions, mentioned how extensive the army search had been. In the West Point vicinity, for example, they had made an all-out effort to find where "George" had stayed overnight, going to all possible hotels, motels, and tourist homes in the area, all without success.

Jacobs mentioned that one-time suspect David Westervelt had then lived in nearby Dumont, New Jersey, and Cavanaugh agreed that if Westervelt was "George," that would certainly explain his not needing a hotel or motel room.

Joe Cavanaugh recalled the excitement when it was discovered that a soldier named "J. T. George" had been in Cox's outfit in Germany, and how that lead, like so many others, had proven nega-tive.

One of Jacobs's written questions concerned Deane Welch: "In what way did Deane Welch arouse the suspicions of the CID that he may have been directly or indirectly involved in the disappear-ance of Dick Cox?"

Cavanaugh's answer: "We put Welch on a polygraph along with several others; he was no more a suspect than any of the others."

In a later conversation, Joe Cavanaugh, with a smile in his voice, related something known at the time only to Joe and his boss. In their desperation, and having exhausted all normal investigative ap-proaches, they had resorted to consulting a psychic, a woman in New Jersey who reportedly had helped certain police searches in the past. This woman, he said, claimed to have seen "George" kill-ing Cox and dumping his body in Delafield Pond. That was the main reason that Delafield had been drained, he said, but at the time they were too embarrassed to tell anyone why they suggested it.

Cavanaugh said he felt both the CID and the FBI investigations had been conducted thoroughly and professionally. He had never heard of the FBI being called off when they were close to finding Cox. Actually, he said, an FBI agent once told him that the FBI had ended its investigation because the failure to find Cox had become an embarrassment, to the Bureau in general and to J. Edgar Hoover in particular.

Jacobs, reviewing the Mansfield phase of his investigation, thought the most interesting item was the story told by Judge Ralph Johns, about the FBI locating Cox and then being told to back off. Of course, Vince Napoli had denied saying it, and Bill McKee had failed to recall any such statement, even though he was apparently at the same table when Johns claimed to have heard it.

With no further corroboration, Jacobs decided the story was destined to remain an unproven rumor, and one that carried but little weight. True or not, of course, the story would never have to be submitted to a court of law. If it *were*, however, what better witness to have on one's side than a respectable judge.

Several weeks later Jacobs dialed yet another name from the investigative files. This time his call was to retired Colonel Henry Harmeling in Beverly, Massachusetts. Harmeling, he remembered, had been the man on duty at Cadet Headquarters as officer-in-charge the night Cox disappeared.

Harmeling, friendly and curious, expressed a strong interest in Jacobs's research. He spoke of the January night Cox turned up missing and said he had a vivid memory of that night and the following morning. Jacobs was impressed by Harmeling's ability to recall many of the specifics, such as calling Cox's mother the next morning to say her son was missing, interviewing Cox's roommates, and notifying Commandant of Cadets Paul Harkins and tactical officer Jeff Irvin.

Henry Harmeling said that over the years he had followed the Cox investigation as best he could. He had heard the rumors of homosexuality playing a part in the mystery and had always wondered if they were true. Then, almost casually, he said he had heard a rumor that the FBI had once located Cox, who was living with a new identity and lifestyle, but had decided not to pursue the matter.

Marshall pricked up his ears. Where, he asked, had Colonel Harmeling heard that rumor, and who had told it to him? Unfortunately, Harmeling said, he couldn't say for sure. As best he could recall, he had heard it from a classmate during one of the West Point reunions he'd attended.

Jacobs had to leave it there. However, he had yet another item to tuck away in his memory bank.

Chapter 11

William K. Hill

Nearly every soldier knows the *Army Times*, a weekly publication sent worldwide with news of interest to soldiers and their families. Many of its readers receive the paper by mail; others simply pick up a copy at their local post exchange.

At the beginning of February 1982, William K. Hill of Valley Station, Kentucky, wrote to the Army Times Publishing Company in Washington. In his letter, Hill implied that he knew something that would solve the mystery surrounding the 1950 disappearance of West Point Cadet Richard Cox.

As a result, on February 5, Russell Jordan, an *Army Times* media representative, phoned the public affairs office at West Point and spoke to Major Tim Carnahan. Jordan told Carnahan of Hill's letter, saying it appeared to be legitimate and not the work of a crank. Major Carnahan said he would relay the information to the local Criminal Investigation Detachment. He then called Brian Jerram, special agent in charge of the CID office at West Point.

Although Carnahan was fairly familiar with the Cox case, Jerram was not, so the first item of business was bringing Jerram up to speed. Carnahan described Cox's disappearance on January 14, 1950, and said the CID, the FBI, and the Military Academy had all conducted lengthy investigations. Nevertheless, Cox was never found, and no information was ever developed to explain what happened to him. Over the years, he said, West Point had received many legitimate inquiries about the case as well as a multitude of nuisance or prank letters. He invited Jerram to review the Cox file in the public affairs office as well as the CID's own material, some of which might still be at West

Point, although most, he suspected, would have been sent to permanent storage. He also gave him Jordan's telephone number at *Army Times*.

Later that day, Jerram spoke to Jordan, who told him that Hill had requested back copies of *Army Times* articles on Cox, specifically mentioning a story that had appeared fifteen years earlier, in 1967. Jordan said this was the first correspondence they had received from Hill. It made him curious. Had there been any recent developments in the Cox case? Jerram assured him there had not. He then asked Jordan to send him a copy of Hill's letter.

On February 8, after receiving a copy of the letter, Brian Jerram called the regional CID headquarters at Fort Meade, Maryland, and spoke to Agent Harry Duket. Duket, who was familiar with the Cox mystery, agreed that someone should talk to Hill and see what he knew. The closest CID office to Valley Station was at Fort Knox, so Duket suggested that Jerram contact Knox directly and ask them to have an agent interview Hill.

Jerram, after giving Major Carnahan a copy of Hill's letter, then briefed the Military Academy Chief of Staff, Colonel Harvey Perritt Jr., both on the letter and on the actions that were being taken. Perritt, coincidentally, had been one of Dick Cox's classmates. Since his 1952 graduation, Harvey Perritt had carved out a fine career, with several key assignments, two tours in Vietnam, and awards that included three Legions of Merit, two Silver Stars, and a Purple Heart. Perritt, nearing the thirty-year mark, was one of the few members of '52 still on active duty; he planned to retire later in the year. For Perritt, it must have been an eerie feeling to hear the nearly forgotten name of his erstwhile classmate—as though a misty ghost, after hiding for three decades, was now peering out of the shadows.

Oddly enough, when Brian Jerram phoned Fort Knox about the letter from William Hill, the CID man he talked to was also named Hill. Special Agent David Hill assured Jerram he was no relation to Sergeant Hill, the man who had written the provocative letter.

David Hill started immediately for Valley Station, a town on Route 31W, the Dixie Highway, about twenty miles north of Fort Knox and midway between Fort Knox and Louisville. He arrived at Hill's home about 5 P.M.

Agent Hill introduced himself, whereupon Sergeant William Hill, rather abruptly, said he couldn't speak to him at the present time because he had made plans for the evening, and the CID man had arrived without an appointment. He was, he said, a retired sergeant first class, formerly assigned to the military police detachment at Fort Knox. Although he couldn't talk right now, he would say this much: He was writing either an article or a book about the disappearance of Cox, and he wanted a guarantee that any information he gave the army would not result in some sort of official interference with his writing. He added that he was being handled by a very large publishing firm but would not state the name of that firm.

The CID man said he'd at least like to know the gist of what Hill planned to write. In response, Hill said he had been stationed with Cox in Germany along with another individual, named George, whom Hill refused to identify any further. Cox, he said, as a cadet, no longer an enlisted man and not yet an officer, had not been subject to military law. Therefore, his only offense had been in not returning to class, as was his option. (This was an error. Cadets, who take an oath as sworn members of the military when they enter West Point, are fully subject to military law. Agent Hill, who did not correct the former sergeant when he made the statement, may or may not have been aware of this.)

The agent asked if Hill knew whether Cox was still alive. Hill replied that the information he had would "lead you to your own conclusion." When he was still in the army as an enlisted man, he said, he had tried to tell what he knew, but he was not listened to or taken seriously. Now, he said, the army would just have to find out what he knew by reading his article.

The CID man, who didn't want to leave it at that, said he'd like to talk some more. Again he was told that further information would be furnished only on condition that the army would not interfere with the publication of any article. Agent Hill said he couldn't make such a promise, but he'd confer with higher authority.

The sergeant, somewhat mysteriously, said he now knew why the army hadn't wanted to listen to his story. He was then asked if the story would bring discredit on the army, and he replied that probably there *would* be discredit because of the army's failure to listen to him in the first place. With that, the conversation ended, but not before an agreement was reached to meet again the following day.

At one o'clock the next afternoon, the CID agent arrived at William Hill's home in Valley Station. The mood was more relaxed, and the two may even have exchanged pleasantries about having the same last name. Whatever the reason, the retired sergeant was now more forthcoming, and he seemingly had set aside his concern about potential army interference.

Over the years, many theories had been advanced to explain Dick Cox's disappearance. The tale now told by Hill was surely one of the most remarkable.

In 1947, Hill said, he, Cox, and an individual nicknamed George had been stationed together in Bamberg, Germany. He did not remember the man's real name, but he assumed this was the same mysterious "George" who had visited Cox. All three of them, however—he, George, and Cox—had been with the Thirteenth Constabulary Squadron in Bamberg. In 1948, the unit, redesignated the Sixth Constabulary Squadron, had moved to Coburg. George, however, had remained in Bamberg, having transferred to the Sixteenth Infantry Regiment of the First Division, which replaced the Thirteenth Constabulary in Bamberg.

Whenever Cox had a couple of days off, Hill said, he would go to Bamberg to visit George. During this period—while Cox was in Coburg and George in Bamberg—the body of a German girl was found in a freight car in Bamberg. She had been strangled with a belt. The Polizei (the German civil police) identified George as a suspect after witnesses placed him with the girl about the time of the murder, and in the vicinity of the rail yard.

Soon it was rumored throughout the Coburg area that George had been the killer, and Hill believed it was Cox who had spread those rumors because the stories began well before the German police had named George as a suspect. Later in 1948, the German police had turned the case over to the military for the prosecution of George, but George was never court-martialed. Instead, he was transferred to Coburg and put on orders to be shipped home.

During the last eleven months Cox was in Coburg, according to Hill, he lived with a German girl named Alice in her apartment. Hill said he often observed George going into Alice's apartment to meet with Cox.

Hill's story continued. Three days before George left Coburg, Hill and a Sergeant Zorn had returned from the border of the Russian zone and found George using a belt to strangle a new recruit in the hallway of the barracks. Hill and Zorn had pulled George off and then roughed him up a bit. While George was in Coburg, he had bragged about having had something to do with the death of a German fräulein and had given a vivid account of events that led to her murder. Hill never heard George actually admit to the killing and had only heard him say that "nobody would ever prove he had killed the girl because the German criminal police could not prosecute him."

Later, Hill said, when Cox turned up missing, and stories circulated about his having testified at a court-martial, the military searched their records but found no evidence of any such testimony. Investigators unfortunately did not check the records of the German police; therefore, they never learned the real identity of George. In Hill's opinion, Cox had participated in the murder of the German girl, or at least had been a witness to it. This involvement had been a factor in his leaving the Military Academy in the company of George.

As they talked, David Hill had been taking copious notes. He then asked the retired sergeant if he would be willing to sign a written statement. William Hill refused, saying this was on the advice of his publisher, who would be handling the magazine article he planned to write. End of conversation.

At West Point, CID man Brian Jerram received Fort Knox's report of the Hill interview. It was yet another fascinating item for his file on Richard Cox. Before putting it away, Jerram made a copy for Major Carnahan in the public affairs office and once more briefed the highly interested Chief of Staff, Cox's classmate Harvey Perritt.

One consequence of the Hill interview was a message sent to Major Carnahan from the Pentagon. One might have thought the tale of a 1948 murder and a possible cover-up would be a principal concern. However, the question to Carnahan dealt only with Hill's threat to embarrass the army by saying he'd been ignored when he tried to give evidence. Was there any indication, the message asked, as to whether Hill was ever interviewed?

On March 8, 1982, Carnahan asked Brian Jerram, at the West Point CID office, if he knew the answer. Jerram said he, of course, had no way of knowing this, but he would try to find out. Jerram called his CID superior, Special Agent Duket at Fort Meade, who advised him to contact the Crime Records Center and have them research the file on Cox.

At the Crime Records Center, a Ms. Dempsey took the call from Jerram, who first asked if she was familiar with the case of Cadet Richard Cox. She surely was. Over the years, she said, she had fielded many requests concerning the case, either from army authorities or the media. Well, then, would she search the files for any interview of Sergeant William K. Hill? And would she also check for a soldier named "George," who allegedly served with Cox in Germany and who was the subject of a murder investigation?

However capable, Dempsey must have groaned. The file, she said, was extremely large. Moreover, it was not computerized or even on microfilm; it consisted of thousands of pages of unsorted documents. It would take her considerable time to go through them, she said. Jerram could only offer his sympathy.

Six weeks later, on April 21, 1982, Dempsey notified Jerram that she finally had completed the search. Except for the present incident, the file had no reference to Sergeant William K. Hill ever having been interviewed. If he had ever tried giving his story to someone in authority, there was no record of it. Several people named "George" had appeared in the file, she said, but there was no evidence of anyone by that name being accused of a murder offense and then being either located, interviewed, or shipped home early to avoid command embarrassment.

A few weeks after this, Mansfield reporter Jim Underwood saw the CID files and the memos concerning Hill. Underwood must have taken Hill somewhat seriously, for when he traveled the country interviewing people for his series in the Mansfield *News Journal*, Underwood went to Valley Station and spent no less than seven hours interviewing Sergeant Hill over a three-day period. The sergeant, with reporter Underwood listening closely and taking notes, had expanded his story on Cox and proposed a whole new scenario, one even more bizarre.

Hill's story, presumably the one he wanted to write (but, in fact, never did), was that in 1947, while he and Cox were in Coburg, their duties brought them into almost daily contact with U.S. and Soviet intelligence agents. Coburg, he said, was a "hot spot" for spying, and the town was "crawling" with both U.S. and Russian agents. Cox, as a member of an intelligence unit, would have been in a position to have had frequent contact with these agents.

On one occasion, according to Hill, Cox had shot and killed a Soviet agent in a border incident at a checkpoint that divided East Germany from West Germany. He and Cox, as part of their constabulary duties, were often assigned to a border patrol. One night, he said, he and Cox accompanied American OSS (Office of Strategic Services) agents to the border, where they were supposed to meet with certain Russians. During the meeting, said Hill, an American interpreter began arguing with one of the Russians and one side opened fire. At that point, he and Cox also began firing, with Cox killing one of the Russians.

Underwood reported what Hill had told him, giving no indication as to whether he believed or disbelieved. He ended that portion of his article by writing that army records showed Cox and Hill serving in Germany at the same time and in the same Constabulary unit but were unclear as to all their assignments. He noted, however, that Cox for a brief time had. been a clerk in an intelligence section.

Reading all this, Marshall Jacobs thought back to his meeting with Frank Sturgis. The ex-CIA man had speculated about a possible Russian angle to the case, perhaps to include an abduction set up by "George," followed either by murder, imprisonment, or by Cox being "turned." Did this story of a border incident add credibility to that theory? At least it suggested a motive, basically one of revenge. If so, did Cox's killing of a Russian trigger a chain of events which ended with his imprisonment in the Soviet Union? Fantastic as it all seemed, there *was* one bit of substantiation—the CIA memo saying an American named Cox had been sighted in Vorkuta.

John Noble, the former Soviet prisoner who had been released from Vorkuta in 1955, seemed like someone who might know. Following his return to the United States, Noble had been questioned for more than six weeks by various government agencies, including the U.S. State Department, the CIA, and the Atomic Energy Commission. He had gone on to become something of a celebrity, making nationwide appearances and lecturing at Harvard's Russian Research Center. Later, he wrote a book on Vorkuta that was condensed in *Reader's Digest* and made into a television drama.

Jacobs reached Noble at his home in Muncy, Pennsylvania. The ex-prisoner still had a remarkable memory about his time in captivity. He told Jacobs that he had been at Camp Number Seven in the Vorkuta area, a desolate spot on a high plain, surrounded on three sides by mountains and open on the fourth side to the Arctic Ocean. There had been two to three hundred camps around Vorkuta, and prisoners were constantly moved from place to place. As he had testified earlier, the Cox he'd heard about in Vorkuta was Homer Cox from Oklahoma, a man who had been released in 1954 and was now deceased. Noble had no knowledge of Richard Cox.

Was it possible, though, that Richard Cox might also have been a Soviet prisoner? Anything was possible, of course. The Russians over the years had kept many Americans prisoner, some from World War II or Korea, and some from as far back as World War I. They were quite capable of abduction. According to Noble, one Vorkuta prisoner, William Verdine, had been an American GI on guard duty near the East German border. After being relieved from his post, he had headed back to his area by taking a shortcut through a no-man's-land, where the Russians grabbed him.

Seizing someone in the States, of course, and then smuggling him out of the country, would have been a different matter and far more difficult. Jacobs was inclined to believe that the Cox in Vorkuta must have been the man from Oklahoma. However, Noble said that Homer Cox was released from Vorkuta in 1954. Then how could one explain the CIA memo about a prisoner named Cox being sighted in Vorkuta in 1956?

Although Marshall Jacobs tended to discredit the "Richard Cox in Vorkuta" theory, the story would not go away. It was widely publicized, for example, by "The Insiders," a group of current and former intelligence officers dedicated to finding evidence about missing Americans who had fallen into Soviet hands.

In late 1992, Michael Van Atta, chairman of "The Insiders," wrote an article headed "West Point Cadet—By 1956 He Appears at Vorkuta Prison Camp." The article included a photo of Dick Cox and a picture of the formerly classified CIA memo. Van Atta urged the U.S. government to pursue the matter, and lest anyone think the theory far-fetched, he added some chilling background material, for example: "On June 8, 1992, Soviet General Volkogonov hand delivered a letter from Boris Yeltsin to Senator Bob Smith (NH) and John Kerry (MA) the leaders of the Senate Select Committee on POW/MIA's. Attached to this letter was a list of 536 American POWs whose names were discovered in secret Soviet archive records as having been kept secretly in the Soviet prison system."

Who else, wondered Jacobs, could throw some light on Sergeant Hill's story? What about Bud Groner? After all, Groner had known Cox the entire time he was in Coburg, and it was at Coburg that most of the things cited by Hill had taken place.

Groner, as it turned out, had been told of Hill by Jim Underwood, and he had been in direct contact with the retired sergeant. Frankly, Groner told Jacobs, he was convinced that Hill didn't know what he was talking about. For example, the story about Cox living off the base with a German girl named Alice was pure bunk.

"Cox never lived off the base—ever," Groner said. "What's more, Hill talked about Cox being stationed in Bamberg. Cox never even *was* in Bamberg!"

Then what about the stories of Cox shooting a Russian border guard and being involved in the killing of a German girl?

"Well, the guy's got a vivid imagination, I'll say that for him. As a matter of fact, when Underwood was here, I called Hill and talked to him. I told Underwood I had ten questions lined up, and when Hill answered them, I'd know whether or not the guy was sincere.

"I asked him, 'Just what months were you in Coburg?' When he told me, it was a time when Cox and I weren't even there, so after that it didn't matter what he said. And when I asked him who his commanding officer was in Headquarters Troop, he gave me the wrong name. He said it was Lieutenant Sanger. When Cox and I were there, it was Lieutenant Byers."

"What about that story of the murder, and the German police having a record of it?" Jacobs asked.

"Underwood wrote and checked on that, and come to think of it, so did Hill. Months later I asked Hill what he'd ever found out from them, and he just said, 'Oh, they didn't have anything.'"

At one point, Groner said, he and Hill compared notes and exchanged letters. He showed Jacobs one of the letters Hill had written. In it, the retired sergeant revealed feelings of extreme bitterness, not only toward the army but also toward the entire military establishment. When he first heard Cox was missing, Hill wrote, "I just naturally assumed he had become disillusioned with the garbage West Point handed out and he just walked off."

Later in the same letter, he said that in 1955, on returning to the States after a tour of duty in Japan and Korea, he "learned that Cox was still missing. The Washington Post, New York Times and Life magazine, had wrote stories about Cox's disappearance and one Almanac had listed Cox's disappearance as among the top 10 unsolved vanishings."

In Hill's opinion, according to the letter, the army CID hadn't tried to solve the mystery because they were only interested in covering up their shortcomings, finding someone to blame, and "avoiding command embarrassment."

Reading the letter, it was clear that Hill was almost paranoiac in his distrust of the military. No wonder he had sought assurance that no one would interfere with what he wrote. No matter, thought Jacobs. Groner, in effect, had put Hill's story to rest. Nevertheless, Jacobs decided to go to Kentucky and question Hill directly.

Hoping to arrange an interview, Jacobs phoned the Hill home in Valley Station. Louisa Hill, who answered the phone, was initially wary, and when Jacobs explained his research project, she became highly suspicious. The German-born Louisa Hill said her husband, retired Sergeant William Hill, had died of a heart attack in August 1983, some year and a half after he'd written that letter to *Army Times*. Before his retirement, she said, he had served in the army for twenty-three years, mostly as a military policeman. Jacobs expressed his regrets and asked if there had been a history of heart trouble. Yes, she said, her husband previously had undergone heart bypass surgery.

Jacobs asked if he might come to see her and perhaps look over her husband's notes. Louisa Hill hesitated. She would have to think about that, she said, and before she agreed to meet with him, she would want to check with her lawyer and her son.

Two weeks later, when Jacobs called again, she said she couldn't let him see her husband's files. During the conversation, which was overall very cordial, she conceded that perhaps her husband had confused Cox with someone else. Jacobs agreed it was possible and thanked her for her time.

Well, Jacobs thought, he might never know what had prompted Hill's story. Were there elements of truth in it, or had Hill, as Groner suggested, merely embellished what he'd read in newspapers and magazines? Certainly there were some obvious flaws in what he'd told both the CID and Jim Underwood.

Hill had said Cox at one time was stationed in Bamberg, which he was not; he had referred to Cox's "last eleven months in Coburg" but Cox had been there less than four; his tale of Cox living off the base in "Alice's apartment" was clearly impossible; and the murder Hill spoke of, with no record in either German or American files, probably never happened.

All in all, Jacobs thought it best to forget the late William K. Hill and go on to something else.

Jacobs still felt he had much to learn about the "real" Richard Cox and his problems with sexual identity. He was willing to try any avenue that might give him a clue. In a Miami newspaper, he read an intriguing article about Gonzalez Regiosa, a psychologist on the faculty of Florida International University in Miami. According to the story, this was a man who often came up with remarkable insights on matters of sexuality.

Jacobs made an appointment to see the professor, and on a Tuesday afternoon, he drove to Florida International's Bay Vista campus, where Gonzalez Regiosa had his office, a rather small, congested room with a desk, filing cabinet, and a few straight chairs. It was reminiscent, Jacobs thought, of some of the cramped spaces he himself had occupied during his years as a teacher.

The Hispanic professor, articulate and highly professional, gave his guest his full attention. Jacobs explained the purpose of his visit, provided background information on the Cox case, and then handed Gonzalez Regiosa several letters written by Dick Cox. In the professor's opinion, a bisexual living in a military environment and struggling with his own sexual identity would have felt severe stress. From what Jacobs said, it appeared that Cox was feeling threatened and pressured—by cadet life, by his mother, by his friends at home, and even by his girlfriend, Betty Timmons. When she wrote of her plan to move to New York to be closer to him, the pressure may have become intense, even though, at the same time, Cox was writing loving letters in return.

Gonzalez Regiosa was particularly interested in the unmailed letter written to Betty Timmons on January 10, 1950, shortly before Cox disappeared. This was the one on which Cox had drawn a figure spitting on the words "United States Military Academy" in the letterhead. After studying the letter, the psychology professor said it indicated tension, pressure, and conflict, but not to a degree that would indicate psychosis. He also said he would "not find the possibility of homosexual behavior the least bit unusual." In his opinion, the letter was written by a troubled person, one faced with a decision, and perhaps with a need to "get out from under." In sum, it was not a happy letter, and clearly it was not written by a happy person.

Having heard the view of a psychologist, Jacobs wondered what handwriting experts would say. He retained the services of GPA, a "graphoanalysis" company based in Miami. Nona Fried and Ronald Cote, after examining several letters written by Richard Cox, wrote a lengthy report, with highlights that said:

> This is a profile of an extremely troubled young man. The first letter reveals that he needed to make an impression, needed to be noticed, to win recognition, to stand out.

His public image . . . was a well-constructed front to cover up and compensate for his inner withdrawal. He could be charming in social situations while remaining emotionally aloof, his fears and anxieties remaining unacknowledged. He wanted to appear different from what he was. . . . Although he was self-absorbed, at the same time he was out of touch with himself.

This young man was confused. He needed his privacy. He was emotionally guarded and needed distance from others. . . . His repressed instinctive needs and feelings were displaced into goal-directed pursuits in which his quick wit and sarcastic barbs covered up his feelings of self-reproach. Yet, through all this there was a searching for self, for his sexual identity. There was an immature attachment to the mother figure. . . . He felt rejected by, or rejection for, the male figure in his early life. He felt much anxiety and tension. He had self-destructive tendencies. His sexual urges were strong and lacking in imagination, warmth, and kindness. . . . He likely had many sexual fantasies in which men and women played a part. . . . He felt dominated by women and, although he allowed them into his life and even sought their friendship, feared them and their power over him. He was angry and confused. . . .

He felt like a martyr. The fear of disapproval to his way of life was a constant factor in his behavior and personality. He clung to past experiences and memories, always continuing to look to authority figures and institutions for guidance.

There was more, all in the same vein. Was it possible to see all that from someone's penmanship? For the first time, Marshall Jacobs felt like an intruder, as though he had invaded Richard Cox's privacy. If the analysts were on target, it explained many things about Dick Cox—an ability to hide his inner feelings, ambivalence toward his mother, confusion over sexual identity, even a desire to escape from the restraints of cadet life, and, when he escaped, to look for an "authority figure" or an "institution" for guidance. Did this indicate a willingness, even as he deserted one rigidly structured authoritative society, the Military Academy, to join an equally structured group such as the CIA?

More and more, Marshall Jacobs felt he was coming to "know" Dick Cox. If only they could meet face to face. Jacobs closed his eyes and pictured Cox standing on his doorstep.

"Come in," he'd say. "Sit down here at the table—make yourself comfortable. Something to drink? Coffee? A soda? I'd offer something stronger, but I understand you're not much of a drinker."

"It seems you know a great deal about me."

"Yes, you might say that. In many ways I know you better than your own family."

"So what do you want from me?"

"I want what everyone wants—an explanation. Perhaps you don't owe anything to me, but you sure owe something to a lot of other folks."

"Let's just say I've got my reasons. For now, forget about the others—what's *your* problem?"

"Well, Dick—may I call you Dick?—it's not really a problem. 'Obsession' might be a better word—always wondering whether you had regrets, whether you'd go back if you could. I've studied you for years, but I still don't understand your motives. You hurt many people, and all my research leads to one word. Why?"

"Frankly, I wouldn't know where to start."

"How about on the night of January 14, 1950? I feel sure, when you left your room that night, that you planned to return. So what happened to change your mind?"

The figure across the table looked long and hard at Jacobs, gave a half-smile, and then slowly, slowly, faded away. Even as a specter, Dick Cox managed to be frustrating.

Suddenly Jacobs realized his imaginary conversation had been with a twenty-two-year-old cadet, and by now Cox would be over sixty. What would he look like by this time? On an impulse, he gave a photo of Cox to a professional artist and asked her to "age" it. A few days later, he received a drawing of a rather haggard elderly man with thinning hair and hollow cheekbones. The face had a haunted look, or was that just Jacobs's imagination? In any case, for future "talking" to Cox, that's the face he would have to visualize.

Marshall Jacobs continued to seek out former cadets who had known Richard Cox, anyone who might have a theory about why he disappeared. One of these was Arthur Webster II, who had been both a classmate of Cox and a fellow member of Cadet Company B-2.

Art Webster, who now lived in Bethesda, Maryland, said his knowledge of the Cox episode was very limited. If he thought of Cox at all, he generally assumed that he had been murdered. Perhaps, he suggested, Cox's body had been tossed into the Hudson

River. Many people thought that, he said, and he pointed out that the Hudson was at its deepest point when it flowed past the Military Academy. Someone once told him, Webster said, that the railroad had used the river to dispose of old railcars, dumping them off barges somewhere near West Point.

From the beginning, Jacobs had believed it would have been nearly impossible for "George" to put Cox's body into the Hudson without being observed. Even if he had, wouldn't the body have come to the surface at some point? Jacobs, of course, had no technical knowledge about the factors that caused a body to rise, so before making any assumptions, he decided to consult some experts.

His first step was to learn the river conditions on the night Cox disappeared. At Jacobs's request, a Dr. Brown of the New York State Bureau of Water Resources in Albany consulted navigational charts derived from a 1957 geological survey. It showed the Hudson near West Point flowing at one to two feet per second, and being deepest between North Dock and Constitution Island, approximately 202 feet. By the time the river reached South Point, it became wider, and the depth was only 138 feet. During World War II, Jacobs was told, the river was used to dispose of certain construction materials.

Next expert to be consulted was J. S. Barnhart, Office of the Dade County Medical Examiner. Jacobs phoned Barnhart, made an appointment, and the next day proceeded to the doctor's office on Bob Hope Road on the campus of the University of Miami Medical School.

Jacobs described the Cox case to Barnhart and told him what he had learned about the Hudson River at West Point. From his research, he told Barnhart, he had also acquired other data, including the air temperature the day Cox disappeared (between thirty-five and forty-four degrees), water temperature (about forty degrees), and Richard Cox's dimensions (five-foot-eight, 165 pounds).

Barnhart couldn't be positive, but he thought that Cox's body would probably have come to the surface. Weighting it down with a few stones, or even a small piece of cement, would not have been enough to keep it submerged unless it somehow became snagged on some underwater obstruction. As to when or where it would have risen, that would, of course, have varied because of prevailing conditions.

This last conversation seemed to clinch it. If Cox was murdered on the night he disappeared, Jacobs felt certain that his body had *not* gone into the river. Similarly, the dragging operation at Lusk

Reservoir and the draining of Delafield Pond had long ago ruled out those places as possibilities, just as the careful ground searches seemed to have eliminated the chance that Cox's body had been buried somewhere on the Military Academy grounds.

All of which left—what? Throughout his investigation, Jacobs had tried to keep an open mind, and he had never rejected murder as a possibility, even when many of the FBI and CID investigators seemed to have ruled it out. In his talks with them, one man had speculated that Cox might have been smuggled off the post in the trunk of a car and later murdered, but most investigators seemed to have concluded that Cox had been a willing deserter.

Jacobs now agreed with those investigators. He believed beyond a reasonable doubt that Dick Cox had left West Point voluntarily. So was he still alive? That, of course, was a different question.

Chapter 12

Murder at Sea

During the course of his research, Marshall Jacobs had been to West Point several times and spent long hours sifting through files and records in the archives, the library, and the local CID office. Occasionally, however, like thousands of other visitors to the Military Academy, he had just roamed the grounds soaking up atmosphere. The museum, Trophy Point, the chapel, the statues and monuments, even the post cemetery—all held a special fascination for someone who appreciated the nation's military heritage.

This visit, however, was different; Jacobs had an appointment to meet with the superintendent. It seemed like a good idea. People at the Academy had been extremely helpful, and it was only fair to thank the man in charge, describe the project, and tell what he had learned to date.

Jacobs flew into Newark airport and rented a car. The drive to West Point took about an hour and a half. When he arrived, he first checked into the Hotel Thayer and then headed for the office of the "Supe," located in the fortresslike Administration Building on Thayer Road.

An aide ushered Jacobs into the imposing, dark-paneled office of Lieutenant General Willard W. Scott, the Military Academy's fifty-second superintendent. General Scott, USMA Class of '48, had graduated a year and a half before Dick Cox disappeared and was only vaguely familiar with the case. He told Jacobs he welcomed the chance to be briefed on it.

Most people, Jacobs had found, were enthralled by his accounting of the Cox case: the disappearance, the extensive efforts of the FBI and CID, the alleged sightings, the false trails, the hundreds of interviews both stateside and abroad. General Scott was no exception. Clearly intrigued, he asked pointed questions and pressed Jacobs for all the details. He ignored the passage of time and the fact that only twenty minutes had been set aside on his schedule. Finally, after more than an hour had passed, Scott's aide-de-camp opened the door and, somewhat embarrassed, reminded the general that his next appointment had been waiting for some time.

Before he left, Jacobs told General Scott that the Academy librarian had asked him, at the conclusion of his project, to donate his research files to the West Point Archives, and he planned to do this. He also assured the general that he would keep West Point informed of any further developments.

Jacobs's next stop was the West Point CID office. He'd been there so many times that he considered the local agents, Bill Capps and Roy Flanders, to be old friends. Bill Capps, he had heard, would be leaving the CID to join the U.S. Secret Service, becoming one of the people guarding the President, and Jacobs wanted to congratulate him. The CID people made Jacobs welcome, and after the initial greetings and handshakes, Roy Flanders invited him into his office.

"Sit down, Marshall," Flanders said. "Have you heard the latest about your friend Cox?"

"My God," Jacobs thought to himself, "don't tell me they've found him!" By now he had a "proprietary interest" in Cox, and much as he hated to admit it, he'd be disappointed if someone solved the mystery before he did. He didn't say this, of course, but merely asked Flanders what he meant.

Flanders called to his secretary. "Would you go out and get that file for me, please?" She returned with a bulging manila folder. Flanders handed it to Jacobs.

"Marshall, I'm going to let you see this and read it, but you can't copy it." Flanders busied himself elsewhere, leaving Jacobs alone with the case file on Richard Cox.

When he opened the folder, he was surprised to see that the first items were all about *him*: his name, address, birth date, social security number, plus memos for the record about his various visits and requests. He guessed that was to be expected, and in a way it was almost flattering.

So what was this "latest" information Flanders had mentioned? Here it was—a memo from a CID agent in California, something involving, of all things, a sensational murder case.

Inspector Ora "Whitey" Guinther, a senior homicide detective in the San Francisco Police Department, had been investigating the murder of Muriel Barnett, a wealthy widow and a prominent West Coast socialite. The principal—in fact, *only*—suspect was Robert Dion Frisbee, a known homosexual who had served as Barnett's secretary and companion, and who apparently had bludgeoned her to death in her cabin on the cruise ship *Royal Viking Star*.

During the investigation and out of the blue, Guinther had received in the mail an envelope containing a faded newspaper clipping, evidently an item someone had been keeping for a considerable length of time. The clipping described the mysterious 1950 disappearance of West Point Cadet Richard Cox, and on it, the anonymous sender had written: "Does the disappearance of this cadet have anything to do with the murder case you are presently investigating?"

Neither Inspector Guinther, nor his partner, Inspector Klotz, had ever heard of the Cox case. Guinther contacted Special Agent Troy Webb at the San Francisco CID office, who hadn't heard of it either. Webb prepared a memo, which he forwarded to West Point, along with the clipping.

Jacobs, learning of this new development, wondered what it might mean. Who had sent the anonymous note, and why? Surely the sender was someone who had a reason to preserve that clipping all these years.

Jacobs saw the name "Frisbee" and wondered if someone was putting him on. After reading further, however, he decided Frisbee was indeed a real person, not a spinning plastic saucer. Moreover, this was no laughing matter. Here was an individual who had committed a murder, and someone he needed to investigate. He couldn't picture Cox as a killer, but if this Frisbee person was involved in Cox's disappearance, perhaps he would turn out to be the mysterious "George." Jacobs phoned San Francisco and talked to Inspector Guinther, the recipient of that cryptic note.

"Whitey" Guinther, ever since he'd received that odd communication, had been curious about its reference to a West Point cadet. The envelope with the clipping, he told Jacobs, had a Massachusetts postmark; other than that, he knew nothing of its origin. He listened with interest when Jacobs described the Cox mystery, agreed there was a possibility that Frisbee and "George" might be the same person, and said he'd be happy to share what he knew of Frisbee's background. As it happened, he knew a great deal.

On May 5, 1927, Robert William Dion, who later became Robert William Dion Frisbee, was born in West Springfield, Massachusetts. At an early age, the boy was introduced to homosexuality, first by an older brother, then by a movie house manager who gave him free admission in exchange for sex. In grammar school, where his main hobby was knitting, his girlish manner made him the target of bullies who called him "sissy" or "momma's boy."

During his teens, he became an avid reader, daydreaming that he was the heroine in romantic adventures. Meanwhile, he continued to have homosexual encounters, always with older men. At a commercial high school, where 95 percent of the students were female, he took a secretarial course, concentrating on typing and shorthand. Then, at age eighteen, he was drafted into the army.

Thanks to his secretarial skills, Robert Dion became an army clerk, maintaining personnel files in an administrative office. While in the service, and in an apparent effort to change his lifestyle, he married a girl named Pauline Hazzar. After his discharge, Dion used the GI Bill to attend hairdressing school, following which he and Pauline moved to Washington, D.C. By this time they both knew the marriage was a disaster; they separated in early 1949. Pauline, a diabetic, developed gangrene poisoning and died soon after. Meanwhile, Dion had been lured to New York by a former lover, a hustler named Joe Dillon.

During the war, Dillon, a merchant seaman, had operated a string of young boys who would go into bars, make eyes at lonely men, and accept invitations to a prey's home or hotel room. Dillon would arrive, flash a fake badge, threaten to arrest the man on a morals charge, but also make it clear he could be bought. At one point he had invited young Dion to join his stable, but the offer was rejected. Now, in 1949, he wanted Robert back in New York as part of a different scam.

As a merchant seaman, Joe Dillon participated in a union collective agreement that required bonus checks to be sent to wives whose husbands were away at sea. Dion, assuming the role of "Mrs. Dillon," collected the checks on Dillon's behalf. Then, in early 1950, Dillon sent Robert Dion to California as an advance man who would start setting up still another illegal operation. Dillon, who had planned to link up with Dion, was arrested in New Orleans, however, and never made it to California.

Next, Robert Dion became a chauffeur, as well as lover, to Dwight Frisbee, a wealthy married bisexual more than twice his age. The older man, who became sincerely fond of Robert, made him his legally adopted son so he'd be eligible to inherit from a family trust. Robert Dion thus became Robert Dion Frisbee.

After Dwight Frisbee's death, and after his inheritance had been frittered away through bad investments, the man now known as Robert Frisbee went to work as a secretary to Philip Barnett, a prominent San Francisco attorney. For the next seventeen years, Frisbee served Barnett and his wife, Muriel, as general handyman, flunky, traveling companion, and drinking partner. Eventually, he and Philip Barnett had a homosexual relationship, presumably with Muriel's knowledge and passive consent.

After Philip Barnett's death from a heart attack, Frisbee remained with Muriel Barnett, serving as companion and secretary. He and the eighty-year-old widow developed what might best be called a mother-son relationship. However, a psychiatrist later described Frisbee during this period as a "subservient go-fer," "a toy poodle," "a court jester." He was, to say the least, an unlikely murderer.

It was a weird case, Guinther said. Robert Frisbee and Muriel Barnett had been on a luxury cruise ship, the *Royal Viking Star*, sharing an eighteen-thousand-dollar penthouse suite, when he murdered her as she slept, smashing in her head with a whiskey bottle. Frisbee had been placed in custody, and when the ship docked in San Francisco, Guinther and his partner had been put in charge of the case. Soon, though, as the killing had occurred on the high seas and not in the state of California, the FBI had assumed jurisdiction and taken over the investigation.

Before long, a new question arose: Had the killing taken place in the United States or in Canada? On the afternoon of the murder, the ship had left Vancouver, British Columbia, and sailed through the Strait of Juan de Fuca, a body of water bisected by the U.S.–Canadian boundary. After a good bit of legal wrangling, and after Frisbee had spent a full year in California jails, it was determined that Muriel Barnett had died while the ship was in Canadian waters. Consequently, Frisbee was given over to Canadian custody. Eventually his trial was held in Vancouver, where he was convicted and sentenced.

Any further details, said Inspector Guinther, would have to be obtained in Canada. Jacobs asked if he had any suggestions, and Guinther, happy to oblige, supplied the name and phone number of a Canadian contact: Sergeant Ken Rehman, Royal Canadian Mounted Police, Victoria, British Columbia.

Over the phone, Sergeant Rehman at first hesitated to say much and sounded rather guarded. When Jacobs described the Cox case and threw in the name of Inspector Guinther, however, Rehman became more receptive, even friendly.

Frisbee had been convicted of first-degree murder, Rehman said, and was presently serving a life sentence in a Canadian prison. Jacobs said he would like to come to Canada to interview the man. Rehman agreed to meet with Jacobs when he arrived. Meanwhile, he would try to find out where Frisbee was incarcerated.

The following month, Jacobs flew from Miami to Denver and then to Vancouver. From there, he took first a bus, then a ferry, and some hours later arrived at Sergeant Rehman's office in Victoria.

Rehman had been doing some checking. After the trial, he said, Frisbee was sent to the federal penitentiary at Kent in the Fraser Valley, a maximum security facility for hardened criminals. At Kent, his cellmate had been a young psychopath who raped and brutalized him. After four months of this, fortunately for Frisbee, a lawyer had won him a transfer to Mountain Prison, a medium-security jail for protective custody inmates. That's where he was now. If Jacobs wanted to talk to him, he probably should work through his lawyer, a man named William Deverell.

Before doing anything further along those lines, Jacobs returned to Vancouver, where he visited the office of the *Vancouver Sun* and asked to see the stories on the Frisbee trial.

And what a trial it was! *Sun* reporter Larry Still, in one front-page story, noted that the case involved a wealthy widow, a luxury liner with a two-thousand-dollar-per-day penthouse suite, a blood-soaked bed, and even a suspect who stood to inherit by means of a secret will. Still called it "a courtroom drama with all the elements of a classy fiction whodunit."

During the six weeks of the trial, the papers had given it maximum coverage and managed to include every lurid detail. Jacobs began piecing together the story of Muriel Collins Barnett, Robert William Frisbee, and their ill-fated cruise on the *Royal Viking Star*.

Frisbee, it appeared, would have preferred separate cabins when he and Muriel Barnett set sail from San Francisco's Embarcadero pier. Muriel, who wanted Frisbee at her beck and call twenty-four hours a day, had said by paying a bit more they could reserve a luxury stateroom. Since she who controlled the purse strings was also able to call the shots, that is what they did. They were assigned to Penthouse Suite Six on the sundeck; one of its previous occupants had been movie star Elizabeth Taylor. It had a large bedroom with twin beds plus an adjoining den with floor-to-ceiling windows, built-in bar, refrigerator, and lounge chairs. The den also opened onto a private balcony.

On Muriel Barnett's last day of life, she and Frisbee rose around nine, had breakfast followed by cocktails, and then went ashore in Victoria. They were accompanied by shipboard acquaintances Max and Thelma Biegert, a pleasant retired couple from Paradise Valley, Arizona, a suburb of Phoenix. Muriel had arranged for a limousine tour, and the driver took the foursome to several Victoria tourist attractions, including the picturesque Fable Cottage and the Butchart Gardens. The group had lunch at Chauney's, an excellent old Victoria restaurant.

At Chauney's, Muriel Barnett and Robert Frisbee continued to punctuate their day with alcohol. Frisbee, over the years, had turned into a confirmed alcoholic, one who drank steadily throughout the day. Muriel Barnett, it appeared, generally followed suit. With their lunch, they had more drinks.

The party returned to the ship around 4:30 that afternoon. Muriel Barnett and Frisbee had one or more cocktails in their room. Muriel, who wanted to rest up for the captain's dinner that evening, had a bath and then went to bed for a brief nap.

Around 6:30, a steward with the improbable name of Michael Georgiou Michael knocked on the door of Penthouse Suite Six. Each day at that time, it was his custom to bring a tray of caviar canapés to the Barnett stateroom. Barnett had told him she liked caviar, and the Penthouse Suite was not without its perks.

Frisbee, responding to the steward's knock, came to the door looking dazed and disoriented. Muriel Barnett, her head bashed in, was lying in a pool of blood. In the cabin bathroom was a bloody liquor bottle, the apparent murder weapon. It appeared someone had tried to wipe it clean. According to Frisbee, he had no recollection whatsoever of what had happened.

At the trial, Frisbee's attorneys tried to establish what they called the "automaton" defense. They admitted he had done the deed but said he wasn't responsible, that he had acted while in a stupefied state somewhat like a sleepwalker. They stressed the fact that he had no criminal record and that any act of violence would be quite out of keeping with his nature. One psychiatrist had used the term "pathologically unassertive" to describe him.

The jury hadn't bought it. No doubt they were swayed by evidence that Frisbee was the beneficiary of a secret will, which Muriel Barnett had indicated she was about to change. Also, it was revealed that Frisbee, in his role of secretary, had handled all of Muriel's checking accounts. Over the years he had been skimming from those accounts rather consistently. To the jury, this made him not only an embezzler but also one who probably feared losing the lion's share of a multimillion-dollar inheritance. It was more than enough to convince them that the killing was premeditated. He was convicted of murder in the first degree and given the maximum sentence: twenty-five years to life.

One of the newspaper articles contained a physical description of Robert Frisbee and a photo. In Jacobs's opinion, he bore a distinct resemblance to Cox's visitor "George." Also, having been born in 1927, he would be about the right age.

After learning all he could from the newspaper files, Jacobs called William Deverell, Frisbee's attorney, who was not only a trial lawyer but also a well-known Canadian novelist. Jacobs mentioned the anonymous note implying a connection between Robert Frisbee and Richard Cox and asked if Deverell could arrange for him to interview his client. If Jacobs's name wasn't on Frisbee's list of preferred visitors, Deverell said, it wouldn't be possible to meet with him. The attorney added, however, that the next time he saw Frisbee, he would tell him about Jacobs and ask if he wanted to see him.

Deverell told Jacobs he would get back to him, or words to that effect. He never did. After waiting several weeks, Jacobs called Deverell again.

"He doesn't want to see you" was the only answer. One of the Canadian policemen said Frisbee was coming up for a parole hearing and probably hesitated to do anything that could rock the boat. Jacobs also heard that Deverell planned to write a book about the Frisbee case and might not want anyone else beating him to the story.* For Jacobs, who didn't want to cause trouble, and sought only to ask what, if anything, Frisbee knew about Dick Cox, it was highly frustrating.

After returning to Miami, Jacobs phoned others connected to the Frisbee trial, including Max Biegert, who had toured Victoria with Muriel Barnett and Robert Frisbee the day of the murder.

* William Deverell's excellent book, *Fatal Cruise: The Trial of Robert Frisbee,* was published in 1991 by the Canadian firm of McClelland & Stewart.

Biegert recalled Frisbee as a pleasant enough individual, albeit somewhat dissipated as a result of his alcoholic lifestyle. Nevertheless, he and his wife, Thelma, had found Frisbee and Barnett to be sociable shipboard companions. Biegert described their day in Victoria, including the lunch at Chauney's and the drinking. Evidently Barnett had been urging Frisbee to cut down on his drinking. Whatever the case, Frisbee had two vodka drinks at lunch but had lied to Barnett, telling her he was having Perrier water. Still, Biegert said, nothing in Frisbee's behavior that day would have caused one to predict the violence that occurred later. Biegert's feeling was that Frisbee had intended to throw Muriel Barnett overboard but, failing to do this, had killed her in the stateroom out of frustration. Later, Frisbee's attorney had contacted the Biegerts, hoping they would testify that Frisbee had been well under the influence of alcohol on the day of the murder. The Biegerts had refused to do so. Finally, Biegert said that though he knew Frisbee was from the East, he knew nothing that might tie him to the missing cadet.

Jacobs next contacted Queen's Counsel Dennis Murray, Assistant Attorney General in British Columbia and chief prosecutor for the Crown in the Frisbee trial. Murray was immediately interested in Jacobs's story about a missing cadet, and he wished Jacobs luck in finding a Frisbee-Cox connection.

Murray asked Jacobs if the cadet was still missing, and Jacobs said he was. In that case, Murray said, he had something that might be of interest. When they were investigating Frisbee's background, he said, they found that when he was living in New York he consorted with people who traded in *false identity papers*—driver's licenses, social security cards, birth certificates, and such.

Here was something tangible, Jacobs thought, something that surely made Frisbee a likely person to have helped Cox. Thinking back to what he knew of Frisbee's life, Jacobs suspected the false identity scheme probably originated with the unsavory Joe Dillon. Frisbee's access to such items raised all sorts of conjectures.

Murray next said that Frisbee had started a diary, actually more of an autobiography, while he was in prison. It had been seized as evidence and was in the public domain. Murray said it might contain something linking Frisbee to Cox, and he offered to send Jacobs a copy, along with a transcript of the trial. Jacobs said he'd appreciate it.

A few days later, a package containing two thick documents arrived at the Jacobs home in Miami. They were marked "Province of British

Columbia, Ministry of Attorney General, Criminal Justice Branch," and were accompanied by a card reading "with the compliments of Dennis Murray."

Robert Frisbee's so-called "diary" was a disjointed, rambling account of a bizarre, troubled lifestyle. It was mostly autobiographical, containing names, places, and events from Frisbee's past. He had told his attorneys, however, that he had hoped to make the diary into a novel; hence he had made up some of the stories and disguised several of the names. Although the writing was often incoherent and frequently vulgar to the point of pornography, at times there were flashes of wit. Most of the diary, however, was devoted to a recounting of various gay experiences.

Describing one point in his early life, for example, Frisbee had written: "My first tangle with an articulate male occurred one evening during this time when a sailor approached me in Times Square and after a drunken overture induced me to accompany him to his room in the Bronx." This was followed by a graphic account of what happened next.

In the very next paragraph Frisbee had written, "Spent much of this time at Sloane's YMCA on 34th Street and met a butcher interested in fresh meat." That reference to Sloane's was interesting. The place had been mentioned in the CID files; a night clerk there had said a man answering Cox's description had appeared, accompanied by a young woman, and had asked about a certain guest.

Jacobs read on. Suddenly the words "Fort Knox" seemed to jump off the page. According to Frisbee, he had been stationed there for most of his time in the service, generally doing clerical work. Jacobs began calculating dates. Frisbee, then called Dion, must have been at the Kentucky army post from mid-1945 until late '46 or early '47. *Dick Cox had taken his basic training at Fort Knox in 1946.* Was it possible the two had met at that time?

Next, on page ninety-seven of the diary, Jacobs read:

As to Jim Fitzsimmons. There was at this time a relationship existing, I am proud to say. I met Jim while cruising the local public park. . . . Jim could have done anything to me and I would hardly have known. Following the losing of my heart, trips to faraway Hartford and then NYC, when I stayed at the Times Square hotel and Jim at the mischievous Sloane House YMCA. [Again, the Sloane House!] Still his beloved in name only as I received mail to Mrs. Jim Fitzsimmons, but the pres-

ence was enough to carry us through the hard times, interrupted by the War only to the extent of the clipping in the local
paper pointed out with glee by mother, who had been reading my naughty letters.

In a further section, Frisbee told of his mother having intercepted
one of his love letters from Jim (the word he used was "stolen")
and of the letter being read both by his mother and his sister. For
the moment, this had put a stop to the affair.

"Jim Fitzsimmons," Jacobs realized, must really be Joe Dillon, the
seaman whose bonus checks had been mailed to Frisbee in the role
of fictitious wife. And Fitzsimmons/Dillon, the apparent creator of
false identity papers, had stayed at the "mischievous" Sloane House.
It all seemed to relate to the Cox mystery, but how? Jacobs read on.

There were many references to Dan Kazakes, a gay lover of
Frisbee's over a prolonged period. One diary entry read, in part: "At
this time I was so confused with my life with Dan and Harry I was
ready to clutch at any outstretched hand." Cox's high school yearbook, Jacobs remembered, said his nickname was "Harry." Did this
entry refer to Cox?

Jacobs finished reading the so-called diary. Many things hinted
at a connection to the Cox mystery, but still he could find nothing
definite. Taken together, however, the pieces surely seemed to add
up:

- The anonymous note and clipping sent to Inspector Guinther
  had implied a Frisbee-Cox connection.
- Frisbee matched the physical description of "George" and,
  having been born in 1927, would have been about the right age.
- Cox and Frisbee had been stationed at Fort Knox at the same
  time.
- Frisbee was in New York City during the winter of '49–'50
  when Cox disappeared, spending much of that time in Greenwich Village, another location known to Cox.
- Two diary entries referred to what Frisbee called "the mischievous Sloane House." This was the YMCA on West Thirty-fourth
  Street, where the CID investigated a possible Cox sighting.
- The diary had referred to someone called by Cox's nickname
  of "Harry."
- If Frisbee was able to provide false papers, there was an obvious link to anyone hoping to establish a new identity.

Despite all this, Jacobs remained stymied. Having been stonewalled in his efforts to meet Frisbee face-to-face, he was back where he had started, with lots of ideas but nothing concrete. Before giving up, however, he decided to try one more thing. It might be a long shot, but maybe not.

The FBI, Jacobs knew, had dedicated much time and effort to the search for Dick Cox, and he assumed they would still like to close the book on him. More recently in San Francisco, other federal agents had spent time on Robert Frisbee. Perhaps he could convince them of a possible Frisbee-Cox connection. If he could, and they decided to follow up, the FBI, unlike Jacobs, should be able to gain access to Frisbee in that Canadian prison.

With the help of a friend on the Miami police force, Jacobs scheduled a meeting with FBI special agent Ed Mall. At the appointed time, he arrived at the FBI building in North Dade County and was escorted to Mall's small, glass-enclosed office. Agent Mall, tall, well-built, with an informal yet highly professional manner, rose, shook hands, and invited his visitor to take a seat. Then, as he himself sat down, Mall reached under his desk and appeared to press a button. Jacobs assumed the meeting was being taped.

During the next hour, Jacobs reviewed for Mall the basic facts in the Cox investigation, including the role played by the FBI. He also went over the Frisbee case point by point, citing the coincidences that seemed to link Frisbee to Cox. Other officials had been most cooperative, he said, and he showed Mall the material sent from Canada by Queen's Counsel Dennis Murray, both the trial transcript and the Frisbee diary. It seemed to him, Jacobs said, that the FBI might want to talk to Frisbee about Cox.

What efforts had Jacobs himself made to arrange a meeting? Three months ago, he said, he had written Frisbee's attorney. After receiving no reply, last month he had written to Frisbee directly. Unfortunately, neither letter had been answered.

If they wanted to pursue it, Jacobs asked, would the FBI be able to see Frisbee? They probably could, Mall said; the Bureau had a good working relationship with the Canadian Mounted Police, and he guessed that would be no problem. Nevertheless, the man might still refuse to cooperate, and since he was already serving a life sentence, there was little they could do to make him talk. Mall suggested that Jacobs continue with his research. At this point, he said, a private citizen probably could accomplish more than could the official agencies.

Mall had been listening carefully to Jacobs through all this, taking notes and occasionally interrupting to ask a clarifying question. After Jacobs finished, however, the agent more or less threw cold water on his suggestion. He would contact Washington and ask about the status of the Cox case, he said, but at this late date he doubted the FBI would still be interested in a missing cadet. Jacobs gave him the FBI's file number on Cox, which Mall wrote down. That was that. Well, Jacobs thought, it had been worth a try.

Marshall Jacobs had now been pursuing Richard Cox for several years in the course of what he liked to call his "research project." Inevitably, as he talked to dozens of witnesses and followed every lead, more and more people became aware of his unusual quest. An article in the Military Academy's *Pointer View*, for example, credited him with keeping the search for Cox alive and listed the possible theories he had explored. Another piece, written for a Miami paper, was picked up by the wire services and distributed nationwide.

Increased publicity was fine by Jacobs: he guessed it might cause new sources of information to come forward. He was right. Del Comstock, a retired CID agent living in Piscataway, New Jersey, called Jacobs after seeing a 1988 article on him in the *New York Daily News*. Comstock said he was a former agent with the Seventeenth CID, once based in Brooklyn. He had been one of the first assigned to the Cox case; other agents he recalled working with were Rex Smith and Joe Cavanaugh.

For Jacobs, it was more evidence of the durability of the Cox mystery. Comstock, despite the passage of time, still remembered the case clearly and was eager to discuss it. Jacobs told him of the various theories that had been offered over the years. Del Comstock listened with interest and then said in his opinion the key to the mystery lay with something that had happened in Germany. Maybe they'd never know what that was. As for that anonymous note received by Inspector Guinther, he speculated that Cox himself might have been the sender.

Comstock went on to say that he'd always felt Cox had left the Academy voluntarily, although he'd never understood how someone who had so much going for him could have given it all up. He wished he'd been able to spend more time on the case. However, in April 1950, three months after Cox disappeared, Comstock had been transferred to France, where he later served as a bodyguard to the first NATO Commander, General Dwight D. Eisenhower. If Jacobs ever wanted to talk more, he'd enjoy hearing from him.

It wasn't only the print media that became interested in Jacobs. In 1989 he was approached by the producers of the Maury Povich television show, *A Current Affair*. They wanted to do a feature story on Cox, and Jacobs agreed to cooperate. Soon his living room was a whirlwind of activity, complete with heavy electrical cables, near-blinding lights, two staring cameras, and a highly professional reporter named Christa Bradford.

The finished program, in Jacobs's opinion, was done well. It began with scenes of West Point—barracks, monuments, cadets marching to class—and Povich saying things had looked much the same in January 1950, when Cox disappeared. This was followed by a segment with the attractive Bradford standing in front of the Hotel Thayer. She said Cox had started out for the hotel on the day he disappeared, intending to have dinner with his mysterious visitor, but had never made it.

The Miami portion of the program showed Marshall Jacobs at work, pictured his many boxes of neatly labeled files, and had him review the mystery and answer questions. Jacobs told the interviewer he accepted two sightings of Cox as valid and thought it possible that Robert Frisbee was Cox's visitor, "George." The program showed a "mug shot" photo of Frisbee and also contained a personal interview with Ernest Shotwell, the man who claimed to have seen Cox in Washington. Talking to the interviewer, Shotwell once again insisted that he had seen Cox in 1952, two years after his disappearance, and that during their meeting Cox had said he was on his way to Germany.

The program concluded with Jacobs saying he would truly like someday to meet Cox in person. If he ever did, he said with a smile, he'd ask him to explain what really happened.

Jacobs, who had been keeping up with Frisbee, learned that there had been a board hearing but that Frisbee's request for parole had been denied. Earlier, one of the Canadian officials had told Jacobs that Frisbee's unwillingness to talk might be related to that upcoming hearing and a desire not to raise any new issues. Now that it was out of the way, Jacobs thought, and Frisbee had nothing to lose, he might be more responsive. Jacobs wrote him again, using a friendly tone he hoped would be persuasive and saying in part: "Although we have never met I feel a strong familiarity with you and a compassion for your circumstances. I would like to institute a line of communication with you, which would in no way be detrimental or threatening to you personally. I feel, at this point in time, that we would have numerous interests worth discussing. I am perfectly willing to visit you at a time you consider convenient. I can assure you that our meeting would in no way put you 'at risk' or in any way jeopardize your position."

This second letter elicited a reply, but unfortunately not one to Jacobs's liking. Frisbee's words were suspicious, a bit hostile, and at the same time rather poignant. Writing from his prison cell, he said that he had turned over Jacobs's first letter to his attorneys and had "left the matter up to their discretion. They did not seem [deem?] it worthy to follow up on." Then, perhaps suspecting that Jacobs was a reporter, he added:

> I do not feel kindly toward the media, as I feel (as do so many of the inmates) that I have been maligned by the Third Estate in a most outrageous fashion.
>
> The Cox matter I have no interest in . . . the idea and the connection is preposterous.
>
> I do not invite personal visits or take telephone calls, but if you will please enlighten me as to who the hell you are, and why you show an interest in my life, then perhaps we could establish some sort of empathy [?] through the mails.

Jacobs decided to leave it at that. He still felt the many coincidences couldn't be explained as pure chance and that there was some sort of connection, perhaps even one unknown to Frisbee.* He had to acknowledge, however, that Frisbee was not "George." The rough, arrogant voice heard on the phone in 1950 by the B-2 charge of quarters was not that of Robert Frisbee, whom everyone described as soft-spoken. Also, Cox had said he'd known his visitor in Germany, and a check of Frisbee's army record showed that he had never served outside the continental United States. That seemed to clinch it.

Although he had given up on turning Frisbee into "George," Jacobs still believed that anyone hoping to find Cox had to start by identifying his visitor.

So, if Frisbee wasn't "George," who was? Once again, Jacobs went over his notes. In both the FBI and CID files, it appeared the most serious "George" candidate had been the former sergeant from New

---

* If there was such a connection, as implied by the writer of that anonymous note, it would remain forever hidden. Frisbee died in prison in 1991.

Jersey, David Myron Westervelt. Both agencies, it would seem, had eventually accepted Westervelt's alibi and concluded he wasn't the one who had visited Cox those two weekends in January 1950.

He knew it was nearly forty years since the authorities had dismissed David Westervelt as a suspect. Nevertheless, Marshall Jacobs decided to examine the evidence one more time.

Chapter 13

David Westervelt

M arshall Jacobs first heard of David Westervelt from Bud
Groner, who thought not only that Westervelt was "George"
but also that he had visited Cox in order to recruit him for some
government agency such as the CIA. At the time, Jacobs had more
or less tabled that theory, with the thought that in time he might
come back to it. Well, since he had exhausted all other ideas, it
seemed the time had come.

Over the years, Jacobs had adopted a filing system that involved
colors. He now went through the FBI and CID files and his own
interview notes, extracting all pages with blue-colored tabs—pages
pertaining to David Myron Westervelt.

One by one, he reviewed the items. First was an army CID
memo from February 1950, telling of an interview in which Bud
Groner urged the agents to check on Westervelt. The next item,
dated a month later on March 21, showed the CID, apparently
following up on Groner's suggestion, questioning Westervelt at
his home in Bergenfield, New Jersey. The CID agents, accompanied by a detective from the Bergenfield police department, had
asked the former sergeant to account for his actions during the
afternoon and evening of Cox's disappearance.

On that day, Westervelt said, he had attended a wheelchair basketball game at the armory in Teaneck, New Jersey. (To support his
story, he'd produced a program from the game, a somewhat unlikely
souvenir.) Initially, he said, he and his wife, Alicia, then living in
Dumont, New Jersey, were supposed to have had dinner with an
aunt and uncle before the game. For some reason they hadn't met
for dinner. Instead, the others had picked them up at their home

around 7:30. He couldn't account for his time before 7:30 on that date, but he thought he'd been home with his wife from about five. Anyhow, he said, they went with his aunt and uncle to the game, which started at eight. After it was over, both couples had gone for something to eat, after which he and his wife had arrived home, probably around 12:30.

The others in the party had supported Westervelt's story, and apparently the agents had accepted it. Nevertheless, that same CID memo indicated a certain degree of lingering suspicion. The army CID, checking on Westervelt with the FBI, had learned of a previous incident when he was arrested for transporting a stolen vehicle across state lines.

Jacobs had read all this before. This time, however, the thought came to him that an FBI arrest, even one far in the past, meant that somewhere a Westervelt file must exist. He therefore wrote the FBI, cited the Freedom of Information Act, and asked for whatever information they had on Westervelt. Then he returned to the files on hand.

The next item was dated March 24, 1950, only three days after the initial Westervelt interview. This one told of his coming to the CID office in New York and taking a polygraph, one judged inconclusive because of "certain mannerisms." On this same occasion, the two cadets who had seen "George" were brought into New York to observe Westervelt unobtrusively as he came into the office. One cadet made a "partial identification," and both said he was the "same type" as the man they had seen. Neither cadet, however, was willing to say for sure that this was the same person.

The final item in the file was from April 1952, two years subsequent to the polygraph test, and told of an interview conducted jointly by the CID and the FBI. Basically, the session covered familiar ground, with Westervelt accounting for his actions at the time of Cox's disappearance. According to the memo, Westervelt said Cox worked for him in Coburg, Germany, as an intelligence clerk for a three-month period, ending in July 1947, when their Constabulary outfit was disbanded. He and Cox were then transferred to different units and never saw each other again. His wife, Alicia, he added, did not know Cox; he had met her after leaving Coburg.

During the questioning, Westervelt said he had been in combat in the Battle of the Bulge and had received the Purple Heart because of frostbitten feet. When the agents asked him about the names used by Cox (Richard, Harry, Dick), he said he was only called "Cox."

Later he used the name "Dick," but when the agents called him on this, he denied having said "Dick." Finally, Westervelt was shown some photos taken in Coburg, and he identified two others who had known Cox: James Duffy of the Bronx and Halstead (Hal) Falch from Brooklyn. So much for the Westervelt material on hand: Now Jacobs waited to see what the FBI would send.

When the file arrived at Jacobs's home, the cover letter stated: "Enclosed are copies of documents from FBI records. Excisions have been made to protect information exempt from disclosure pursuant to Title 5, United States Code, Section 552 and/or Section 552a. . . . Pursuant to your request 84 pages were reviewed and 48 pages are being released."

Seven weeks later, six more pages came in the mail, along with a covering note: "The material now being released was originally referred to another Government agency for consultation regarding the release of their information. The release of the enclosed documents completes the processing of your request by the FBI."

As with the Cox files he'd received earlier, excised pages tended to heighten his curiosity. He'd always had a great deal of respect for the FBI. He still did, in fact; the federal agents he'd met, just like the CID agents of his acquaintance, were hardworking, patriotic, honest guys. He was not a suspicious person by nature, and he had little use for conspiracy theories. That was for the media, or for entertainment people like Oliver Stone, many of whom had an ax to grind. Nevertheless, all those deleted pages—165 from the original files, now another 30—would make *anyone* suspicious. What in the world were these people hiding? And why? He wondered if the excised items might not be far more interesting than the pages that *were* released. Despite all that, the new pages at least allowed him to put together a good picture of David Westervelt's early life.

Westervelt's parents, including a father who was a marine colonel, were divorced by the time he was a teenager. Young David attended public schools in New York City and, later, after having had behavior problems, was enrolled in Oakdale Military Academy in New Jersey. In 1943, at age seventeen, he falsified his age and tried to enlist in the army. When his true age was discovered, however, he was rejected. Later that year, on October 21, 1943, he and another man, a sailor, stole a car, abandoned it when it had ignition problems, then stole a second car, and drove it from New Jersey into New York. Crossing state lines turned the theft into a federal offense. When pursued by the police, they tried fleeing, but a train at a railroad crossing suddenly blocked their way. The car ended up in a ditch, and they were apprehended. Westervelt, although not in the service, was found to be wearing the uniform and insignia of an army second lieutenant.

David Westervelt and his companion were charged by the FBI after being fingerprinted and photographed. Westervelt at the time was described as five-foot-eleven, 140 pounds, slender build, light brown hair, gray eyes, with a triangular five-inch burn scar inside his right shin.

In the FBI file was a 1960 memo summarizing the case and its disposition. Significantly, the memo was prepared in response to a request for background information, the type of request that might have been made if Westervelt was being considered for some type of security clearance. The memo read as follows:

> On October 21, 1943, David Myron Westervelt and another individual were arrested by the United States Military Police at Camp Shanks, New York, after abandoning a stolen Ford. Westervelt was dressed in the uniform of the United States Army although he was not in the Armed Forces.
>
> Westervelt when interviewed stated he was born April 15, 1926, in New York City. He admitted the illegal wearing of the uniform and also participating in the theft and interstate transportation of two automobiles.
>
> The facts in the case were presented to the United States Attorney, Southern District of New York, who declined prosecution and released the subjects to the Chief of Police, Hackensack, New Jersey.
>
> On October 29, 1943, Westervelt was sentenced to two years' probation by the Bergen County Court. His probation would be suspended upon his entering the armed forces at the age of eighteen.

Also in the file was a copy of an April 1950 job application in which Westervelt wrote that he had received the Purple Heart because of a shrapnel wound in his right leg. It seemed he'd always been something of a poseur, as a youth showing off in the uniform of an army lieutenant, and later claiming a shrapnel wound (rather than frozen feet) as the basis for his Purple Heart. Maybe he'd even used that scar on his right leg as "evidence" of the alleged shrapnel wound. In that 1952 FBI interview, however, he'd prudently given the more prosaic and less dramatic true reason for the Purple

Heart, his frostbitten feet. Over the years, Jacobs thought, Westervelt's actions had been consistent with how the braggart "George" might have behaved.

In that same application, submitted to Consolidated Film Industries of Fort Lee, New Jersey, Westervelt had listed, under "previous technical training," "polygraph operator." Well now—wasn't this the fellow who had been given a polygraph test by the CID with "inconclusive results"? And hadn't the uncertainty been attributed to "certain mannerisms"? And wouldn't someone trained on the polygraph have known how to invalidate the test? It seemed that things were starting to fall into place.

In one of the interviews, Westervelt had mentioned Halstead (Hal) Falch from Brooklyn and Jim Duffy from New York. On that employment application, which Jacobs was finding quite helpful, Westervelt had given Falch as a reference and listed for him an address in Brooklyn.

A Brooklyn phone book showed a Falch living at the address on the application. It turned out to be the home of Falch's mother. Incredibly, after a passage of nearly forty years, when Jacobs made the call, it was the right Hal Falch, the former soldier from Coburg, who picked up the phone.

Jacobs introduced himself and explained his lengthy, determined effort to solve the mysterious disappearance of Richard Cox. Falch well remembered Cox and Westervelt and said he'd be happy to help. Although he worked in Brooklyn, Falch said, he and his wife now lived in Lake Hopatcong, New Jersey. He'd just happened to be at his mother's when the phone rang.

When they later met at Falch's home in Lake Hopatcong, Falch began by telling Jacobs of a weird personal experience. It was in the latter half of 1950, he said, but he couldn't pinpoint it exactly. He'd been married in July 1950, and it was sometime after that, so it must have been between six months and a year after Cox disappeared that Falch had received a puzzling phone call.

Jacobs, all ears, asked him to continue. Well, said Falch, it was a man's voice, a voice with no particular accent. The caller identified himself as a sailor, then said he knew "all about Dick Cox" and asked if Falch would like to find out what happened to his friend. Falch, wondering how the caller even knew he was acquainted with Cox, said of course he would like to learn what happened.

The sailor then said he'd get back to Falch and let him know where they could meet—maybe somewhere around Times Square.

At the time, Falch said, he wasn't sure what to do, so he phoned David Westervelt, who also knew Cox, and asked him what he recommended. Westervelt suggested he call the FBI, which is what he did. The FBI asked him, when the man called back, to agree to the meeting, anytime, anyplace. They, of course, would be on hand to back him up. Strangely enough, however, the supposed sailor never made the second call.

It was an intriguing story. How had the stranger known about Falch being acquainted with Cox? And why had he never called back? And why, for that matter, would a sailor have the information?

Thinking "sailor," Jacobs remembered the *Batory* theory, about Cox being kidnapped and smuggled aboard a Polish spy ship, but he felt sure any *Batory* crewman would have had a pronounced accent. The only other sailor "connection" in the case was Robert Frisbee's friend, Joe Dillon, who'd been in the merchant marine. Dillon, in fact, had been in New York in 1950, presumably selling false identity papers. Of course, if Dillon *had* made the call, he could have learned Falch's name only from Cox himself—interesting thought.

The conversation shifted to David Westervelt. "He's dead, you know," said Falch. No, Jacobs hadn't known. Falch elaborated. Westervelt, he said, had died in 1969 of leukemia. He was in Mt. Sinai Hospital in New York, and Falch had visited him there not long before he passed away. He and "Skippy," as he called Westervelt, had been good army buddies, and for years they'd managed to keep in touch, even though Westervelt was often away for long periods.

Why was that? Well, Falch said, he was pretty sure Westervelt was working for the government, probably the CIA, not on the regular payroll, but as what they called a "contract employee." Westervelt would suddenly get these calls, after which he'd pack a bag and disappear for weeks or even months. Once, for example, he'd gone to Guatemala for a considerable period.* Jacobs speculated, Could the deleted pages in Westervelt's FBI file be related to a CIA application? He and Falch kicked around the idea and decided it made sense. Falch went on to say, however, that as far as his covert assignments went, Westervelt was always close-mouthed

---

* The CIA's long history of Guatemalan involvement includes not only "Operation Success," the 1954 overthrow of the Arbenz government, but later use, officially unconfirmed, of that country as a military training base for Cuban exiles.

and never told anyone, not even Alicia, what he was doing during those times.

Alicia, was that Westervelt's foreign-born wife? Yes, Falch said, her maiden name was Alicia Weiss. She was a Russian, and during the war she'd been seized and brought to Germany as a slave laborer. She'd been in a displaced persons camp when Westervelt first met her, and later she worked for the army as a secretary and interpreter. When she was around Westervelt, he said, she always acted submissive, and Falch felt sure she'd have backed up any Westervelt alibi without asking questions. The marriage had ended in divorce, Falch said, and in his opinion she married Westervelt only so she could get to America.

For Jacobs, needless to say, the name Alicia brought to mind the story of a confused Dick Cox running into the hallway and shouting, "Is that you, Alice?" Could "Alicia" have been "Alice"?

Falch tried to remember what else he knew of Alicia. Once, he said, while she and Westervelt were still living in Germany, she had received notice from the Russian government that she was a Russian national and, as such, should return immediately to Russia. They had ignored the notice and apparently heard nothing further.

Alicia's story ended tragically, Falch said. She had remarried, and at some point she shot and killed her second husband, then committed suicide by turning the gun on herself.

With Falch's help, Jacobs next contacted Jim Duffy, the other man from Coburg, who now lived in Howell, New Jersey. Once again, just as he'd done with Falch, Jacobs went through the story of the Cox case. By this time, when he discussed with anyone the events leading up to and following Cox's disappearance, he was able to include some of his own theories and tentative conclusions.

As Jacobs described what he always called his "research project," Duffy, an outgoing, self-confident ex-New Yorker, became more and more interested. He said he remembered quite a bit about Cox, Westervelt, and their time together in Coburg; he'd be happy to talk and give Jacobs whatever he thought might help. Duffy was also pleased when Jacobs offered to put him in touch with the other Coburg veteran, Bud Groner.

In Coburg, Duffy said, he was in a supply job while Cox was working as an intelligence clerk. He and Cox often socialized, going out drinking—but only beer. He remembered Cox dating girls, and he'd never seen any indication of homosexuality.

Duffy remembered that Cox had worked for Westervelt, and, in his opinion, Westervelt often intimidated Cox. Duffy never could understand why Cox put up with it. To tell the truth, Duffy said, he was never impressed by Cox as a soldier. He remembered him as having much too passive an attitude, and he'd been surprised when he heard Cox had entered West Point.

Jacobs told Duffy about "George" and also told him of Westervelt's alibi for the night of Cox's disappearance. Duffy agreed with what Groner had said, that Westervelt could well have been Cox's visitor. The physical description matched, and Westervelt was always a neat dresser, with a cocky, "wise guy" attitude. Speaking of physical description, he said Westervelt had prominent buck teeth, with a pronounced overbite. Cox, he said, thought he looked like a squirrel and used to refer to him as "Westy-nuts."

Duffy said he had met Westervelt's wife, Alicia, and he thought she was dominated by her husband. Like Falch, he thought she would have done what Westervelt said and backed up any story about his actions on the day Cox disappeared.

While Duffy told Jacobs a good bit of what he remembered from those days in Coburg, he told even more in a long letter he wrote to Bud Groner. In the letter, he told of first meeting Westervelt in Marburg, where Westervelt, then only a private first class, had conducted close-order drill "as though he were General Patton." Later, Duffy wrote, "he started chewing me out about something—me being Irish, a former sergeant, and from 'Hell's Kitchen,' a bad combination. I stepped out of the formation and was getting ready to deck him when some of the other guys stopped me. . . . We more or less got along after that."

Later in the letter, referring to Cox, Duffy wrote:

> I do remember quite clearly the last time I saw him, outside of saying goodbye, of course. About two nights before I shipped home I was on guard duty patrolling the back fence. Dick Cox and a few other G.I.'s were with some Frauleins outside the fence near my post. When they were coming back into camp, Cox, who knew me, asked if they could climb over the fence. I went to the other end of my post and let them climb over. They were having a good time with those German girls, so I had a hard time accepting that homosexual allegation, and I thought Marshall Jacobs was barking up the wrong tree.

I was acquainted with Cox only a short time, I never really knew him that well but he never showed that side of himself to me. Of course in those days it was rare or else we were all very naive. . . .

As for Westervelt, when I first read the description of Cox's visitor, blond, about five ten, wearing a trench coat (if I remember correctly) he was the trench coat type if I ever saw one, and an ex-Ranger—he was the first one I thought of. I really can't recall if I mentioned this to the FBI agents when they questioned me, in all probability not. For the simple reason I couldn't see Westervelt overpowering Cox. Physically there was no comparison. As I remember, Cox was a pretty well built kid, whereas Westervelt was a cream puff. . . . [But] now that I look back, I saw W. on a few occasions really talk down to Cox and he took it without a murmur. I used to say to myself "why don't he bust him in the mouth and put this guy in his place" but he never did while I was in Coburg. I really felt sorry for Cox during those days.

Later in the letter, Duffy mentioned being surprised one evening when Hal Falch, Westervelt, and Westervelt's wife, Alicia, all appeared at his door. They talked about Cox, he said, but no one had any ideas, and Westervelt never mentioned having been questioned by the FBI.

After talking to Duffy, Jacobs thought again of his conversation with Hal Falch, especially Falch's remark about Westervelt having once been in Guatemala. That brought to mind Cuban refugees, their failed 1961 attempt to overthrow Fidel Castro, and the persistent stories linking the CIA to military training in Guatemala.

If Westervelt was in Guatemala, Jacobs presumed he'd been one of the trainers. For that matter, maybe Cox had been there, too. He felt certain the CIA wouldn't tell him anything, so maybe he'd try confirming the CIA–Guatemala connection on his own.*

Jacobs made a trip to Miami's Cuban section, known to the locals as "Little Havana," where there was a small private museum financed by Bay of Pigs veterans, a proud group whose members were still bitter over their failure to overthrow Fidel

---

* Despite requests under the Freedom of Information Act, according to Peter Kornbluh, director of the Cuba documentation project at the National Security Archive, the CIA's "internal record of the disaster remains hidden in its secret archives—unavailable for historical research." ("The CIA's Cuban Cover-Up," *New York Times*, April 16, 1996.)

Castro. Many still blamed the U.S. government for not giving them greater support at the crucial moment.

The museum caretaker, when Jacobs interviewed him, was suspicious of an outsider asking questions. Jacobs assured him he was there only as a private citizen, and the man began to unbend. Even then, however, his answers were terse.

"When you were preparing for the Bay of Pigs invasion, did you train in Guatemala?"

"Yes."

"Who were your instructors?"

"CIA."

"Do you remember any of their names?"

"No, we never used names." That was about all Jacobs was going to get, but for his purposes, it was enough.

Returning to his conversation with Falch, Jacobs recalled his saying that Westervelt, after divorcing Alicia, had remarried and had then died in 1969. After several hours of digging, Jacobs found the obituary notice in the Hackensack *Record* of August 6, 1969: "New Milford—David M. Westervelt, 44, of 688 Stockton St., died yesterday in Mt. Sinai Hospital, New York City, after a brief illness. An Army veteran of World War II, he lived in Bergenfield before coming here 13 years ago. . . . Surviving are his widow, Gloria; three sons, Pieter, Keith and Brian, all at home, and his parents, Mr. and Mrs. Herbert L. Meyer." (Evidently Herbert Meyer was David Westervelt's stepfather.)

Using the address from the obituary notice, Jacobs found Gloria Westervelt's phone number. When he called, she wasn't interested in either Jacobs's project or in Dick Cox, and not too happy about answering questions. Her husband, David, she said, had died several years ago, in 1969, and was buried in the George Washington Memorial Park cemetery in Paramus, New Jersey.

Did he ever discuss Cox? Well, she remembered David and Hal Falch talking about the case, and David once told her he was surprised that the investigation was still going on. Jacobs told her about his research and then asked a direct question: "Was your husband CIA?"

After a long pause, Westervelt's widow simply said, "Draw your own conclusions." Jacobs asked if they might meet in person, and Gloria Westervelt, still suspicious, said she'd have to think about it.

A few weeks later, Jacobs visited Westervelt's grave in Paramus and took a photo of the headstone. Then, wanting to close the loop, he visited New York's Mt. Sinai Hospital to verify the date of death.

Down in the hospital basement, where medical records were kept, Jacobs was asked, "Are you a family member? Are you a relative? Do you have a power of attorney?" If not, he was told, the hospital was unable to release any information. Undaunted, Jacobs waited a few days and tried again, this time by phone. He called on a Saturday, thinking a weekend record clerk, probably a part-time employee, perhaps bored and looking for something to do, might be less officious. This time he was deliberately devious.

"Look, he said, "I'm trying to check on an old army buddy of mine. His name was David Westervelt, and I heard he died in Mt. Sinai back in 1969."

"Let me check," said a cheerful feminine voice. A few minutes later the clerk returned to the phone, saying she'd found the record. "Your information was wrong," she said. "Your friend didn't die in '69. Our records show he was treated here in 1981."

"Thank you," said Jacobs. Now what? Was the young woman mistaken? He waited a couple of weeks and called again, once more on a weekend. He used the same ruse, that he was trying to verify the death of an army buddy.

A different clerk, equally helpful, and perhaps equally happy for something to break the weekend monotony, came up with the same information. His friend Westervelt had been treated at Mt. Sinai in 1981, so obviously he couldn't have died in 1969.

"Well," Jacobs said, "Westervelt isn't that common a name, but even so, I wonder if we might be talking about two different people."

"Well, the man I'm talking about," she said, "was a David M. Westervelt who was born on April 15, 1926."

Bingo! It was the same birthdate. "Thank you very much," Jacobs said. Did this mean Westervelt was still alive? And if he was, then who was buried in Paramus?

Jacobs wrote the Mt. Sinai Hospital administrator and asked for clarification. In due time, he received a letter saying:

Dear Mr. Jacobs:
I have investigated the matter regarding David Myron Westervelt's actual date of expiration. [Expiration? Sounds like a magazine subscription, Jacobs thought.] After reviewing Mr. Westervelt's medical record, it indicates that Mr. Westervelt ex-

pired at the Mt. Sinai Hospital in 1969. There was an error in our patient fiche which has been corrected.

My apologies for any inconvenience and confusions this may have caused you. If you have any questions, please contact me at [phone number].

The letter was signed: Teresa McGregor, Director, Medical Records Department. Jacobs called and talked to McGregor, who assured him it had been a clerical error. Personally, he wasn't so sure. He thought *someone* had been treated there in 1981. Perhaps a CIA person, unwilling to use his own identity, had borrowed Westervelt's. And was it possible that person was Cox?

Now, more than ever, Jacobs wanted to meet with Westervelt's family. However, several months had passed since that one phone conversation, and when Jacobs called again, he found that the Westervelts no longer lived in New Milford. Jacobs phoned Hal Falch, who said he'd lost touch with the family, but he thought they were still living in northern New Jersey, probably somewhere around Teaneck or Hackensack.

Jacobs began leafing through phone books and dialing people named Westervelt. Then came a lucky break, as a woman said she wasn't the one he wanted, but she knew of a young man named Westervelt who was working in a nearby garden-shop nursery.

Jacobs called the nursery and said he was looking for the family of David Myron Westervelt. "That was my father," said the young man who answered. He and his mother, he said, were now living in Hasbrouck Heights. He told Jacobs the number.

Somewhat reluctantly, when he reached her by phone, Gloria Westervelt consented to a meeting, agreeing only when he told her he'd ask Hal Falch to be there too. Her boys, she said, still referred to him as "Uncle Hal."

Jacobs's meeting with Westervelt's widow took place in the Sheraton Hotel in Hasbrouck Heights and lasted about three hours. On hand were Gloria Westervelt, Hal Falch, and two of Westervelt's three sons, Pieter and Keith.

When Jacobs described his extensive investigation and told what he knew of Westervelt's background, Gloria Westervelt became upset, saying, "You know a great deal about me, and I know nothing about you." She even wondered how Jacobs had located her son Keith at the nursery, since he worked there only part-time. Had Jacobs been lingering close by and watching him? Jacobs hastened to explain how a woman named Westervelt had told him of meeting Keith.

Gloria, a bit mollified, said she and David Westervelt were married in 1958, and she knew very little of his earlier life. David, she said, was a tight-lipped person who talked very little of his past, although she knew he had fought in the Battle of the Bulge and had been wounded by shrapnel. Jacobs made no comment; in the presence of Westervelt's family, it would be both mean and pointless to debunk the shrapnel story.

David once told her, Gloria continued, that their marriage was a "new beginning" for him, a "starting over." She had met his first wife, Alicia, also called "Lydia," but, like Falch, hadn't cared for her. She didn't know the whereabouts of Joe Russell, Westervelt's uncle, the man who'd been with him that night at the basketball game. She did know, however, that Joe and his wife, Jean, had divorced and that Jean had since died.

The Westervelt family knew very little about the circumstances of Cox's disappearance, so Jacobs now related the story in detail. The boys, Pieter and Keith, were quite interested in the mystery, but both they and their mother wondered why Jacobs suspected a Westervelt connection.

Jacobs explained his reasoning. The files, he said, showed Westervelt being questioned several times as a result of his (a) knowing Cox, (b) living close to West Point, and (c) being named by others, such as Bud Groner, as the person most resembling Cox's visitor. Jacobs then explained the Freedom of Information Act, which had allowed him to learn these things. Gloria Westervelt said she understood. However, as far as she knew, David had never been to West Point.

When the meeting broke up, Gloria told Jacobs that she now felt much better about him and was actually quite glad that they had met.

Upon reflection, Marshall Jacobs now believed he had a workable scenario for the events of January 1950. Maybe it wasn't exactly the way things happened, but it *was* a sequence that fit the known facts:

David Westervelt, who may or may not have used the name "George," comes to the Academy on Saturday afternoon, January 7, calls the Company B-2 orderly room, says he's "just up here for a little while and wants to take Cox to dinner."

"Up here" implies he's from somewhere south of West Point, such as Dumont. Intensive searches had failed to discover an overnight stay by "George" at any nearby hotel, motel, or tourist home. Westervelt, living in Dumont, about an hour's drive away, obviously could have visited two days in a row without requiring overnight lodging.

Cox meets Westervelt in Grant Hall and recognizes him. Although Cox signs out for Dining Privileges, he and his visitor do *not* go to the Hotel Thayer. Instead, Cox returns to his room after taking several drinks; says his visitor "made" him do so and also made him promise to meet again the following day. (Here we remember Jim Duffy's telling of Westervelt's ability to "intimidate" Cox.) By missing supper formation and not having gone to the Hotel Thayer, Cox has committed an honor violation. Later, he alters the entry in the B-2 departure log, making it appear he'd been back in time for supper formation.

The following Saturday, January 14, Westervelt arrives unexpectedly and again invites Cox to dinner. Jacobs knew that the West Point staff psychologist and others had considered it unusual for one man to visit another on consecutive weekends. Jacobs didn't believe, however, as suggested by Frank Sturgis, that the visitor came there to "set Cox up" for something. Similarly, he disagreed with Bud Groner's contention that Westervelt went twice to West Point, intending from the start to recruit Cox for the CIA.

In Jacobs's opinion, there was a simpler explanation for the return visit. On the previous weekend, Cox, after having several drinks, probably "unloaded," telling about his lack of desire for a military career, his hatred of cadet life, perhaps even his sexual hang-ups. Westervelt, because of his intelligence background, has already been approached by the CIA. Over the next few days, he thinks about Cox in that connection. True to form, he's eager to play the "big shot." He returns to West Point the following Saturday with a "solution" to Cox's problems.

Returning to the scenario: It is now 5 P.M. on January 14. Cox signs out for Dining Privileges at the Hotel Thayer, tells his roommate Welch he'll be "back early." At this point he fully intends to return. However, when Westervelt suggests going off post for a few drinks, Cox agrees. The idea might even be Cox's—earlier that day he'd suggested to Deane Welch that after taps they sneak off to Newburgh, but Welch had discouraged the idea.

Cox has been feeling tremendous pressures. His distaste for a military career has been steadily increasing, but he fears the reaction of his strong-willed mother were he to resign. Everyone expects him to marry his girlfriend, Betty, and she even plans on coming to New York to be near him. Meanwhile, he continues to struggle with his own sexual orientation.

At this point, Cox, whose low alcoholic tolerance is well known, is becoming intoxicated. He tells his visitor that by passing up dinner at the hotel in favor of off-post drinking, he has committed a second honor violation. What can he do? He's too proud to accept the consequences, possibly including dismissal and going home in disgrace.

Suddenly, as if by magic, he's given an opportunity to solve his problems. Perhaps his visitor says, "Come home with me. I know where you can get a job easily—they're recruiting heavily for that new intelligence agency." Cox drunkenly nods consent, and they drive south to New Jersey.

Westervelt was to have had dinner with an aunt and uncle, but he's not back in time. He *is* home, however, by 7:30, when the others arrive to drive him and Alicia to the basketball game. Alicia supports his story that he was home from five o'clock onward, and to bolster his alibi for the evening, he retains the program from the game.

Here, unfortunately, Jacobs's scenario came to a halt. He was satisfied that he had "transported" Cox from West Point to somewhere in New Jersey or New York, but he couldn't say for sure what happened next. By this time, however, Marshall Jacobs had amassed a multitude of clues. They resembled, he thought, a handful of loose beads. Perhaps, if he persisted, he'd eventually string them together.

Chapter 14

The Spymaster

To know someone well, he'd always heard, you had to "walk a mile in his moccasins." Now Marshall Jacobs tried putting himself into Dick Cox's moccasins, not at the confused, impulsive moment he deserted the Military Academy, but several hours later, on the "morning after" of January 15, 1950.

No doubt he awoke somewhere in the greater New York area, perhaps even in Westervelt's home in Dumont. What was it like when he opened his eyes that morning? Was there a momentary feeling of panic, a sudden sensation of "what have I done?" Or, remembering the usually phlegmatic Cox, was there, instead, an acceptance, even a pleasant sense of relief? He had, after all, escaped the immediate pressures and problems. Now, coolly and dispassionately, and without the distracting rigors of cadet life, he could think about the future.

Even so, wouldn't Cox's first thoughts have been of home and family, especially concern for his mother? Surely he knew how worried she'd be when she learned of his disappearance. When Jacobs interviewed Cox's roommates, they both expressed strong doubts about Cox still being alive. The reason, of course, was that they couldn't believe Cox would have let his mother suffer all these years. He would have felt compelled, whatever the cost, to get word to her that he was safe. Others had said the same thing—that a loving son and brother would have called home at the first opportunity.

That made sense. The Coxes were a close-knit family, and Minnie Cox was an outstanding parent, a loving, protective, strong-willed matriarchal figure, respected and appreciated not only by the family but by everyone in Mansfield. Apparently there was also a special bond between Minnie and Richard, her youngest, the boy on whom she'd always doted. For proof, one only had to read his many affectionate letters, written to her both from Germany and from West Point. Further evidence came from the way he called her by her first name, indicating a special personal relationship. Always it was "Minnie" or "Min" rather than "Mother" or "Mom." In other words, if Dick Cox was alive, feeling as he did about his mother, how could he have failed to contact her?

Then again, despite the protestations of love, there were some disquieting contradictions in the relationship, enough to raise a nagging doubt. For example, Jacobs remembered a chance remark of Joe Groner's from the time Groner flew to Ohio to meet with the Cox family soon after Dick's disappearance. Describing Minnie Cox to Jacobs, Groner said she "was a very nice person. Kind. Not at all the way Dick painted her." What did that mean? Deep down, did Dick view his mother with mixed emotions? Was there some sort of ambivalence, of love coupled with resentment? Jacobs was no psychologist, but he did remember hearing of Cox's annoyance when his mother secured a West Point Congressional appointment for him, thus making superfluous the Regular Army appointment he'd won on his own. There was also that story of the work crew accident, when Dick's arm was slashed open by a scythe. The wound was bleeding profusely, but Minnie, the devout Christian Scientist, only "read over him." By the time a friendly neighbor got him to a doctor, the cut had become infected. He still carried a prominent scar as a physical reminder of the incident. Perhaps there was an emotional scar as well.

Yes, the relationship between son and mother was far more complex than it appeared on the surface, particularly in light of Cox's ability to hide his true feelings. On Dick's part, of course, clearly there was love and a desire to please. Taking it a step further, however, wasn't there also an outright fear of *dis*pleasing? Earlier, when he considered leaving the Academy, he hadn't worried about the loss of a military career, hadn't worried about his girlfriend—who'd have been delighted to have him home—no, he'd worried only over what his mother would feel.

Jacobs recalled what Cox had written Betty Timmons; "I asked Minnie what she'd think—or do—if I'd give this place the boot it deserves." Those were the words, it seemed to Jacobs, of a young man strongly influenced by a dominant mother and fearful of her reactions. Even if such a man decided to call home, what could he have said? "Hey, Min, I quit the Academy. I violated the honor system and I can't go back." That would have been a blow to *any* proud parent, and especially to this one.

Even worse, however, for a woman steeped in the ultraconservative culture of 1950 Mansfield, would have been, "Min, I can't stay at West Point and I can't marry Betty. Sorry, but it seems I'm a homosexual." One can only imagine how Cox would have hated saying *that* to his mother. The shame and embarrassment would have been overwhelming, and someone as proud as Dick Cox might well have been unable to make the call.

Jacobs paused. Putting it all together, it seemed quite possible, even probable, that Dick Cox, on the day he left, and on every day thereafter, would *not* have called home. This was all conjecture, of course, and Jacobs wanted no part of psychobabble. Nevertheless, despite what people said about Cox as a loving son, there was also evidence of a resentful Cox, a cold, distant figure, lacking concern for people or places from the past. As one of his Mansfield acquaintances put it, he was "the kind of guy who could have left it all behind and never looked back."

On that January morning, it seemed, Cox had two choices: One, he could return to West Point, confess to an honor violation, resign, then return to Mansfield with head hung low, perhaps to work for his mother in the insurance business. Alternatively, he could start a new life, seek a new identity, and let the old Richard Cox fade into oblivion.

Jacobs knew he'd have a hard time piecing together the rest of Dick Cox's life. To help, however, he had three fairly good milestones or benchmarks: 1950 in New York City, 1952 in Washington, D.C., and 1960 in Melbourne, Florida.

First was New York City. There had been numerous early sightings of Cox in metropolitan New York—in Greenwich Village, at the Sloane House YMCA, at one or more restaurants or nightclubs. Not all of these could be accepted at face value, of course, but the sheer number of sightings made it likely that at least one or two were valid. It seemed that Cox initially lost himself somewhere in New York's vastness. Naturally, he would have needed help during this time, perhaps from Westervelt, perhaps from someone he'd met earlier—maybe even a homosexual acquaintance. And during this period, he doubtless pondered Westervelt's suggestion about applying to the Central Intelligence Agency. On the one hand, he couldn't just walk up to a recruiter, saying, "Hello, my name is Cox and I'm looking for a job. Oh, by the way, I just deserted from the Military Academy, so the U.S. Army and the FBI are both looking for me." On the other hand, one *could* put out cautious feelers with the help of an insider such as Westervelt. These were the early days of the CIA, an exciting organization, headed largely by idealistic but pragmatic veterans of Bill Donovan's wartime OSS (Office of Strategic Services). They had come to recognize the realities of Cold War intelligence gathering, and to do the job they had to enlist promising talent, wherever that talent might be found, and without worrying too much about past histories. Also, a strong rivalry existed between J. Edgar Hoover's FBI and the fledgling CIA. A new candidate, one seeking anonymity, could easily have been brought on board without notifying Hoover's people. They might even have had a measure of satisfaction in spiting Hoover by doing just that.

If Cox approached the CIA while he was in New York, there would have been a necessary delay while he was checked out or "vetted." Once accepted by the agency, he would then have undergone training somewhere near Washington.

That brought Jacobs to the second benchmark, the 1952 appearance by Cox at the Greyhound Post Restaurant in the nation's capital. There Cox had been positively identified by his friend Ernest Shotwell, and in their brief conversation he had said he was on his way to Germany.

It seemed likely, when Cox ran into Shotwell, that he was heading overseas after having completed some type of training program. It wasn't hard to guess what the program might have been in 1950 or 1951. Former CIA Director William Colby, writing of those early days, said in 1950, when he joined the agency, he was assigned to OPC (Office of Policy Coordination), the "Agency's paramilitary, propaganda, and political-action arm." It became his job, he wrote, to help organize European "stay-behind" teams, since "in the event the Russians succeeded in taking over any or all of the countries of the Continent, the OPC wanted to be in a position to activate well-armed and well-organized partisan uprisings against the occupiers." And unlike World War II, "we intended to have that resistance capability in place before the occupation, indeed even before an invasion."*

---

*Honorable Men: My Life in the CIA, New York: Simon and Schuster, 1978.

Cox, a bright young man who had served in Germany, would have been a good candidate for a "stay-behind" team. Moreover, it would have been an ideal situation for someone wanting to forget the past and think only of the future.

So far, Marshall Jacobs's deductions about Cox and the CIA, while logical, were still unproven. What he needed now was some way of confirming them. Who would be in a position to do this? He had started by doing the obvious—writing the CIA, citing the Freedom of Information Act, and requesting the files on Richard Cox. The result was pure frustration. After months of delay, assurances that nothing was available, and a general runaround, he had been given an irrelevant single page, one referring to *Homer* Cox of Oklahoma, at the time a prisoner in the Soviet gulag.

He might as well accept it: Straightforward queries were almost useless. What he needed was a "source," someone with access to the CIA's inner workings. But where could he find such a person? It couldn't be someone still on active duty, presumably silenced by official policy. Even if he could, Jacobs wouldn't ask such a person to risk his or her job by violating security. No, he probably needed to find a former employee, preferably a retiree, someone who still had connections at Langley, and perhaps still owed a few favors. Jacobs thought of Frank Sturgis, the cooperative ex-CIA man he'd met earlier. Sturgis, however, saddled with the stigma of Watergate, had become a "nonperson" as far as the Agency was concerned. For that matter, Sturgis probably hadn't been high enough in the organization to have had the right kind of contacts. For Jacobs, the only thing to do was wait and hope something turned up.

He had finished breakfast and, over a second cup of coffee, was reading the morning paper. An item with "CIA" in the heading caught Marshall Jacobs's eye. It was an interview with Walter Robinson, a retired senior CIA official now living somewhere in central Florida, and evidently a well-known figure in the intelligence community. Robinson, according to the article, had been with the Agency since the early days and had worked closely with such men as Allen Dulles, William Casey, and Richard Helms. He spoke several languages and had served with distinction all over the world, including Europe, South America, and the Far East. Some of his exploits had become CIA legend. He was not only a man who had served the nation well but also a fascinating figure.

In the interview, however, Robinson showed that he could also be sharply critical and outspoken about the American intelligence establishment. He referred to the way the CIA had been losing credibility with Congress and the White House, citing disputes over the budget, the construction of an unauthorized office building, and a running feud between a certain CIA director and the head of the congressional oversight committee. He was, moreover, outraged about the Iran-Contra fiasco as well as other episodes in which he felt the Agency had acted ineptly or had been kept in the dark by the administration.

Walter Robinson, it seemed, was a bit of a maverick, someone who knew the spy game inside and out and had no illusions about its seamier aspects. "When I started in the business," he told the interviewer, "my boss told me that secret intelligence operations were a vital ingredient of national security but—like certain bodily functions—best not performed in public."

Perhaps this was the man Jacobs needed to meet. There was a big "if," however. Would he be willing to sit still while Jacobs told him the story of Richard Cox? The first problem, of course, was trying to find him; he doubted an ex-spy would be listed in the phone book. On a hunch, Jacobs called the newspaper. He spoke to the interviewer and was given a phone number he might try. He did.

"Hello, I know you don't know me, but my name is Marshall Jacobs, and I'm calling from Miami. Is this Mr. Robinson?"

"Yes."

"I'm calling about a research project of mine, one concerning a West Point cadet who disappeared some forty years ago. I think you might be able to help me. Would it be possible for us to get together?"

Robinson sounded dubious. Jacobs had encountered that type of reaction before. As always, however, he kept talking, saying he'd be willing to come whenever and wherever Robinson said.

Finally the ex-spymaster, perhaps a little amused, agreed to meet with Jacobs, while saying he didn't really see the point to it. Nevertheless, he suggested Jacobs drive to Orlando, check into a hotel, and give him a call. They agreed on a mutually convenient date.

The following week, on the agreed-upon day, Jacobs left home, tape recorder and notebook in hand. It was a pleasant day for a drive, and as he headed north on I-95, he wondered if this would be another fruitless interview. For some reason, however, this time he felt optimistic.

Near Orlando, he turned onto I-4, and a few miles later found the exit near the Sheraton Hotel, an attractive pink building just off the interstate. Jacobs checked into the Sheraton and, from his room, called the number he'd been given.

"Hello, Mr. Robinson, I'm at the Sheraton. If you'll give me directions, I'll head out to your place."

"No. Stay where you are. I'll come pick you up." Robinson arrived at the hotel some time later. He and Jacobs introduced themselves and shook hands. Then, almost in silence, Robinson drove to what appeared to be an upper-middle-class Orlando neighborhood, turned down one of the streets, and stopped at a house halfway down the block.

Robinson, like Jacobs, was dressed in slacks and a sport shirt. The ex-CIA official—short, thick-bodied, with dark eyebrows, a strong nose, a closely cropped fringe on either side of his head but little on top—wore thick, rimless glasses. His features were heavy, almost coarse—somewhere between Ernest Borgnine and Mikhail Gorbachev. The overall impression was one of strength and quiet self-confidence.

They entered the house. Although the place was fully furnished, it seemed void of personal touches. There was no one else around, and Robinson, although presumably the host, made no move to offer refreshments of any kind. Jacobs had the feeling that this wasn't really Robinson's home—that perhaps this was one of those "safe houses" he'd read about.

Robinson and Jacobs seated themselves in heavy wooden chairs at a long table. Now, what was this all about? As he'd done so many times before, Jacobs launched into the story of Richard Cox—the Mansfield boyhood, the service in Germany, the days at the Stewart Field prep school, the time as a cadet. He then described Cox's visitor "George," the events surrounding the disappearance, and the extensive army and FBI searches that had followed. By this time he had told the story so often that the narrative rolled off his tongue; it was almost like turning on a record.

Then, before going into his own theory, about Cox joining the CIA, Jacobs described some of the other ideas that had been advanced. One held that Cox had been seized by communist agents, smuggled out of the country on a Polish spy ship, the *Batory*, and eventually imprisoned at Vorkuta.

Jacobs reached into his briefcase and took out the CIA document that told of someone named Cox being sighted in a Soviet prison camp. He handed it to Robinson, who read it carefully.

Jacobs asked Robinson if he thought the document was genuine and whether the contents were plausible. "Oh, it's genuine all right, and quite plausible, even to the mention of Lieutenant Colonel Hamblen, the West Point liaison officer. Matter of fact, I knew Hamblen—he's now a retired brigadier general."

"What about the *Batory*," Jacobs asked, "the spy ship that was used to smuggle out Gerhard Eisler?"

He, of course, knew of Gerhard Eisler and was well aware of Eisler's having been a communist agent. Cautiously, Robinson said he also knew of the *Batory*, but he couldn't say whether it was actually a spy ship.

Jacobs next told Robinson about "George's" story of killing a pregnant German girl, adding that Cox had told people he'd once been a witness at a court-martial. A retired sergeant named Hill, Jacobs said, had taken those two facts and woven them into a rambling tale in which he claimed an American GI had killed a German girl, the army had covered it up, and the Germans, in turn, had not only failed to prosecute but also not even owned a record of the event.

"Personally, I'm skeptical of all this," Jacobs said. "I wonder, though, what you think of it."

Robinson said one thing rang true. In 1947, when Cox was overseas, the German police wouldn't have been able to try an American soldier. They would have been obliged to turn him over to the Americans for prosecution. The cover-up sounded fishy, of course, and the story broke down completely when Hill said the Germans had no record of the crime. German civil authorities and newspapers keep excellent files, Robinson said, and any such killing surely would have been recorded.

"Now to change the subject to my theory," said Jacobs. "Let me ask you, was the CIA recruiting heavily in 1949 and '50?"

"Affirmative."

"Well, then, isn't it possible that Cox left West Point voluntarily and became associated with the CIA?"

"Negative. As you describe him, he was a capable young man with a bright future. Frankly, with what he had going for him, I can't imagine him leaving West Point voluntarily."

Then Jacobs said, "If I told you Cadet Cox was bisexual, would that make a difference?"

"Wait—stop right there!" Robinson understood immediately the implications of Cox being homosexual, especially back in 1950. He would have lived in constant fear of being "outed," either by a fellow cadet or by someone back home. In such a case, starting a new life in some obscure CIA assignment would have had a strong appeal.

"That changes everything," Robinson said. Jacobs was startled by the suddenness of the response. Obviously, the other's interest had picked up. He'd like to know more, he said. Jacobs had piqued his curiosity. He might look into the story, and possibly he'd be able to learn something. By now, he was mostly out of the loop back at Langley, but he still had a few chits he might call in. If he did, he'd let Jacobs know and set up another meeting. That was that. It all ended cordially, and Robinson drove Jacobs back to his hotel.

As they parted, Robinson said, "Possibly we'll get together again." To Jacobs, it sounded like a polite brush-off, a "don't call us, we'll call you." He suspected he'd never hear from Walter Robinson.

In the weeks that followed, as Jacobs pursued his research in other directions, he almost forgot his meeting with Robinson. Occasionally, however, he'd come across the CIA man's name in either a book or a newspaper article: Robinson testifying before a congressional committee; Robinson praised—or criticized—for some action taken either when he was in Germany or when he was chief of station at a major overseas post; Robinson speaking out on the administration's handling of national defense. He might officially be retired, but plainly he still had lots of opinions and lots of energy.

Jacobs had to admire the man. Although their meeting hadn't produced anything tangible, he was happy he'd at least made the other's acquaintance. At that meeting, of course, Jacobs had done most of the talking, and Robinson had spoken only briefly of himself. What little he'd said (when Jacobs mentioned the possibility of Cox going to Germany) had concerned the chaos in postwar Germany when Robinson first joined the CIA.

At the time, Jacobs had wondered if Cox and Robinson might have met during that period. Later, he saw how unlikely that would have been. By 1952 the Agency had mushroomed; some fourteen hundred people were said to be on the CIA payroll in Germany alone.

Jacobs turned to his third "benchmark," the 1960 sighting of Cox in Melbourne, Florida, by a man who turned out to be an FBI informant. Something about that report had always bothered him. He thought Cox's reference to Castro "not being around much longer" was understandable, particularly if he knew there were Cubans training in Guatemala for some future action. However, why would Cox have asked a stranger, a man he met at a bar, to introduce him to certain local figures?

Thinking it over, Jacobs recalled that the people Cox sought out were shady characters who didn't want their names mentioned to the FBI. Therein, perhaps, lay the explanation. The CIA, both before and after the Bay of Pigs invasion, had been involved in anti-Castro schemes. According to author Evan Thomas, President Kennedy and his brother Bobby, the attorney general, relentlessly prodded the CIA to "get rid" of Castro. In fact, RFK once "chewed out" a CIA executive in the cabinet room "for sitting on his ass and not doing anything about getting rid of Castro and the Castro regime."* Some of the resulting schemes, it appeared, had contemplated the use of underworld figures, the type of people Cox was looking to meet when he asked the man in that Melbourne bar to make some introductions. With that in mind, Jacobs now thought his third benchmark rang true.

It had been nearly eight months since Jacobs had met with Robinson, and he'd given up on hearing anything further. Then the phone rang. It was Robinson.

"I think we should meet again. Can you come to Orlando?"

"Certainly," Jacobs said. It appeared Robinson had learned something. Whatever it was, it also appeared he didn't want to discuss it over the phone.

Once again Jacobs drove to Orlando, checked into the Sheraton, and called the number he'd been given. This time Robinson said he'd meet with Jacobs in his hotel room.

The CIA man arrived, made himself comfortable, and said, "I'm going to tell you something." First, though, he said he himself would have to remain anonymous. Jacobs agreed.

"Well, I found your man."

Jacobs felt the butterflies gather in his stomach. These were the words he'd been waiting to hear all these years. Did it mean he'd finally meet Cox and solve the mystery?

Robinson said he had a certain amount of information, but it was fragmentary. He'd tell what he could, but Jacobs was not to ask the

*The Very Best Men—Four Who Dared: The Early Years of the CIA. New York: Simon and Schuster, 1995.

source or even inquire about Robinson's reasons for telling him these things.

Jacobs nodded. He still felt a bit numb. Then the other man began. "Following World War II," he said, "we were having a great many problems with the Russians. Special training schools were established for undercover or covert actions and there was a great deal of maneuvering people around." Cox, he said, for many years lived and worked in Europe, mostly in Germany, in the intelligence field. He did not name Cox's employer.

"Besides being in Germany," Robinson said, "he may have served as a contact point at a central location in France." Robinson continued to sound vague. Jacobs didn't know whether this was on purpose. Suddenly, however, he became more specific.

"One of Cox's tasks was getting people out from behind the Iron Curtain. These were members of the scientific community; some were Russians and some were individuals who had been taken captive by the Russians.

"Cox, I think, has seen a lot, has probably been scared a lot, but has still maintained a West Point sense of duty. His work has been secret—and significant. It appears the people he helped were important to the Russians' nuclear capability, and getting them out caused those operations to shut down for a time. However, where these persons are now, or who they are, I have no idea."

As for Cox's role, Robinson thought it might have been something illegal, which would explain why it was necessary to get him out of Europe. In any case, he said, something about his activities was still being hushed up, and it looked like one government agency was hiding him from another agency.

"It's an immensely complicated situation," he said. "At this particular time, his only problem is what he knows. And the more *you* dive into it, the more you know what he knows, the more it puts you in a particular situation."

Robinson gave Jacobs a meaningful look. Was this an implied threat? Would Jacobs be putting himself in danger if he pursued this?

"Really?" said Jacobs, trying to sound unconcerned. Later he decided this was merely Robinson's way of telling him to back off. At that instant, however, it was unnerving.

"On the other hand," Robinson continued, "while I don't know what your investigative abilities are, I doubt you'd find out much more anyhow."

"But Cox came back to this country, you say?"

"Yes, he's been living out west, in the mountainous Panhandle region of northern Idaho—not far from the little town of Kellogg." Jacobs had heard there was right-wing militia activity in that area, but he had no idea as to whether that had anything to do with Cox.

"Right now," Robinson said, "you'll find him at NIH [National Institutes of Health] in Bethesda, Maryland. Notice he was put into a federal facility rather than a regular hospital. Now the bad news. Unfortunately he has cancer, and it's terminal."

Jacobs, trying to recover from this, the latest shock, asked what kind of cancer. Robinson pointed to his upper chest.

"Thoracic?"

"Yes, thoracic. For all I know, he may be dead right now."

"Can I see him?"

"No, Marshall. He knows about you, and knows about the publicity you've stirred up. But—and this is definite—you are *not* to try contacting him."

Jacobs said he understood. Cox at this late date, and on what might be his deathbed, would see no reason to break the silence merely to satisfy someone's curiosity.

Before they parted, Robinson reminded Jacobs of his promise to maintain his anonymity.* He had made certain commitments, he said, and that was all he was going to say on the matter. Jacobs was not to ask for any further explanation. They shook hands, and Robinson left. This second meeting would be their last, and it had been made clear that further contacts would not be welcome.

As he drove home, Jacobs couldn't tell how much of what he'd heard had been factual and what was inference. Robinson had mixed the two and managed to create a blurry mélange. It was all very confusing, and maybe that was the idea. In any case, Jacobs had learned the essentials. Cox, although he might soon be dead, was at this moment alive. As a cadet, he had been under various pressures, and it was hard to say which had caused him to disappear. At least, however, when he left West Point to assume a new identity, he had left voluntarily.

Jacobs decided he had learned all he was going to, and he accepted the fact that neither he nor anyone else would ever know the full story. It was gratifying, nevertheless, to know that Cox had lived an honorable, patriotic life in the service of his country. Rich-

*Robinson is not his real name, and to this day, Jacobs honors his promise.

ard Colvin Cox was a complex, talented individual, and Jacobs would have liked to have met him and to have had a long talk. This was not to be. All the same, the research project, which along the way had turned into an obsession, could justly be called a success. Marshall Jacobs had "found" Dick Cox and brought him back from oblivion. The files could be closed.

Epilogue

In writing the story of Richard Cox, I have relied heavily on Marshall Jacobs's voluminous files and interview tapes. I've also spent many hours talking to Marshall himself to flesh out this account of his "research project." I'm deeply grateful for his cooperation, which remained cheerful even when I annoyed him by playing devil's advocate and challenging his assertions. At such times, I might add, he was always quick to back up his conclusions.

"Why," I'd ask, "do you believe Shotwell saw Cox in '52, and if he did, why did he wait until '54 to come forward? And why should we believe the informer's story about meeting Cox in a Florida bar? Didn't he just read about Cox in a magazine article? And wasn't he just trying to make points with his FBI contact? And why on earth would Walter Robinson have told you so much?"

Jacobs was always ready to come back at me, both about the sightings he considered valid and the truthfulness of "Walter Robinson." If Shotwell was just a publicity seeker, Jacobs said, he *would* have come forward earlier. Obviously, since he spoke up only after seeing that article in *Coronet*, he was telling the truth—and the polygraph backed him up. As for the man in Florida, why would anyone in 1960 have resurrected a Cox story out of thin air? By that time the case was old hat, the FBI had pretty much lost interest, and the informer would have had little to gain. Finally, Jacobs said he believed Robinson gave him what he did merely to shut him up. If Cox was indeed being kept under wraps, it was counterproductive to have someone like Jacobs running around and keeping the story alive.

I had to admit his conclusions made sense. Marshall Jacobs can be justifiably proud for bringing the story to closure. In addition to thanking Jacobs, I must also express my appreciation to the people at West Point, including Alan Aimone in the Library's Special Collections area, Bruce Bell in the Public Affairs Office, Suzanne Christoff and Judy Sibley in the Archives, and Jay Olejniczak in the Office of the Association of Graduates. Let me also thank Don McKeon, my capable editor at Brassey's, who has been consistently helpful and encouraging.

Today, Marshall Jacobs, who still lives in Miami, teaches English to Hispanics in adult education classes. He has also been heavily involved with a Stephen Spielberg project, interviewing and filming Holocaust survivors to preserve their stories for posterity.

In conclusion, let me offer a hope that those who knew Richard Cox will be pleased with this account and with the knowledge that he lived a productive, patriotic life. His mother, Minnie, unfortunately, although living to the age of ninety-six, died in a Mansfield nursing home without ever learning the fate of her son.

About the Author

Colonel Harry J. Maihafer is a 1949 graduate of the U.S. Military Academy and holds a master's degree in journalism from the University of Missouri. A former infantry officer and retired banker, he is the author of *From the Hudson to the Yalu: West Point '49 in the Korean War* and *Brave Decisions: Moral Courage from the Revolutionary War to Desert Storm* (Brassey's, 1995). His articles have appeared in *The Wall Street Journal, Military History, U.S. Naval Institute Proceedings, Military Review,* and other publications. He and his wife live in Nashville, Tennessee.